SURVIVAL

BY HEIDE AND ROBERT EGERT-BUDIK

T0354923

NORTH AMERICAN
Editorial Assistance: Mary Coons
MaryCoons@usinternet.com

EUROPEAN
Editorial Assistance: Theresa Egert Lorenz
Theresa.Egert-Lorenz@gmx.de

Cover design by:
jts
Phoenix AZ

Order this book online at www.trafford.com
or email orders@trafford.com

Most Trafford titles are also available at major online book retailers.

Printed in Victoria, BC, Canada.

ISBN: 978-1-4251-4010-6 (sc)
ISBN: 978-1-4251-4011-3 (eb)

Our mission is to efficiently provide the world's finest, most comprehensive book publishing service, enabling every author to experience success. To find out how to publish your book, your way, and have it available worldwide, visit us online at www.trafford.com

Trafford rev. 1/26/10

 www.trafford.com

North America & international
toll-free: 1 888 232 4444 (USA & Canada)
phone: 250 383 6864 ♦ fax: 812 355 4082

CONTENTS

PROLOGUE

FUTURE GENERATIONS: This is letter two [book] of the series NO LEFT TURN. It is dedicated to our children, their children, and the generations to follow. You may ask why we bother to do this? In addition to sharing with you the lessons we learned through experience, you know - trial and error, we feel a strong responsibility to think about things beyond our lifetime, beyond our children's lifetime and beyond their children's lifetime. We truly believe that we have both the right and the obligation because the sum of the horrors and violence of today's world outweighs the lesser amount of relative good that occurs. Yes, we do want to be two of the *good guys and good gals!* And, we want each of you to join us.

The Revolutionary War, setting the stage for the creation of the U. S. A., has evolved into a series of successive phases. Beginning circa 1860s, Lincoln decided to war with the Southern states. They only desired to exercise self-determination and create their own country and government. As part of the war effort, Lincoln deliberately violated the Constitution. His death ironically ended the Supreme Court taking final action. What did the Supreme Court say? We talk with an expert:

Professor David Cole, Georgetown University Law Center, noted in the Nation magazine that the very name, USA PATRIOT Act, "implies that those who question its sweeping new powers of surveillance, detention and prosecution are traitors." In the U. S. Supreme Court's decision in Ex Parte Milligan, [771 US 2 (1866)] the court ruled that President Abraham Lincoln violated the

Constitution when he suspended the writ of habeas corpus, subjecting many dissenters to military tribunals while civilian courts were operating normally. The court said, "the Constitution of the United States is a law for rulers and people, equally in war and in peace, and covers with the shield of its protection all classes of men, at all times, and under all circumstances." Further the court said, "The court also recognized that this nation "has no right to expect that it will always have wise and human rulers, sincerely attached to the principles of the Constitution.""

We must ask our self whether today we have *"wise and human rulers"?* In view of the remarks made by President Bush that *"the Constitution is just a piece of paper"*, it appears the answer is no. In view of the fact, often noted by the press, that government enjoys a rating at the level of used car salesmen, it seems we must now decide for our self what happens next and what do we do? Is it time to go? If so, where? This begins a counter-revolutionary action that results today in our government having been taken over by elite groups of radicals. We can expect from this time on that those opposing this new form of our government will be labeled *"revolutionaries"*. We believe that in fact we are the successors to the revolutionary war patriots – yet others will call us counter-counter-revolutionaries. But so be it if that is a part of the price to regaining our freedom.

For the purpose of clarity we present the following analogy cast within the judicial court system. Imagine God looking down from above with a great view of the courtroom. Here is the cast of characters: The judge is played by the *Constitution,* the attorneys for plaintive and defendant are the *Radical Right and Left Ideologies,* the jury box consists of *middle class Americans,* and the observers are the elite power brokers, lobbyists and special interests. The Constitution [judge] and the ideologies [attorneys'] have been in chamber cleaning up a few technical matters. The Constitution [judge] states, *"We'll begin with opening statements [think of the wannabe candidates practicing their rhetoric early for the 2008 presidential sweepstakes], and I need to caution you [the people] that these are not statements of fact but rather statements about what each ideology thinks the facts are and what they will endeavor to prove during the course of the trial. These statements [rhetoric and spin]* <u>*are not*</u> *to be considered by you [the people] to contain evidence. All of that comes later on. So listen closely but keep an*

open [critical] mind because a lot is still coming down the pike."
The trial begins with the prosecution and you can select either
ideology for that position with the other ideology being the
defendant. The lead prosecutor stands and moves to the
lectern. He nods to the jury [you and us], identifies himself and
his case [ideology] and the circus begins. The witnesses are
called in turn and sworn in to an oath promising to speak the
truth, the whole truth and nothing but the truth, so help them
God. God looking at this circus likely labels this as *"The
Garden of Earthly Delights"* and the home of the seven deadly
sins. Notice the utter darkness of evil, darker even than the
darkest moonless night, but then it is always the darkest and
coldest before the light of a new day.

SURVIVAL is the how and, therefore, the key to the series
NO LEFT TURN. While the prospects of our government
returning to honesty, integrity and behaving according to the
Constitution, is nil to none, there is a silver lining. We will
explore how the overblown egos, insatiable greed, lust for even
more power, and zealous efforts to promote ascendancy, by our
so called leaders, to achieve their vision for America, to
promote their views on the socialism to fascism spectrum, and
to use the levers of government to achieve these ridiculous,
even evil, goals. People have always wanted to trust and have
confidence in their leaders as a natural consequence of newly
found independence. Our leaders have squandered what trust
and faith people once felt toward them. Listening to them is
like answering the phone and experiencing the disgusting
telemarketing annoyances, or watching a TV commercial from
ambulance chasing attorneys. Having been sold out by our
leaders to the extent and nature that they fostered upon us is a
living hell. It is the people that carry the burden of
government's unworthy and dishonest goals. Some of us, in
time, will arrive in hell, but there is no justification for
government to deliberately make living our lives on earth a
living hell so that they can have their utopian dream.

Throughout our history, with the exception of the two wars
with Great Britain, most other violent confrontations were
avoidable. During our darkest time, when we needed
statesmen - not political hacks, we found America wanting.
Instead of statesmanship solving our problems, our great
leaders, on their own, substituted their opinions. Their
opinions became the basis of their purpose, and their purpose

was molded by their sense of what is best for them. Thus was born the evil of *"legacy"* that to this day haunts us and taunts us, causing us to pay a high price, an unnecessary high price. Is it any wonder that today we find but 14% of *'the people'* expressing confidence in our Congress and 27% in our president?

In **SURVIVAL** we delve deeply into how to turn political corruption and malfeasance to our benefit and how to profit from that knowledge. We know from experience that politicians are beyond redemption. We know from physics, *"for every force there is an equal and opposite force."* It is that *blood-letting* corruption that we will tap into. Corruption lives on the feasting that occurs in creating **winners and losers** by government, business and society. We can follow this unconstitutional behavior [money-payoffs] in both directions, from where it comes, who acts as intermediary, to who benefits, and its final repository. The corrupt leaders are clearly visible as they are the self appointed *"intermediaries or agents"* that we will label ***"the corruptors"***. They are the ones identified in **BETRAYERS** as those who cheated the people by usurping the intent of the Constitution and betraying the faith and trust of the people. It is those corrupt acts that reveal a gold mine to those with the knowledge to recognize the truth. What are these truths?

Governmental corruption at the highest level is a continuous occurrence. The **corruptors** at this high level control and manipulate the people and their businesses through laws, rules and regulation. They skim off the top, money and power, for their use. They rule like Royalty, enjoying the spoils of their efforts. We also know who the losers are.

Businesses participate in corporate corruption, for example – the looting of Enron and MCI – back dating options awarded top executives by the companies they manage, monster pay and retirement packages – luxurious working and living conditions – with the *left-over* trickling down to workers and consumers.

The *'People'* have brought back the **'gotcha'** society. They emulate business and government as they try to cheat other people, businesses, government, and ultimately end up cheating themselves. The betrayers have destroyed and continue to destroy our American culture. It is evidenced in the uncivil behavior that we see around this sick attitude, driving us toward social, economic and political *uncivil war*. Uncivil warfare between society, business and government is clearly **not** a zero sum war. In the end, **"we all"** are the losers. **Survival** will tell you how to actually survive and profit from these circumstances and provide you with a Principality to wait out this period of insanity. How?

> Keep your mouth shut
> Gas and sales tax anomalies
> Oppressive labor management regulation
> Free labor vs. Wage labor
> Home schooling vs. Government propaganda
> Keep your mouth shut
> Owning real estate vs. renting
> Discipline vs. the social habit to shop until you drop
> Buy low and sell high vs. buy high and sell low, aka keeping up with the Joneses
> Voting for individualism vs. voting for the lesser of two evils
> Making your own decision vs. buying into the government line
> Keep your mouth shut
> Understanding both sides of an issue vs. going with the herd mentality
> Private business vs. public business
> Non-employer vs. Employer business - identify camouflaged lies and other deceptions
> Never act as dumb as government thinks you are
> Keep your mouth shut
> Keep your mouth shut and look, listen, think and act!

SURVIVAL

WELCOME BACK FUTURE GENERATIONS: Survival of individuals and families will be determined more by the quality of their survival plan and their courage than by the amount of resources they have accumulated. It is not difficult to imagine an event, either domestic or foreign, in which a survival plan is everything. Most recently are 9/11, Katrina and Rita. Survival rates for those events were determined almost exclusively by the planning to deal with such catastrophe, not the number and volume of available resources. True, after one survives, then those resources become vital. If one does not survive then the resources become part of the decedents' estate. Survival is therefore paramount.

We never make rules for others, only ourselves. We try to play by the rules we impose upon our selves and in doing so we make the effort to minimize the harm that often accompanies the rules passed down to us. We stay alert to recognize each crisis by knowing our history. We know that the do-gooders will seize all opportunities to further impose regulations upon us and lead with large doses of compulsion, propaganda and damn the peoples' feelings. Yet, each crises carries with it a *silver lining* and it is this opportunity that we desire to recognize and utilize.

FUTURE GENERATIONS: Survival is the most important book in the "NO LEFT TURN" series. We make the point that individualism is most significant in our lives and that the family is the cornerstone of our society. Government is that which must be guarded against and protected from. The human nature driving the political view of government is that, if we already have more evil government than necessary – our greed demands that we have more.

MINI-REVIEW OF "BETRAYERS"

1] The world is an *illusion,* presented courtesy of government, media, politicians, political and special interest, schools, church, et al.

2] One evil of this illusion is the creation of an addictive co-dependent relationship between people and their government.

3] America began its empire building with the Mexican War and continued it through the Civil War and into the 1898 war with Spain. This early empire building had as its purpose land expansion and retainment.

4] Woodrow Wilson changed the nature of empire expansion by entering WWI on the side of the Allies. He preempted an armistice that would have come about naturally through combatant exhaustion and prolonged stalemate. He thus changed the purpose of empire from land expansion to the expansion of influence and power with global as the ultimate sphere. His slogan *"make the world safe for democracy"* was a farce and as such failed, done in by the Paris Treaty of 1919. It is a part of the *illusion,* a myth then and a myth today.

5] Bad envy is taught to the public through the propaganda emanating from the various voices of government and media and is still force-fed in public schools to this day. The primary vehicle for this propaganda is dominant ideology with emphasis on sub issues such as class warfare, rich versus poor, and necessity of huge welfare programs to correct the mismanagement of government in not permitting people to act as free people.

6] Public education, being nationalized circa 1850 and socialized in 1976, doomed education as we seniors knew it. There is no free discussion or level playing fields as all sides of issues are not included in public school curricula. This denies children the opportunity to know, discuss, compare and understand these issues as the truth normally lies somewhere between them.

7] Government compulsion immediately emerged following the creation of our government. This compulsion is intended to introduce fear to coerce people to obey laws made by man for man, and thus are inconsistent with natural law.

8] Government, all branches, is progressively waging war on defining the intent of the Constitution and in so doing is stealing from the people. The freedoms outlined in the Constitution speak directly to government and tells government what it *shall never do*. In essence, the Constitution is driven into *exile* and its voice gagged and muted.

9] People have recourse, when they feel their government is violating the Constitution, to change that form of government by creating a new form of government. Intentional violation by government of the Constitution is defined as treasonous. There is not yet a majority support for this as people remain addicted to *government dole*.

10] Two major parties have become so involved in running the daily lives of the people that they can now be labeled as the *"Mommy"* and *"Daddy"* party. People cling to these political parties like a child clings to a security blanket.

11] Government statistics, produced to justify reasons for making decisions, lack credibility and honesty as expressed by both economists and people. For decades successive administrations have watered down the data to create the illusion of *"don't worry, everything is fine"*. Will there be a day of reckoning? Likely. When today's inflation and unemployment rates were refigured using the formulas from the 70's, inflation was 8 to 10% and unemployment closer to 10 to 12%. What will be the final result?

12] During Greenspan's 18-year run as chairman of the Federal Reserve, the domestic purchasing power of the dollar fell 50% - by the end of this decade it likely will fall another 25% or more. Think of your savings, IRA's and 401-k's and factor this in when arriving at the amount of money you will need to retire comfortably.

13] Waste, fraud and abuse in government are all illegal and immoral. Congress in making laws that tend to favor one group over another, execute sweetheart contracts, accept bribes from lobbyists and flaunt the Constitution, saying that it is just a piece of paper. This behavior permits us to label the federal government as the largest, meanest and most dangerous *"organized crime family"*.

14] Education, justice, taxes, spending, to name a few, are all far too important to entrust to leaders of government as their lust for personal aggrandizement, placed ahead of caring for the people and the country, is evil and another form of treasonous behavior in regards to the sanctity of our Constitution.

15] Broad sense tells us, wage labor is truly a form of slave labor. We have set our thoughts out in a later section.

Politicians seldom rise to the satiation point of their lustful desires through a free competitive process. The explanation is that the political deck of cards is stacked against free enterprise process as the route to political governance. Successful politicians reach the apex of corruptibility when they master the art of illusion and deception of sociopathic and psychopathic behavior. History shows that over centuries Empires first become corrupt and then decay and rot from the inside until they collapse. Sometimes they fall with but a whimper, but normally they fall with a loud bang, heard round the world, and then they are history. How ours will end we do not know. When it will end we also do not know. Regardless of the manner of the fall, the survivors will be those who planned well: that is, they have a detailed survival plan. For survivor's we present "Enlightenment".

ENLIGHTENMENT

FUTURE GENERATIONS: To better prepare for this section we reprint excerpts of Washington's farewell address to set this stage of learning.

GEORGE WASHINGTON, September 19, 1796

"Though, in reviewing the incidents of my Administration, I am unconscious of intentional error - I am nevertheless too

sensible of my defects not to think it probable that I may have committed many errors. Whatever they may be I fervently beseech the Almighty to avert or mitigate the evils to which they may tend. I shall also carry with me the hope that my country will never cease to view them with indulgence; and that after forty-five years of my life dedicated to its service, with an upright zeal, the faults of incompetent abilities will be consigned to oblivion, as myself must soon be to the mansions of rest.

Relying on its kindness in this as in other things, and actuated by that fervent love towards it, which is so natural to a man, who views in it the native soil of himself and his progenitors for several generations; I anticipate with pleasing expectation that retreat, in which I promise myself to realize, without alloy, the sweet enjoyment of partaking, in the midst of my fellow-citizens, the benign influence of good laws under a free government, the ever favorite object of my heart, and the happy reward, as I trust, of our mutual cares, labours, and dangers."

SLAVE is a common word but often misunderstood. In our American Heritage Dictionary, we find: 1. One bound in servitude to a person or household as an instrument of labor; 2. One who is submissive or subject to a specified person or influence; 3. One whose condition is likened to that of slavery.

1. Yesteryear: During the period of slavery in which blacks were brought to America to primarily work the plantations they were bound to the wealthy Southerners who owned these plantations. *This year:* Workers are bound to employers and government. Yes there are many exceptions to this statement, but in general we do see a similarity.

2. Yesteryear: The early slave was submissive and subject specifically to the person who owned him/her and the influence of the US government in recognizing slavery as legal. *This year:* The worker is submissive to a supervisor or employer and is subject to the US government in matters of wages, benefits, safety and other conditions.

3. The worker is also likened to the slave in the following areas. Just as the slave owner provided healthcare, education, housing, food, clothing and other necessities these functions have been usurped by government(s) and are administered

partly through businesses as employers of these worker-slaves. The plantation owner providing for the slave was inadequate. The employer and government providing for the worker are also inadequate.

We do from time to time find ourselves enslaved to our emotions and addictions. This type of slavery is probably the most painful and lasting. Many black slaves of years past developed emotional bitterness and hatred toward their masters and all white people, while simultaneously whites developed emotional bias and discrimination toward blacks and their culture. Today it is not so much a black / white circumstance. The emotional slavery today is the addiction to government, their rhetoric, their broken promises and failure to exact from them responsibility even for their oath of office. This emotional slavery will be with us forever or until the masters have been tamed by the slaves.

ASCENDANCY
[Rise Above All Others]

With the advantage of hindsight, a rather clear picture emerges of the substance of American ascendancy. We are not certain of the moment when it began, but it seems very probable that it emerged at about the time of George Washington's death. In his farewell address, above, he warned of avoiding the silliness that held the European attention.

The Federalists clamored for a stronger central government while the Agrarians took a *live and let live* attitude. It is thus anticipated that within each group there were those visualizing America ascending to the pinnacle of power and prestige among all nations of the world. To those who visualized such, it seems logical that at every opportunity an attempt to seize and capitalize on the moments would be in order. When we look into that crystal ball and view past events, we can better understand the "WHY" of what happened.

The Revolutionary War and the War of 1812 were both waged against Great Britain, first to gain independence and then to defend it. This was followed by the war with Mexico, which was clearly a *land grab.* This war was a clear attack on peoples' right to *self-determination* that today our government so proudly claims as a right for others but not for us.

In 1861 the Southern states, later to be named the *Confederacy*, exercised what they believed to be their just rights of *self-determination*. As we all know, at that point the North declared war on the South and coined the battle cry *save the Union*. In reality it was little more than a poorly disguised power grab by Washington to continue ascendancy as their private goal. What is in doubt is whether this was a socialist or a fascist war, or maybe neither. We say *private goal* as there is absolutely no documentation to conclude otherwise or that the people approved. The wars that followed can best be described as *wars-of-opportunity* in support of ascendancy.

Jefferson's presidential victory over Hamilton may have been the signal for those individuals of power – wealth – opportunity and driven by *out-of-this-world* egos and legacies to forge alliances that ultimately would be passed down through successive generations. It is not of your usual conspiracy theories but actually a normal and logical outgrowth of the driving force of certain types of individuals under a selected set of circumstances. At their worst, these individuals were misguided in their belief that they were patriots and it was their given right and responsibility to compete for ascendancy in the political, economic and social spheres of mankind; and the cost was justified by the ends. We were unable to find any evidence that a referendum of the people or even an amendment was considered, so we must believe that the anti-Constitutionalists of the period just took it upon themselves to do it.

These so-called patriotic feelings drove them to actively promote ascendancy, without regard for *live and let live*. That the majority of the people did not sanction ascendancy and would never sanction such actions was never in question or doubt. For the illusion of Empire to be attained, means it had to find a way to bypass or go around the people by denying them knowledge of these actions. This meant that the people must be made to believe – to believe that supporting such actions – was something other than what was actually planned. This deception found fertile ground in the idea of illusion and co-dependency, in which the people *would not* see truth and would willingly give back their Constitutional rights and freedoms in exchange for false promises.

We know that for man to act in a manner of beguilement, he must possess the emotional belief that *good outweighs bad*. This is the typical process known to mankind of first deceiving oneself into believing that wrong is right, and then it is possible to lie in the most convincing of manners – not recognizing the lie that they tell. This attitude is reinforced by people of authority and respect telling them that they are the chosen to lead the people – that they know better than the masses of what is good, for we of the masses are considered incompetent to do what is best for ourselves. To look for the evidence of such misrepresentation, look no further than Harvard, Yale, Princeton, Stanford, and in England, Oxford and Cambridge to name a few of the worst.

Today's politics of lies and deception, as we daily view it, is the answer to the earlier question of "HOW". You can lead a lemming to water but you cannot keep it from marching headlong into it and drowning.

The remaining wars were only *"wars of opportunity"* in support of this *thing* known as ascendancy, but also known today as *super-power* or worse yet, *Empire*. If these men and women of misguided power and motivation had not existed, we can only guess at what circumstances we would all be living in. But we can understand the *cost* of ascendancy in terms of human, financial and opportunity costs. If this deception began as we assumed, then we place the human cost at hundreds of millions of lives lost or denied their rights and opportunities – the financial cost well in excess of tens of trillions of dollars – and opportunity cost well beyond five trillion dollars. And, worst of all, there is no indication this pattern of dilemma has run its course. The end will be the same death throes as for all preceding Empires.

EVIL OF ENVY

Struggling with ENVY is one historical pinnacle of morality that transcends all ideologies – the Tenth Commandment. *"Thou shalt not covet thy neighbor's house, thy neighbor's wife, nor his manservant, nor his maidservant, nor his ox, nor his ass, nor anything that is thy neighbor's."* This moral demand not to envy is the key to peace and prosperity for any people, culture or nation. The future of any civilization depends on finding and applying an antidote to the corrosive social poisons of envy and envy appeasement. Those leaders who find their power through use of and appeal to envy and its appeasement, destroy our culture, morality and drive our politics downward into sewers of disasters, **must** be removed. It is this that addicts people belonging to the co-dependency system.

EXAMPLES OF HOW DECEIT AND DECEPTION WARP REASON

DECEIT with a capital consequence. Government, actually the Labor department, has so confused and distorted the Consumer Price Index [CPI] that everyone from Joe Six-pack to Harvard MBA's step lightly for fear of repercussion from telling the truth. In reality we have three CPI indexes. 1] *Core* index **excludes** food and energy. 2] *Headline* index **includes** food and energy. This index is used to adjust government retiree pensions, etc. and, 3] *Real* rate is what you look at each time you open your monthly utility or credit card statements, or when you go shopping at the mall. Review: the *core rate* is used to make government appear efficient. The *headline rate* is used to adjust cost of living increases. The *real rate* is what *Joe Six-pack* pays at the check out.

For example: January 2006 rates came in as follows; *core rate +0.30%, headline rate +0.70%, the real rate,* the one you pay, is between *+0.80% to +1.25%* depending upon the economist you listen to.

We have wondered for some time how to describe where the radical Left is actually heading. To label their goal *'communism'* is inadequate and ripe for argument. Yet, the Left aided in part by the Right is, we believe, moving to someplace far removed from the original intent of the Constitution, democracy, freedom/liberty and right to property. The federal government and the states, the other 50 entities, are moving toward all powerful political regime(s). When the above has been achieved, we will have parts of communism and fascism, parts of democracy, parts of totalitarianism, and parts of tyranny. At a later date, much later, a label will be coined to define this monster. For the present we are left with this definition. We have an evil government and it is attempting to operate under another name. Sometimes it is known as radical socialism and at other times radical fascism. It passes the levers of power back and forth, somewhat like a ping-pong game.

FUTURE GENERATIONS: We pause here to share with you the opinions of others relative to this matter.

Saturday, February 25, 2006: Second amendment rights. The Wyoming Tribune Eagle carried a front-page lead article regarding efforts to eliminate the need for special permits to carry concealed weapons. If this bill becomes law then anyone can pack concealed heat [their phrase]. We quote directly from the article posted by Ben Neary, Associated Press, one succinct paragraph that shares with us the views of others. *"It means people in Wyoming can exercise an unalienable right,"* said bill sponsor Rep. Becket Hinckley, R-Cheyenne. *"An unalienable right to protect yourselves from the bad guys. And, although it may seem a little outdated, an unalienable right to protect yourselves from a government that a lot of people in Wyoming don't trust."*

Monday, March 13, 2006, USA Today: COST-EFFECTIVE 'OUTSOURCING' GROWS. The use of independent contractors to handle customer service calls from their homes is soaring as companies look to cut costs – and more employees seek jobs that allow them to work remotely. It is estimated that today [2006] 112,000 are working from their homes and that by 2010 that number will be about 328,342. [Editor comment: Will you be one of them?]

Monday, March 13, 2006. USA Today: SURVEY FINDS MORE INFORMATION KEPT FROM PUBLIC. Local, State and federal government agencies are keeping more information secret from the public, making it harder for citizens to keep tabs on what elected officials and bureaucrats are doing, an investigation by the Associated Press shows. [Editor comment: Does this also mean the end of the *"Freedom of Information Act"?* Is this a harbinger of what is in store for us in the future, say globalization?]

FEBRUARY 2006: Sandra Day O'Connor, former supreme-court justice, retired recently. She saw fit to leave, with the public a warning about attacks on courts for alleged liberal bias. She said that the US is in danger of edging towards dictatorship [a ruler having absolute authority and jurisdiction over the government of a state, especially one that is considered tyrannical or oppressive] by contributing to a climate of violence against judges and endanger the freedoms of all Americans.

MARCH 2006: Supreme Court justice Scalia offered the thought that decisions of a moral nature are probably best made by the people, not the courts.

POSTMODERNISM. From the 1976 edition of The American Heritage Dictionary of the English Language, we look at what postmodernism has done to the word *freedom*.

FREEDOM 1. *The condition of being free of restraints. 2. Liberty of the person from slavery, oppression, or incarceration. 3. a. Political independence. 3. b. Possession of civil rights, immunity from the arbitrary exercise of authority. 4. Exemption from unpleasant or onerous conditions. 5. The capacity to exercise choice: free will. 6. Facility, as of motion. 7. Originality of style or conception. 8. Frankness. 9. a. Boldness; impertinence. 9. b. An instance of improper boldness, a liberty. 10. Unrestricted use or access. 11. The right of enjoying all of the privileges of membership or citizenship.*

When these definitions are compared to the current circumstances that Americans are forced to live under, imposed upon them by their government, then it really is not possible to say that one is free. As each freedom is taken from us, it is done with great explanation as to its need for *National Security* or *fighting terrorism*, and served up with the connotation that if one is unwilling to acknowledge National Security or fighting terrorism as national goals then that person is not a patriot. This, of course, takes us back to labeling, claims making and constructionism. For government and/or its apologists and supporters to label one a traitor for questioning an act of the government that clearly takes away not only freedom, but also privacy in violation of the Constitution and by coercion attempts to shut one up, is impractical and illegal. Government having taken our fourth amendment rights from us only had to pass an amendment to repeal the fourth amendment. Of course, that would risk the lie being seen in the light of day. Incidentally, when I entered *freedom* into the web and asked for the definition, I received a definition that is word for word as my 1976 dictionary. As our minds wandered it caused us to look up *semantic* that produced the definition, pertaining to meaning, especially meaning in language. So is that the correct name of the game we are forced to play?

Be advised that not all is lost. In actuality, knowledge of the threat and assets available to us is enough to carry the day. So, with excitement, we delve into the threats that stand in our way.

SURVIVAL: THREATS AGAINST

FUTURE GENERATIONS: We go into detail regarding *"construction of government"* for this is how we got to where we find our selves in 2006-2007.

CONSTRUCTION OF GOVERNMENT

We discussed this issue in BETRAYERS, but it is so important we feel that it should be reviewed here. In this section the ideas and thoughts presented will be woven into a simple concept. Text and images have become the medium that has the greatest influence on society. The human senses are targeted daily through all means of information and disinformation dissemination. As a text is read and studied, it is not really possible to understand the mind and reality of the writer to the full extent. The same is true of this text. You cannot understand our minds and our perception of reality unless you follow up with, first, reading the text, second, discussing it in detail with us, and finally, how we have successfully deconstructed what the bourgeoisie created with their influence on and of the People's Government.

Social sciences and opinions have become the arbiter of public truth. We don't appeal to religious beliefs any more and we don't appeal to tradition. When the time comes to make policy, we turn to science. We thus tend to see science as a sacrosanct area. It has only been since the middle of the 20th century that sociologists have felt comfortable in deconstructing the scientific enterprise.

We live in a social setting where we are constantly negotiating the nature of truth, where claims and counterclaims are made in the public forum, and whereby the use of media and information allows us to think about and promote our own ideas of right and wrong. We are all moral entrepreneurs as we promote our own ideas of deviance and non-deviance through our actions, thoughts, and speech. We communicate to others what we think is deviant and what we think is ok. How society accepts this, is determined by the relative labeling and claims making within the power structures of society. Some people and some groups have managed to put themselves into positions where their views on what is deviant are accepted. We must always question definitions of deviance. We must always deconstruct these questions, never let a question just sit. The most important job that each of us has as a member of society and as a social being, around questions of deviance, is to ask the question, what is deviant? Why is it deviant? Whose interests are being preserved by the maintenance of these ideas?

Talking about interests leads us into asking the question, *"can we put names and faces to the otherwise invisible government and people?"* Sure we can, if only we give the matter serious thought. The faces of those who control government are the wealthy, those already powerful, those whose lust for greater power over others is so great it cannot be denied, those who feel compelled to say and do that which will guarantee them a place in the history books or even their face on a mountain. They are elected politicians [in all three branches of government], senior bureaucrats, military leaders, old New England Wealth and the new wealth in the entire country. They are known to all of us as the elite.

Probably the best example of constructionism is *Ascendancy* as outlined above. It started slowly, but by the beginning of the 20th century it had been fully embraced by the Right and Left. This effort remained unknown to the general public coming to light only at the end of the 20th and beginning of the 21st century. The goal of those who believed in the theory of *Ascendancy* clearly is best defined as *'to gain political power'*. This is a very sophisticated process and first required gaining the attention and support of the media. This was the labeling process and it includes those oldies but goodies such as *'make the world safe for democracy'* and *'spread democracy throughout the world.'* Those slogans are pure bull-crap!

This accomplishment was joined by *claims making* and making common-cause with the population. The masses would provide the funding [taxes] and the human assets [military personnel] who would eagerly come forth to fight and die for *'ascendancy'*. Regrettably, they never understood the true nature of the purpose as it was successfully shrouded in *illusion*. With the people bound together with leaders that lived primarily for *ascendancy,* it was easy to lead them from one war into another and yet another. The lesson here is that democracies really are not what they profess to be. Democracies seldom produce statesmen, but always produce men of greed and envy. Democracies can become evil and seek ends that are inconsistent with Constitutions and the peoples true beliefs. But the people like what they hear and follow like sheep. The end is yet to be played out.

The forthcoming 2008 presidential election will offer two candidates, one promoting socialism and the other fascism, but nowhere to be seen or heard is anyone running to defend our freedoms and our Constitution. What are we to do? We can consider boycotting the election, like throwing a party and no one comes, or how about a real honest-to-goodness *wake,* as we bury Freedom and liberty. Maybe that will get their attention. We can, by the millions, organize and demonstrate first in front of our state capitals and then with tens of millions arrive in the sewer we call DC and make our demands upon government of what we desire. For specifics on these demands, see a modern day Declaration and proposed 28th amendment set forth at the end of this book.

FUTURE GENERATIONS: We have told you that we are devoted to studying the relationship of the people with your government. We defined this relationship as an addictive co-dependency system. We have also told you that our writings are initiatives for the individual to gain freedom and liberty. We, therefore, must understand what freedom is. The next step is to make demands upon our government and politicians and be prepared to shed our blood if necessary. We do not believe that you, our children, grand children, great grand children, brothers and sisters, neighbors and friends will follow any government order to fire upon us, to demagogue us to save your skin but lose your soul. We believe and pray that you will see what we see and fulfill the promises that we failed, and by that failure, failed you.

POWER OVER PEOPLE

FUTURE GENERATIONS: HOW AN ILLUSIONARY IDEA GETS INTO ONES HEAD: The first to get into Robert's head was from his father. When he was young and still in public school, his dad was a staunch free trader and self-responsibility advocate. That part of his dad's lessons stayed with Robert. In the 1930s, FDR began to promote the American Socialist Party ideology. His dad at first resisted, not trusting FDR, as a great many did not in those days. His dad ultimately succumbed and changed. By the time of his death, he was a full-fledged liberal socialist, a victim of co-dependency. Initially Robert bought into it, but quickly questioned it and then found by his own research that his dad was very wrong.

POWER OVER PEOPLE

How do others get into our heads? This story is to share with you how remarkable a man FDR was and how he could make you believe something that you knew was not true but you bought into it regardless. He spoke to people who were fearful and scared for their future. For many people of that era, he was the most magnetic man they ever listened to. The apparent wisdom and extent of his knowledge came across as impressive, and as for plausibility, he had no equal. He spoke of many so-called facts and truths that people could not deny. They could not or did not seek their own counsel to judge his authenticity. FDR talked and smiled – talked and smiled till people no longer were sure of what they held as truth or believed. It came to the point that people could not see the truth for all the obfuscation of the perpetually repeated ideology. It wasn't that they were convinced against their own beliefs as much as having been persuaded to believe an illusion. They stopped thinking and let FDR do their thinking for them. Ultimately, having bought FDR's ideology, people would see truth through FDR's eyes as so many now were, so to speak, reading from his page. Never had one man made believers out of people who in their hearts new better. Today, presidential historians write about FDR with glowing praise as if he walked on water. Just last week a presidential historian, on TV, referenced FDR's speech, *"all we have to fear is fear itself."* The attribution laid the authorship of that sound bite to FDR – but the truth is that FDR borrowed it from an earlier speech by another - and to make it even worse, I bet that the presidential historian knew that. Information is skewed for they have no access to the feelings of the people who lived through those years, only the writings of those before them that also were skewed.

CHILDREN – WHO TEACHES THEM VALUES?

A child's formative years begin at birth and begin to max out at about the 7th or 8th grade. Their teenage high school years are now formed, and the behavior in their later teens will reflect what they learned during those formative years.

Many parents believe that it is fine to leave their children with day care and the schools for them to imprint **their** values on children's minds. If as a parent, you were concerned about who the people are that have ultimate control over how the schools are run, what they are expected to learn, how they are instructed to manage your child's education and you found that background checks revealed the following rap sheets about them, would you be surprised? This group is comprised of 535 men and women who have convinced us they are the best for the position of representing us in DC. Did we make a mistake?

Spousal abuse – 36
Fraud arrests – 7
Bad checks – 19
Two or more business bankruptcies – 117
Hard time for assault – 3
Bad credit, can't get a credit card – 71

Arrested on drug related charges – 14
Arrests for shoplifting – 8
Currently defendant in lawsuit - 21
DUI's – 84

Would you engage an organization whose members' life style and personal conduct are as revealed above, for managing and controlling your children's minds, during their formative years? Do you see defiance as a legitimate subject to be taught in our schools or on school grounds?

For many, looking toward the future is like looking into a tunnel where there is no light at the end. Politicians continue to make official statements that omit pertinent facts that might tend to reflect adversely upon their performance, and present other information clearly designed to enhance their own contributions to the accomplishment of responsibilities. In other words – they are lying.

FUTURE GENERATIONS: If faced with having to work into your 70's, then, considering the stresses associated with your job, it makes perfect sense that you take the initiative and decide for yourself what you want to do. The 21st century will favor the person with knowledge, who selects a manner of taking income that provides wealth, and in turn, is the means to gain significantly greater freedom and liberty than previously enjoyed. That is precisely what we talk about and are prepared to teach to those who want out of the grind, and have the determination and discipline to manage their own lives.

WHO WILL ASK THE TOUGH QUESTIONS?

NO LEFT TURN questions much of what has been written about the events that transpired since ratification of the Constitution, and is presented by leaders and government to the people as the dominant ideology of our time. Our sole purpose was to uncover the truth of the nature of the relationship between *we-the-people* and our federal government, who is supreme and who is to fear whom. We do not intend to judge the ENDS that have driven the MEANS of government action, as there is insufficient documentation available. Many documents are missing, destroyed, revised or sealed.

Rather, our concern is to find the truth as to how America, founded as a Republic, and recognizing individuals and families as its strength, could, as we enter the 21st century, be best described as a socialist democracy – with periods of fascism - realizing that politically minded groups and varied special interests have displaced the individual and the family. These groups and interests appear to be vacuous entities, producing not a cohesive strength but a Balkanization between groups and interests that government skillfully uses to drain the strength of American families through misuse of its resources and the institutionalizing of *waste-fraud-abuse* as a perpetual way of life for government operation.

The door to free labor does not open simply by knocking. You must, in fact, break down the door as an obstacle to your intent. What is your intent? To seize those Constitutional rights held out to you from the creator – to grasp and hold for your life those two jewels of the Constitution – freedom and liberty. To do this, you must first inventory your assets and skills.

And finally, the mind provides each of us with an *override* for those behaviors that many refer to as addictions or weaknesses. As humans we are susceptible to being tempted by wrong, when we know it for what it is. It is the mind's *override* that allows people to follow the dictates of a conscience.

DEMOGRAPHICS

FUTURE GENERATIONS: Definition: Study of the characteristics of human populations such as size, growth, density, distribution and vital statistics.

SIZE: Today's world population is six billion plus people and growing.

GROWTH: The population of the world continues to grow at accelerating speed. In America, the birth rate is at replacement level and increases in the total population are from immigrants. American rate of population growth is not alarming if drawn from overpopulated countries. In countries that offer free trade and free enterprise we find that such items as money and freedom tend to go to those places that offer the best return on their desires. In those countries it is documented that when anything is produced in excess that the value of each item decreases. What is yet to be discovered is how the world will handle the continued large increase in human population. The neglect of the world regarding mass murders of civilians, especially in the LD, less developed countries, does not appear to be encouraging for the future attitude of excess populations.

DENSITY: A large number of countries with very high birth rates also have large populations that create increases in the population density. Countries like India, Indonesia and many third world countries, particularly Africa, continue to grow at birth rates of 6 – 7 children per woman. The replacement rate is 2.5 children per woman.

DISTRIBUTION: During the 20th century, America's population migration reversed the trend of originally settling in rural areas and found people leaving the farm and going to the cities for jobs. The next wave of migration was to the suburbs to escape crime and density in the cities. Then the convenience of the interstate highway system inspired industries to also move to the suburbs. The current wave is away from the cities and suburbs and back to the rural and less populated areas. Those that can afford it choose areas that are recreational and resort in nature.

VITAL STATISTICS: Many governments, including America, are faced with the great challenge of the graying of the population. Seventeen percent of Americans are presently over 60; by 2020, 25% will be. In Germany, the proportion over 60 will rise to 30% from 22%. In Japan, it will go to 31% from 20%. And the problem will get worse as time passes.

Governments have a mind-boggling un-funded pension liability. The OEC (Organization for Economic Cooperation) reports that the shortfall in America amounts to 43% of the value of the economy's annual output (GDP). In Germany, it is 160%; in Japan, it is 200%; in Canada, 250%.

Alan Auerbach, economist, University of California, argues that if current spending trends continue, "*the tax burden would be very close to absorbing almost all of the lifetime income of individuals.*"

DEMOGRAPHICS ARE A TIME BOMB WAITING TO GO OFF! The question facing the Congress and the Administration is not whether spending and taxes should be reduced, but how and when. If spending is not brought under control by government, the market will eventually force a reduction. This will occur when government needs to borrow more money than investors believe is wise, then refuse to buy the government bonds.

To reduce the percentage of GDP required to fund spending, the economy must be growing. This will mean a reduction in taxes to provide incentives for entrepreneurs to make the effort to create wealth as opposed to protecting wealth from confiscation by government.

Population growths are like tidal waves, they just keep coming, and will eventually become tsunamis. Unless humanity makes some wise changes, we all might be swept aside by this human tidal wave.

FUTURE GENERATIONS: The above is a time bomb in the making. Developed countries are aging and third world countries have a population explosion. Going forward from this point the future of America will be bright and for some time appear unlimited in its growth. Many of our friends will unfortunately be left behind. But the countries budget time bomb is ticking. We need preparation, planning, skill development, confidence and alertness to deal with the challenge this presents to conduct a safe and peaceful life.

Peeking into our draft of the next book we see that globalization will indeed be kind to the elite of all countries producing for them record wealth. In the wealthy countries it will be those in the middle class and lower class that will find life difficult. It will take several decades for wages to equalize between workers of the emerging and developed countries. Workers in the developed countries will find their wages stagnant or in decline in terms of buying power and standard of living. We currently see the working class in America and

Western Europe attempting to maintain their standard of living by borrowing more and using ATMs to subsidize a life style that eventually they could lose.

Consumer confidence has the greatest impact on the economy out of any of the numerous conditions that influence it. When consumers fear for their job or their future, they tend to stop spending and begin saving. When they stop spending, business slows down the rate of purchase from suppliers declines. Inventories begin to build up. As inventories build up, manufacturers begin to cut back production. As production is cut back, employees are furloughed. As profits begin to contract, stock prices begin to fall. When people begin to protect their money instead of investing it or spending it, the market begins to run out of buyers for products, services and the stock itself. When the buyers dry up, the process accelerates and begins to feed upon itself. More fear, anxiety, lack of confidence emerges again feeding the process. When this process begins, it is almost impossible to stop it before it has run its course and it produces extreme changes in the flow of capital. If you stopped spending now you would not even be close to the first one's out the door, but, you would avoid the disaster that will befall those who spend to the bitter end. There are investors and contrarians refusing to follow the herd. They know that herd mentality is like a herd of buffalos, which continues racing ahead and ultimately plunges over a precipice, or for investors like lemmings, drowned in a sea of debt.

Demographics in itself will be the causal agent in massive capital flows moving from one favored special interest group or activity to another. Anticipating that movement correctly will create real winners.

Now we will look at a real catch 22. The US economy is 2/3 individuals' consumer spending. The savings rate for individuals is about 0%. In Germany, it is over 10% and Japan closer to 22%. When consumer confidence falls and consumer spending declines, the markets go bananas. They know that a decline in consumer spending for a prolonged period of time would precipitate a recession. It is argued that if people saved more, there would be greater capital in America to invest in business and create jobs. If consumers increased their savings rate to 10%, this feared drop in spending would logically follow.

We can't have it both ways. We are faced with a trade-off. Figure out that event and anticipate where the capital will flow next and what area it will abandon. The fortunate and less fortunate will find themselves traveling in opposite directions – dictated by their individual character traits.

LESS FORTUNATE

Fortunate: Occurring by good fortune or favorable chance.

Dear ....,

The issues of equality/inequality – wealth/poverty – fortunate/less fortunate have been thoroughly discussed in the media and by politicians. We wish to add our 2 cents worth and in doing so will piggy-back on the *fortunate/less fortunate* issue. The first question to answer is, *"what is it that the less fortunate have less of than the fortunate"?*

Money, wealth, good looks, good fortune – baa, baa, black sheep. The answer to the question lies in what is the difference between them that results in success or failure. The fortunate understand that *if you do not know that you do not know you are essentially ignorant.* If you know that you don't know and decline to take action on that knowledge, you are stupid. If you know that you don't know and eliminate that problem through determination, courage and desire, act intelligently on this new knowledge, you become a member of the *"fortunate"*. As so often written that low intelligence does not make one automatically lower class, for many are in the upper class. How did this happen? Assuming that we know we don't know and are determined to learn, we take inventory of our assets [intellectual and character] and determine who and what is the greatest obstacle to our becoming fortunate. You don't have to be a rocket scientist to know that government takes 50% of your gross income in taxes of various forms or that government squanders from 25 % to 40 % of its tax income on legal waste, fraud and abuse. Therefore, contrary to opinion, you must consider tax consequences in planning for your life. This should lead you to the issue of wage labor versus free labor. As Aristotle said, wage labor is no different than slavery.

If they choose free labor they then must decide how they wish to take income, as all income is not taxed the same. Only the blind will fail to see that free labor is of itself begging for the opportunity of acting as a business or better known as 'safe-haven.' Behold, they find that there are two types of business when measured by people issues, *employer versus non-employer*. If a business has no employer, it is known as a pass-through entity, it is exposed much less to regulation from Labor, Treasury, and HHS departments. They have a choice of private or public traded activities. Your regulator is more state than federal as the SEC could care less about you. And finally, remember the adage, *follow the money*. Money taken from us by government as taxes must pass through numerous agencies and levels of government. This journey exposes tax money to a large number of what we call *'highway-men'*. We all know about corrupt politicians, lobbyists, and special interests. We have now gone full circle and return to the less fortunate. Follow the corruption and you will do fine. This is the major argument offered as to why many Americans of means have achieved their wealth and position. The argument is usually framed by referring to those that are not fortunate as the *"less fortunate."* The argument is then offered that the lack of good fortune is a major obstacle in the failure of so many in not achieving success.

The above is essentially the text of a letter to an editor that failed to make publication.

Inherent in each of us is a will to fail. Our first contact with this issue will occur early in our childhood. A frequent example is the temptation to give up, especially in the matter of our education. So many of us would rather play sports or engage in other extra curricular or social activities. A partner in this failure is mom and dad who fail to instill discipline and determination to succeed in their children. This is why when government replaces the parents in nurturing the child it is referred to as government-sponsored child abuse. Success still comes the old fashioned way: *"it is earned"*.

The message that comes through loud and clear is that the less fortunate, have *less* determination, *less* willingness to make the effort, *less* confidence in themselves, *more* willingness to give up and let others do for them, *more* inclined to blame others than themselves, and *more* willing to accept failure than to engage the struggle. It seems that they do not want to succeed; they feel more comfortable with mediocrity or even failure. Their efforts seem to focus on escaping from freedom.

Those among us who succeed do so because *we* will not give up or quit. The successful are no stranger to failure. There are two types of failure; the failure of not trying and the failure of trying, then failing, but getting back up and trying again, until they get it right. Those who refuse to give up eventually win often enough to be successful. For more information on this subject, we recommend *'The Will to Fail'* by Dorthea Brand. It is excellent reading.

A middle-class still exists within the general population, however, with increasing difficulty. The elite have excused themselves from behaving pursuant to the dominant ideology. For them it is *"do as I say – not as I do"*. The top of the general population in terms of power remains the governments and their key supporters and lobbyists. With the corruption within the upper levels, to include outright bribery and lying, a forceful downward pressure of violence and defiance exists. Simultaneously, street crime perpetrators place the same extreme pressures creating a forceful upward pressure of temptation. This means that the more ethical center of the general population is being squeezed from both directions. Their temptations to do as the others do is very great and becoming more difficult to resist. This means that those who truly are the more righteous must find a way to disassociate from the general population and its undesirable behavior.

It seems that many of the people born into the street life grow up as thugs, muggers and cons in urban areas. Their life is the street so they become extremely street wise. They live on and by street law literally surviving by this knowledge of the street. Most expect that in time they will stand before a sentencing judge and find out how much hard time they must serve before they get out and get back in touch with their customers. They are street-wise and world-stupid. On the other hand there are those either born with a silver spoon stuck in their mouth or up their rear; they are of the new rich. They are worldly wise and street stupid. They believe that they can cut corners, trim a little truth from the facts or run off at the mouth and get out of trouble. That is why they never expect to face a sentencing judge and when they do they panic. Justice is far from blind. It sees and hears everything and sentences according to abstract connections and corrupt compassion.

TAXATION WITH REPRESENTATION

The Sixteenth Amendment ratified on February 3, 1913 established the right of government to lay and collect taxes on income, from whatever source derived. Taxation with representation has grown topsy-turvy with over 40,000 pages of instructions. The Sixteenth Amendment exploded upon the country in a manner not unlike the "*big-bang*" theory of the universe. It continues to grow exponentially. It is the principal money machine for government to bankroll its welfare/warfare state. In reality, voters elect their representatives but these representatives then represent their personal ideological interest and the interest of those who keep them in office. When representative government is compared to taxation without representation, the totality of political deceit and deception is clear. Representative government today isn't working. More often than not, the Sixteenth Amendment is in conflict with the Fourteenth Amendment, which reads in part, "*No State shall make or enforce any laws which shall abridge the privileges or immunities of citizens of the United States; nor shall any state deprive any person of life, liberty or property, without due process of law; nor deny to any person within its jurisdiction the equal protection of the laws.*" Again, you do not have to play this game only as government wishes you to. How you play the game is your choice. How much of this paragraph did you learn in high school?

Representative government over the past several decades has introduced new language into the tax equation. In the last half of the 20th century the buzzword was entitlement. When this concept became discredited, ideologic politicians needed a new buzzword to replace entitlement that would evoke both compassion and guilt. The word that emerged was targeted as in targeted tax reform. It works this way. The progressive tax system, in the name of fairness, is targeted to levy higher taxes on the rich and then, when tax reductions are provided, tax breaks are targeted to selected groups known as the deserving. Marx called this ideology socialism. With the exception of Ivy League universities, schools do not advertise that they teach socialism. This teaching begins in grade school and is seldom debated, identified or published. It just happens like when the rain falls or sun rises. Does your high school teach you about taxes and give you any idea of how you could proceed to learn to do your own taxes? For schools to ignore the issue of income taxes in the student education is like giving the government a blank check or a credit card with unlimited balances to plunder wealth from your personal account. Remember, legislators are like adult children in a candy shop – they want some of everything – but you must buy it for them.

Government, having established both the concept of "entitlement" and "targeted," has attempted to legitimize the concept and the use of these ideas. For example, can you the citizen-taxpayer state that you have an entitlement to a percent, maybe 90%, of the money that you labor for? There is nothing written that says that you may not. Can you, again as a citizen-taxpayer, target certain sections of the tax code that offer you a more favorable treatment? The tax code often actually sets forth in detail how you may do exactly that! It is difficult, when working eight hours a day to support yourself, but to then donate 40% or more of your labor to another's claim, does seem a bit much. This does not really wash with "the pursuit of happiness" or "the equal protection amendment."

FUTURE GENERATIONS: If you do not know the choices open to you, then you don't know that you don't know. Some will believe that the income tax is just another form of government robbing the rich to buy the vote of the poor. So, what does government cost the average taxpayer? But wait, first we must learn about...

Are you getting what you pay for? Earlier we told you to watch where the money comes from, where it goes and who is the intermediary. Then you see opportunities to capitalize on everything from government corruption to stupidity and malfeasance. Following are some of the obvious.

THE TRUE COST OF GOVERNMENT PART I. For the purpose of this discussion only, let us agree that the true cost of government to the wage labor worker is the present cost born by that individual, minus the cost if he had been a "free labor entrepreneur" managing his own affairs. For example: The nation's 72 million [wage labor] families break down by income thus: 30% earn less than $30,000; 45% earn between $30,000 and $75,000; and 25% earn over $75,000. One who earns $30,000 and pays Social Security and Medicare taxes, at the combined payroll tax rate of 15.3% the annual tax paid would be $4,590; at the $75,000 income they would pay $11,475. At approximately age 65-67, the Social Security benefits would be paid according to the taxes paid; individuals covered by Medicare receive benefits in a manner equal to all other participants. The national average, monthly Social Security benefit is $804 or $9,648 annually. Upon the death of the individual, a surviving spouse would receive 55% of the spouse's benefit. However, each of us does not own or control our accounts, they are paid by the compassion of government and can be taken back by them. On the other hand...

If government had conceived the program as one in which each wage labor workers' payroll taxes plus the employers contribution were required to be invested, through certified private firms, then the government would be regulating and managing the investment firms instead of using the program for political purposes and regulating the individual. But what is the true cost? If you had invested your own money from age 18 to age 65 you would be a millionaire. Subtract your net worth from one or two million and that is called, opportunity cost. So, how do you like those cookies?

Middle-class wage labor pays 50% [plus or minus a couple of points] of their gross income to governments at all levels. Tax freedom day for 2001 was July 7th. The average wage labor works 1800 hours per year, minus holidays and leave. It takes 900 [actually the first 900] hours worked to pay this tax load. That is also part of the true cost of wage labor and the dominant ideology.

THE TRUE COST OF GOVERNMENT PART II. Everything that enters your body, your home or office is taxed and regulated by one government or another. The food you eat, the liquids you drink, the clothes you wear, the car you drive, furnishings for home and office, everything – absolutely everything is taxed. Even the air we breathe is no longer free. Almost everything that we purchase bears a sales tax. Much of what we eat and drink carries a tax. Every service we arrange bears a tax. Even government service carries an additional tax called overhead. All of the taxes paid by business are collected from the consumer through an increase in price. When all of this is added up, we find that those at the bottom pay zero tax, many at the top pay little or no tax, and the remainder pay, percentage of income, the burden of taxes. Actually the top 2% pay 56% of the taxes and benefit only 2% of government services. Middle-class America has absolutely no idea of the extent of their tax burden. They tend to focus on those taxes that they pay in their individual federal and state income taxes. But below those numbers lies all of the above taxes that are passed on to them, sight unseen, to be levied against the income of those who either do not care or do not know.

Low income individuals are continuously being dropped from the income tax rolls – that is, the obligation to pay tax. All of the goods and services consumed by these people are taxed, except that these users do not pay the tax. The tax is re-allocated to be paid by those remaining on the tax rolls.

An interesting comment was made by Eric Fry in the May 18, 2006 issue of the "Rude Awakening" when he stated, "Out here in the real world we refer to the fruits of our labor as 'earnings.' But on Capitol Hill, politicians recognize these same fruits as 'taxable gains'. We believe we deserve our earnings by virtue of the fact that we worked hard to produce them. But the politicians believe that they deserve our earnings by virtue of the fact that they have already spent them."

To that we add that the federal deficit and the debt should not be published as so many dollars per capita or for each family. Why? Government has absolutely no intention of repaying those debts and deficits. Therefore, why don't we divide the national debt by 537, the number of elected officials holding the authority to tax. There is no language in the Constitution speaking to progressive tax rates – the

Constitution speaks specifically to equality among individuals. So maybe we should apportion the budget equally and send everyone a bill.

That insane idea of windfall profits tax has had a new breath of life put into it by Senators Clinton and Schumer of the Peoples Republic of New York. Now Mongolia is touting the idea. In countries that nationalize, read as, confiscate and steal, the foreign companies should totally destroy the mines and the equipment, pack their bags and come home.

FUTURE GENERATIONS: It is choice time for you. Anyone can find reasons to quarrel with the numbers we used in the above calculations. You must substitute, as appropriate, the numbers that represent your situation and find your own answers. You can do either/or, but you cannot do both at the same time. You are either a wage labor person or a free labor person. Do you prefer to invest your own money? If so, there are ways in which this can be arranged. To achieve this, you must accept free labor as your course and learn and understand how to calculate information using the financial bank as a calculator.

DETERMINING WHICH STATUTES YOU WISH TO COMPLY WITH. If you own a home and hold title in your own name and then wish to sell the property, your transaction is governed by real estate statues. If title to that same house is held in the name of a partnership, corporation, or Limited Liability Company, and is the only asset of that business, a sale of the entire business would be treated as a personal property transaction and be governed by personal property statues.

TIME VALUE OF MONEY. Would you rather have $1000 today or wait and receive it 5 years from now? That, in short, is the time value of money. The best way to understand and value money is by how much it will buy in goods and services. Inflation decreases the value of money over time. That is one reason why debt can sometimes be nice. You pay the debt at a later time with devalued dollars. Understanding this lesson permits you to understand how and why you must change your labor from wage to free. When you do this, you change from working for money, to money working for you. Time is your ally. Use it wisely.

BEFORE-TAX DOLLARS versus AFTER-TAX DOLLARS. When you receive your annual W-2, it shows your gross income [wage labor] for tax purposes. This is before-tax dollars. Therefore, we can accept that before-tax dollars have yet to have the tax paid on it. You complete your form 1040, listing income, deductions and exemptions, and arrive at a number known as taxable income. You then calculate the tax owed on that income, and when you pay that tax, the amount left is after-tax dollars. For example, say that your taxable income is $30,000 and your tax rate is 15%. Your tax owed is $4,500 leaving you with $25,500 from the original $30,000 of taxable income. This is after-tax dollars. So, what do you do with this money?

For wage labor people, another name for after-tax dollars is discretionary for the purchase of things necessary and things that make you feel good. That the average middle class [wage labor] worker has savings of only a few thousand dollars suggests that they tend to spend each year most if not all of their after-tax dollars. So, each year they must create new after-tax dollars by paying the tax on each years taxable [wage labor] income. We can either think of this as a merry-go-round or take a $535 billion deficit and apportion it equally among Congress and ask them what they each plan to do about their share.

FUTURE GENERATIONS: What is significant about after-tax dollars is that those dollars are never taxed again; they are free of government taxes forever. However, the money those dollars earn when invested, be it interest or dividends, are taxable. After-tax dollars combined with intellectual currency are both beyond governments reach. The secret of why some [free labor] become wealthy and so many [wage labor] remain poor is the manner in which income is taken, and therefore, the manner in which before-tax income is re-characterized to after-tax income, often without out-of-pocket expense. When we say that after-tax dollars are forever free of tax, do not confuse that with being free from future confiscation – that is why, as your wealth increases, you must diversify not only the investment itself, but what jurisdiction governs the safety and security of that money. Recently President George W. Bush, in promoting his tax cut stated, *"No American should* *have to pay more than one-third of their income to government in taxes."*

TARGETING LONG-TERM HEALTH CARE ANOMALIES. As we grow older, we all worry about the possibility of a health problem that will result in long-term health care at very high cost. Insurance costs for protection are, for many, beyond their means, and today's health insurance including Medicare may be forced to continue to ration coverage. Available to the free labor individual is the use of real property investments. Assume, that at age twenty-five you purchased a rental property for $150,000 and took a traditional thirty-year loan. At the end of twenty-nine years the property has been fully depreciated reducing your basis to about the original 20% allocation for the land. In thirty years, the loan is paid off and you own the property free and clear. In forty years, you would be sixty-five, the property has appreciated and would have a value of $400,000 or more. If you sell your property, you would have a $250,000 gain and $120,000 depreciation recovery on which you would have to pay taxes. Historically, it is financially beneficial to hold real estate for extensive time periods.

Unfortunately, at age sixty-five one of the spouses requires expensive long-term care. What are your options? 1). You can refinance the property back to 80% loan to value [LTV] which will make available to you at least $320,000 in loan proceeds. Borrowed money is not taxable. 2). You can sell the property on an installment sale with annual installments sufficient to cover the medical costs. Your business owns the property and is the responsible party under your medical/long-term care reimbursement plan. Installment sales are income to the business and the cost of long-term care is an expense.

TARGETING SALES TAX ANOMALIES. We will again use the example of the wage labor and free labor comparison. Each purchases the same dollar amount of supplies on which is paid a sales tax. Each, therefore, pays the price of the purchase plus the appropriate sales tax, to the supplier for the purchase. For the wage labor worker, the purchase is paid from after-tax dollars. The wage labor worker had to first convert before-tax dollars to after-tax dollars by paying income tax on the before tax dollars at the appropriate tax rate for that person. For the free labor individual, the purchase is paid from before-tax dollars because this purchase of supplies met the test of normal, necessary and reasonable and therefore is a business expense. The expense offsets a similar amount of before-tax income that reduces this taxpayer's tax consequences.

FUTURE GENERATIONS: Note that for each wage labor purchase the state collects a sales tax. Sales taxes are not normally deductible by wage labor individuals on their form 1040. Free labor business people pay the sales tax but are entitled to take the tax as a business deduction and receive a tax refund based upon the total purchase price. State sales tax rates are always less, as a percentage, than the income tax rate that averages about 15%. The federal and state income tax loses an amount equal to the appropriate rate times the dollar amount spent on normal, necessary and reasonable expenses. In return the state collects a sales tax at the appropriate rate. Who loses? The state and federal income tax is reduced so they both lose. The wage labor employee loses. Who wins? The free labor entrepreneur wins and the tax preparer wins.

TARGETING PAYROLL TAX PROGRAM ANOMALIES. Most readers of this book have or are almost qualified for eligibility under Social Security and Medicare. It requires 40 quarters of coverage or 10 years to qualify. Individuals putting in 40 quarters are entitled to the identical Medicare benefits as someone who has put in 40 years, or 160 quarters, of coverage. No increase in benefits accrues after the 40 quarters of qualification. In this anomaly the latter pay 4X the tax of the former.

Social Security coverage is 40 quarters and entitles the payer to a small monthly stipend when he reaches retirement age. It is not intended recipients will ever be able to get all of their money back. This program takes from workers according to their means and redistributes to other workers according to their needs. The free labor entrepreneur will recognize that it is not necessary that he continue to take income as wage labor, that he can restructure his activities and take his income in other manners and different circumstances, which does not always subject the income to payroll taxes.

A free labor entrepreneur may, in raising his children, engage their services as employees of the business, assuming that their services are normal, necessary and reasonable. When you choose to do this you should then review the section in the tax code dealing with children under 14 and children over 14 to understand the tax consequences. You should also check with the SSA, Social Security Administration, to determine the minimum amount the child must earn each quarter to receive credit for a quarter of coverage. And finally, make sure you know what the minimum wage is so that you may consider that information in determining how much money the child will earn. Your children should have their 40 quarters necessary for coverage by the time they are 18 years of age or at least by the time they have finished college.

TARGETING LISTED PROPERTY ANOMALIES. Listed property is essentially those items of personal property that can be used with equal ease for either personal or business use. For such property, the law allows MACRS depreciation and first year expensing deductions only if business use exceeds 50%. If business use of listed property falls to 50% or less during the alternative straight-line recovery period, you must recapture first year expensing and accelerated MACRS deductions.

Listed property includes autos weighing 6000 pounds or less, trucks [with some exceptions], cellular phones, computers and peripheral equipment, boats, airplanes, and any photographic, sound, or video recording equipment that could be used for entertainment or recreational purposes. Taxpayers must keep complete records to document use of listed equipment.

ECONOMIC GROWTH AND TAX RELIEF RECONCILIATION ACT OF 2001 is proud to announce the birth of the first known tax deception and taxpayer gouging provision of the 21st century. Effective in 2010, the *"carry over basis"* rules providing for inheritors to use current fair market value of the date of death as the inheritor's tax basis dies a quiet death. Thereafter, the inheritor must establish, by going back to the original purchase of the property, and determine the basis. When people wake up in 2010, after this *"Rip Van Winkle"* type sleep, they will find this nightmare facing them. For some, government is a *"love-hate"* relationship; for others it is just one more crime by government against its own people.

LEGAL TAX FRAUD [?] Employers act as surrogate tax collectors under mandate of government. The ones that most people are familiar with are income tax and payroll tax withholding. Business obtains money to pay their income taxes by a number of methods; it is built into the cost of the product or service, through decrease in shareholder or private owners stock, through lower employee benefits and wages, and by reducing the size or quality of their product or service. Therefore, customers, employees and shareholders ultimately carry this burden. Utilities provide service into your home; TV, telephone, electric, gas, water, sewer, etc. and all carry a seldom noticed tax. There is literally nothing in life that is free of tax, not the water you drink, not the air you breath. You suffer the burden of tax for air as industry is mandated by law [EPA] to bear the cost of preventing pollutants [not to exceed a legal limit] from entering the air that you breath. This cost is passed on to you in higher costs for electric generators, refineries for gas and heating oil or smelters for iron and aluminum. Businesses without employees are, of course, not required to withhold from employees, even ghost employees.

FUTURE GENERATIONS: Keep in mind our earlier discussions on wage labor and free labor, and before-tax dollars and after-tax dollars. Free labor pays their normal, necessary and reasonable costs out of before-tax dollars. In the discussion on gas and sales tax, you learned that free labor actually earns a tax refund [in addition to the rebate of tax paid on that product or service]. Follow closely how tax collection goes around in a circle, and when it reaches the end, it is wage labor, buying and paying for normal, necessary and reasonable items from after-tax dollars, paying a very large percentage of their income in taxes.

We use the gas tax scenario as an example. Gas taxes, when collected, are placed into a trust fund for building and maintaining roads and bridges. Free labor and wage labor all pay gas tax on the purchase and consumption of gasoline. For wage labor, that is the end of story. For free labor, the total cost, including the same gas tax that you paid, is deducted as a normal, necessary and reasonable expense. This tax deduction against income results in a tax break that exceeds the amount of the gas tax paid. The highway trust fund retains gas tax collections. The income tax collections are reduced by the amount of the deduction at the particular rate for that business, which invariably will exceed the amount of gas tax paid. Two hands in one pocket and one wonders if each knows what the other is doing.

In essence, it is only people who purchase goods and services with after-tax dollars that carry – as a percentage of income - the burden of taxes in America. These are wage labor employees/consumers. The entire maze of tax laws intentionally places this burden on wage labor. Middle class wage labor pays the taxes that are returned to them as benefits from a benevolent government in various forms of aid and assistance to special interest groups. Remember the "old saw" that the hand is quicker than the eye? Tax legislation is truly the government's version of main-street "three-card-monty". When your local politician – you know, the one that you say is honest while the others are questionable – just used your money to fund the special benefits for you and others that acted as an inducement to you to vote for that local politician. In other words, you have been scammed, but you feel so good about what they did for [to] you. They used your money to bribe you into giving them your vote; you are a victim of psychopathic behavior.

FUTURE GENERATIONS: Wouldn't it be keen if politicians' salaries were tied to performance. They stand before the microphone and berate the salary and benefits private enterprise awards to CEOs and staffers. So the kettle calls the pot black – so what else is new? A greater example of hypocrisy, created through the art of lies – lies that they really believe the people should be trained to accept. Federal pay is overly generous, their sweetheart retirement and health plans have a noxious odor, they wallow in uncontrolled travel and office costs. We need these A.. H.... like we need a hole in our head. Lies, cheats, adultery, fornication, criminally inclined, psychopathic, sociopathic, more lies all leading to destroying our due diligence through co-dependency. They have addicted people to co-dependency by creating through lies false negative readings having the same affect on peoples' minds that HIV has on our natural immune system.

Here is what we do! Everyone begin and continue writing letters and sending email to all politicians damning them for their lies and deceptions, stop voting, stop listening to their lies, declare them person non grata and in your mind declare them irrelevant and dangerous to your life, liberty and pursuit of happiness. Guess we got a bit excited – talking about this subject makes one's blood boil – sorry about that! Start with the current budget – add an inflation amount – and you have created next year's budget. If the government exceeds the budget, each elected politician has their salary reduced by 5%. If however they manage to come in 5% under budget they receive their scheduled raise. Quickly two things would occur. Pork spending would disappear and government expenditures, by line item, would be subjected to prioritizing to determine those expenses that fail the test of *are they really needed*. The other alternative is to make it a capital offense for the government to spend these ridiculous amounts. At least understand that government spending is too important an item to be left to known thieves and should be determined by the people.

THE CO-DEPENDENCY CONSPIRACY GAME

Government is clearly the dominant partner in this co-dependency with each of us be it individually or collectively. They and only they write and enforce the rules between the two parties. In any game victory goes to those who understand the rules and are quick to change the direction of their lives. In the next section we will go in depth into *"the risks and rules of winning or losing"*.

The point we want to make is that government regulations have enveloped our rights to life, liberty and the pursuit of happiness whereby they are strictly controlled in terms of the who, what, where, when, how and why. We therefore must do with our lives what government decrees. That may be fine with you, but for us it is a big no-no.

POSTSCRIPT: Recently we received the property tax bill for our property in Lake County, Illinois. There were three separate line items pertaining to Lake County's solution to past pension plan miscalculation regarding the true cost of employee retirement and health care benefits. A separate line item advised us of our share of Lake County employee benefits for that year included within the assessment of our property that is designated for specific worker category pension reserves. Simultaneously we have been greeted with a 50%

increase in our [HOA] condo owner's association monthly assessment. This of course, significantly impacted our bottom line by reducing the net profit to the owner. After reviewing our due diligence we concluded that this circumstance shall continue to grow out of control. Therefore the *"FOR SALE"* sign has gone up on this property.

We can distinguish between a tax preparer and tax firms, advertising on TV, that defend against tax audits. If you are to be audited look in your yellow pages under tax preparer and see if behind their name the designation EA is included. EA indicates that that person is an *enrolled agent*, a designation available only after passing extensive testing by the IRS. This is a good place to begin searching.

Maricopa County, Arizona, where we live, now shows on their property tax statement, again by line number, our cost for each new bond issue approved by the voters and our cost for preexisting bond issues for which delayed payment was approved. On our tax assessment, the cost to us for the bond expenses comes to about $350 for tax year 2007. In 2000 when we purchased our home, our annual property tax was only about $400. Now it is closer to $750. Another "FOR SALE" sign goes up.

DILEMMA!

Dilemma: *A situation that requires one to choose between two equally balanced alternatives; a predicament that seemingly defies a satisfactory solution.*

FUTURE GENERATIONS: As we look forward we find our selves confronting the elements of a predicament for which there are no obviously safe answers. This includes political ideology, social ideology and economic ideology. We look at each separately.

POLITICAL IDEOLOGY

The two parties in America, earlier labeled as the *"Mommy"* and the *"Daddy"*, have through the generations grown to act like spoiled children. Behavior has consequences and in this case business and society have emulated and followed in the footsteps of government.

American political ideology has become like one huge *dysfunctional* family. Government's unwillingness to act in a reasonable, respectable and moral manner as set forth in the Constitution, has made itself the enemy of individuals and by taxing and regulating the slave masters of workers. Government no longer commands the respect of the people for they now pander to and bribe the people for votes and support. The fighting among themselves and with outside groups has become reminiscent to the way siblings and cousins contest an inheritance, total irrationality. For decades voters have been confronted with voting for the devil we know or the devil we don't, always ending up with a devil. Some base their decision on which is the lesser of two evils, guaranteeing that the winner will be evil. If we desire to vote for true statesmen of honesty and integrity, we will not find them on the ballot. When there are no choices that satisfy our need, namely that they will defend the Constitution against all threats foreign and domestic and swear an oath to do the same and you suspect that they will deliberately fail in this oath to do thus, then we should not vote for any candidate. Eventually there will be so few votes cast in a general election that maybe the idiotic ideological panderers will get the message. It is shameful that people can no longer trust their government – that we must look upon government as a great enemy of people and their freedom – that we are consigned to living in fear of government.

SOCIAL IDEOLOGY

Observing the 2006 American society, it seems more and more like peeking through the windows of an insane asylum [aka nut house] and at times you can't tell the inmates from their guards. When laws were no longer made for the good of all and government began to make laws giving special treatment for some, including themselves and not others, they cleverly positioned themselves at the top of the favored group and gave themselves favors that no other group is permitted to share. They call it freedom - we call it corruption.

When we look at our churches we are shocked by the crimes of sex perpetrated on children. When we look at our public schools we are shocked and distressed at the shooting and bombing episodes, the gangs with their intimidation of others, and drugs and sex pandering to others. Say nothing of the failure to produce children [leave no child behind] that can't read or write or add and subtract up to a par. Who is really left behind? This has raised the question among many parents and students whether going into debt for $100,000, more or less, in student loans is worth the degree or the paper it is written on.

ECONOMIC IDEOLOGY

Economic ideology in America has its own dilemma in today's world. Are we a socialist country or are we a country of individual capitalists in a fascist world? Americans are a very compassionate people always ready to help those in need of assistance. Since FDR's time the government has taken on the task of identifying those among us who are in need of assistance. Those groups have grown into millions and millions: the addicted, the single mothers, those below the poverty line, the elderly, and ad infinitum.

Huge sums of money are needed. Through taxation this money comes out of the pockets of those who create wealth and goes to the needy via our elected representatives. What a wonderful opportunity they created for buying votes and at the same time presenting themselves as the saviors of the poor and needy. The economy needs to be kept in high gear at all times to produce the taxes to finance this socialist extravaganza. This dilemma is an outgrowth of the failure of ideology, sociology and economy to come to a reasonable and financially doable compromise.

During that same time, if you worked for wages, you experienced little real gain compared to the CPI [consumer price index], which itself is seriously questioned as to accuracy. People have been swept up and away with what is called the *wealth effect*. Many actually did enjoy the benefits of the wealth effect as they had increased their wealth dramatically during that time. But most others felt the wealth effect directly from seeing others spend and buy and felt that they also were entitled to spend and buy. Having no savings to match the urge to buy things they did not really need, they had to find a source of other money. Enter the money-lender who with interest rates being artificially low continued to reduce criteria for qualification until one only had to have a warm body to get a loan. When government encourages people to buy things they don't need with money they don't have, it is a pathway to poverty.

The latest projections from the government agencies that track the Social Security and Medicare trust funds is: the drop dead date for Medicare is now 2018 and for Social Security

2040. Where will government get the added payroll taxes to continue this program? Some of it will come from the legal and illegal immigrants crossing the Southern border into the US. Some will come from reduced benefits. Some will come from extending the age at which one can begin to receive payments and some will come from an increase in the payroll tax rate. It would seem that a reasonable person would recognize that this train, the SS and Medicare DC Express, is out of control. But how many will have the will or courage to step aside and not be run down?

FUTURE GENERATIONS: Please take a hard look at the issues above. We believe these issues are presented true and correct. Believing is of course not really the same as knowing. Therefore, exercise your own due diligence and decide for yourself what is correct. Then act upon that knowledge.

We must ask ourselves the question: If a president, without Congressional consent or dissent, knowingly violates the Constitution, does that rise to high crimes and misdemeanors? If the answer is yes then what is the crime that Congress is guilty of and does that also rise to the level of high crime and misdemeanor?

If your answer is yes then who was guilty, when:

Lincoln suspended habeas corpus, which the Supreme Court later ruled was a violation of the Constitution.

McKinley took us into a war that had no relationship to his Constitutional authority to provide for the common defense.

Wilson took us into a war that had no relationship to his Constitutional authority to provide for the common defense.

FDR of course lured the Japanese into attacking so that he could have plausible deniability when he took us into a war, that 2/3 of the people absolutely did not want.

Is Bush guilty of deliberate violation of the Constitution? If yes, he should be impeached and if found guilty punished accordingly.

The big question is how long will we take this behavior before we act to correct it?

FUTURE GENERATIONS: We recently had the 5th anniversary of 9-11-2001 and TV was all over this subject. They are remembering and honoring those who died and those responders that heroically met the challenge. That was good and great. However, those who failed America received a free pass. If you know anything about the Constitution you know that the number one responsibility of government is to *"provide for the common defense."* This failure stands alone as THE priority of government. For when government fails, many of us do not survive, but pay the ultimate price. The horror of this irony is that we gloss over the fact that the president and vice-president and senate and house failed us in providing for the common defense fulfilling their oath of office and commitment to. The president is the commander-in-chief and the Congress is charged with due diligence and oversight of the departments and separate agencies of government. For two hundred years our government has failed in their primary responsibility to the people and the country. We have special holidays to honor those who did good and our slimy politicians use this opportunity to make claim to the greatness of government in *responding* to these atrocities, yet any sane and reasonable person should know the truth. Again, with 9/11 we had the blue ribbon investigation. It did some fault-finding, blaming, and tons of demagogue and spin control. Why do they do this? The answer is clearly – so that we will let our memory of who failed us fade away. This act has been repeated for over 200 years. This misguided attempt to become the biggest, best, richest country has also made us the most corrupt and self centered, dysfunctional culture among civilized people. To achieve this status of Empire government lied while developing the most violent of military capabilities, the greediest of peaceful purpose and the useless killing of our best young men and women. For over two years politicians have talked their way into being honored, when in truth they were only our most successful failures. Every two years they stand for re-election and brag about their, and we quote, *"SUCCESSFUL FAILURES"*. Are the idiots that elect these people any better than the ones they elected or are they all cut from the same cloth? It is clear that at least people should be aware that, to ignore the lessons of history is to sow the seed of another tragic repeat of history.

PERSONAL DILEMMAS

The business of America is business. We forget who said that first, but let us think about it. All of us seek the means to protect wealth from all forms of corruption and crime, from where ever to whom ever. We shudder to think that others now have access to our financial privacy. We see the dollar falling out of bed, yet we are not sure of what best to do. Terrorism is no longer just a threat to our bodies. It is a greater threat to our financial security and privacy. In the name of terrorism and security the government has stripped us of many of the remaining freedoms granted to us. Now that knowledge of our financial circumstances is virtually public information, how do we protect our assets from the grubby hands of those who would take it? So where do we put our money to protect it from government, terrorists, lawsuits and our locals who practice crime and corruption? Reminds me of the guy who puts his money and gold into a piece of PVC, seals the ends and buries it in his back yard. It sure beats the old tin can.

SURVIVAL: ASSETS AND IDEAS

UNDERSTANDING FREEDOM

FREEDOM IS OF COURSE NOT *FREE*

FUTURE GENERATIONS: The creators of our independence then formed a government they termed a *"republic."* What did they envision that *"republican"* model of government would be? By and large, they believed it would be government by free election, with those elected restricted to terms of office; it would be a government answerable to a virtuous citizenry, which would be capable of governing itself.

Madison, in Federalist 39, summed it up in a way that his countrymen would understand. A political regime is a republic only when the government's power is derived entirely from the People and said: *"administered by persons holding their offices during pleasure, for a limited period, or during good behavior."* Thus, the essence of republics is self-government, accountability, and limited terms. This presentation of the idea of Individualism is based upon the words, thoughts and ideas of George Washington. We state those values in today's terms as; good character, high morality, creative intellectual curiosity, and the courage to stand as one. If you develop and cultivate those values, the success that comes your way will, by those who envy you, label you as the fortunate. This then sets the stage for them to refer to themselves and others as the less fortunate. Be reminded that when asked what it is the less fortunate have less of than the fortunate, the answer is those very same values you cultivated from the words of George Washington.

The idea of freedom first was studied during the late *"Enlightenment,"* which hosted a counter-culture, centered in the little duchy of Weimar and featuring Goethe, Schiller and other luminaries of the time. The German romantics and their followers were convinced that the mechanistic philosophies developed in the wake of the Newtonian achievement were both incomplete and misleading. They returned to the book of nature wherein they found mystery and transcendental powers, powers of an essentially aesthetic character grounded in freedom. In Goethe's Faust and in Schiller's Letters on the Aesthetic Education of Man, freedom is offered as the very definition of our humanity. One of Emmanuel Kant's last contributions was an essay titled, *"Was Ist Aufklarung?"* *("What is Enlightenment"?)* He answers his question in one word: freedom. He developed a moral theory based on the powers of a rational being, a theory that placed such a being outside the natural realm of causation and within the intelligible realm of freedom.

FUTURE GENERATIONS: We find alternatives that allow us to checkmate the continuing reduction of freedom by deconstructing the conflict between the workers and elite. By being neither a master [employer] nor a slave [employee], we place ourselves beyond the main sphere of struggle within our society. As the master weaves his web of laws and regulations to control the slave, the thinker, being small and nimble, quickly moves to a safer place and effectively remains outside of the master/slave sphere. The thinker desires power, but different power than that lusted for by the bourgeoisie. The thinker wants the power to control his life [leave me alone] and the power and strength to resist the desire to control others [God syndrome]. The relationship between thinkers is best described as a mutually beneficial cooperation.

The sanctity of contracts has always been an important facet in creating a stable society in the business as well as the social realm. Specifically, it deals with the person who is vague, sneaky and subtly devious; who engages others and receives something of value. But then does not produce the goods or services the other party anticipated. In America, the original contract covering the whole nation was the Constitution and the Bill of Rights. A concept, something called a *social contract,*" has gained popularity and meaning beyond its just cause. The social contract is alleged to be a contract between the People and government. Who ratifies this contract and with what authority is it ratified? They communicate their offers, usually during election campaigning, declaring that if elected they will do such and such. For the People, ratification of these promises comes from the vote of the majority. The People, through this ratification, are expected to give up certain rights in exchange for what government offers. If it is true that certain inalienable rights were granted to each of us individually by our creator, it then becomes questionable how the majority can give away something that was not theirs to begin with. A contract also requires that a consideration be made and given by both parties to the contract. We have already raised the question as to the right of the majority to give what is not theirs, but belonging to the minority. Government, as the party making the offer, in its use of spin, rhetoric and ideology presents its offer in such a vague manner that there can never be a consensus of just what, if anything, government offered. At best, individuals would declare this contract void in the private sector. However, politics is a life unto itself.

FUTURE GENERATIONS: In the political arena, the sanctity of the contract is turned on its head. Politicians will make promises, *"when I am elected [president, senator, Congressperson] I will do this or do that and will not do such and such."* The politician is offering something, and in return is asking People to pay for that something [a promise] with their vote. The politician is really defrauding the voter of his vote because the politician, in wording his promise in a vague but suggestive manner, has no honest intention of delivering on his promise, at least not in the manner he suggests. In the private sector, there is an implied contract between the two parties, and if either party has a grievance, they may seek remedy through the court.

The politician, having accepted your vote and assuming that he won the election, will then turn to his own agenda and lobby among his peers for something entirely different than what was suggested to you, the voter. If the politician when he or she is pandering for your vote, receiving it and ultimately wins it should be viewed between you and the elected. Therefore it also carries the implied status of a *"power of attorney,"* which is another way of looking at representative government. The only way that *"power of attorney"* can be revoked is through a recall, impeachment or his / her failure to be re-elected. The behavior of politicians is really immoral, but by today's values is considered the norm. For a definition of this act, we can turn to Plato's *"Republic."* Plato said that when leaders lie [that includes deception and legal posturing] that the leaders defraud the People and betray the country. Those are strong and heady words but deserving of everyone's thought.

Neither the masses, with only body and labor to sell in the market, nor the elite, with only dominant ideology to sell, will survive very far into the 21st century. Workers will understand that intelligence is valued higher than labor, and that the dominant ideology is a fraud intended to keep them down on the farm. They will understand that they no longer need the elite to provide them with jobs and they will find that they have, in their own hands, the capital, intelligence and labor to function independently, inside and yet outside of the nation state. It then is only a matter of time until everyone realizes that *"the emperor has no clothes;"* the whole set-up is plain and simple fraud against the People. As this becomes common knowledge, the exodus of the *"freedom entrepreneur"* from mainstream business models and paradigms will turn into a flood, an intellectual revolt against their cruel masters. Maybe Marx was on to something; he just didn't have all of the information necessary to create the final part of the puzzle that is to play out in the 21st century.

The social contract is binding upon every man, woman, and child; therefore, it must be obeyed. But obeying specific rules applies only to those who have placed themselves into a position where the rules apply to them. For example, if your product is knowledge, it is difficult to imagine that you would incur violation of rules regarding product liability. Or, if you choose to be a sole-entrepreneur, that is a person who operates a for-profit activity without the use of employees, you can't be regulated by the Department of Labor. Excluding the fact that even a sole-entrepreneur is for labor law purpose considered an employee, the rules and regulations of the Department of Labor, such as the payment of unemployment taxes will not apply to your situation. Therefore, your choice of product and service, choice of how you organize your activities, type of business entities under state laws, operating as a sole-entrepreneur, acting as a principal in your own interest, all combined with the necessary knowledge to eliminate intermediaries [honest (?) brokers] will put you well beyond coverage of the most onerous and confiscatory laws, rules and regulations.

FUTURE GENERATIONS: Your predecessors understood that to go where few have gone, demands all of their mental and physical strength. Thus, a plan must be made based upon knowledge and solid facts, executed with determination and courage. When success comes, it will become a threat to the ignorant ones left behind. What is it that they desire to escape from? Could it be schools that don't educate, healthcare and retirement programs that are either under funded or over extended, a morality that is deteriorating, or, man's law that is often in opposition to natural law?

This causes the same distress among adults over which laws should prevail, as their children are faced with in public schools. A fiscal policy that leaves them with only 50% of the dollars they earn with which to manage their lives while the other 50% is being redistributed to others who have made successful claims upon your physical and intellectual labor. Could it be a political system in which the candidate that lies with audacity, raises money from those whose political soul will be won over, and then be proclaimed the greatest and therefore winner? Or is it simply contempt for the ignorance of the majority and the evil of government? Regardless, you have decided to escape from it, whatever and however you choose to define it.

FUTURE GENERATIONS: Here we want to use the analogy of the space shuttle. Each launch will be aborted and delayed until the preparations are as near perfect as man can make them. The same is true for you when you finally launch into your sphere. Let's make this fun and give our sphere a name. Let's name it *"freedom,"* as that is what we seek in the galaxy of countries.

We might think of ourselves as a *"Noah"* as we decide what to take with us on our ark named *"freedom."* We think that the first item needs to be possession of the right attitude, values and personality. Let's take the essence of George Washington's words. His words, prophetically, proved to be the antithesis of today's government. Washington introduced us to good character, high morals, creative intellectual curiosity, and stand-alone courage. We must first acquire and then load aboard the ark *"freedom"* these values.

The process of letting the fascist/socialist sphere spin off into its own destiny and creating your separate freedom sphere requires that you understand, and with honesty, judge your self. In judging yourself, you must not succumb to the oldest temptation of man – wanting a certain result so badly that you fail to notice contradictions in the information being used to judge it.

You must decide if you truly possess those four characteristics of good character, high morals, creative intellectual curiosity, and stand-alone courage. If you fail the self-honesty test, that is, deceive yourself, through rationalization and denial into believing that you have these qualities, you later will find yourself living as a fish out of water. You will not understand why, with all of your effort and determination, you do not find the success and happiness that you seek. Better then that you stay with the majority. There you can succeed without the above qualities, and the monopoly of mediocrity will protect you.

FUTURE GENERATIONS: Take the time to evaluate the text of the politicians, bureaucrats, journalists, activist, et al, from the standpoint of how they go about communicating their dominant ideology. Before you proceed, you must succeed in recognizing precisely what the elite is talking about, and how they are presenting their ideas for the purpose of persuading you to buy into their dominant ideology. Following is an outline that will help you evaluate the information/disinformation that the public is constantly bombarded with.

Now, compare the above paragraph with this reality. No matter what age group you fall into, there are likely to be some very large bills looming in your future. If you are concerned about how you will pay them, you have good reason for your concern. Around the globe, some of the most important goals of individuals, such as a comfortable retirement, a new home, health care and children's education are increasingly impacted by changing demographics, cultural trends, and the prospects of fewer benefits from government at greater cost to all. Many of the programs now offered or proposed by governments are already demographically terminal. Specifically, the future cost of these programs, as presently provided, plus politically inspired increases in benefits, will, in a decade or two, demand such high tax rates from workers that the very soundness of the economy is threatened. This means that future administrations will have no choice but to reform the systems, and the first and best, from the standpoint of absolute dollars, will be to reduce benefits and pass more of the costs onto the people, especially the rich. Consider the implications of the growing elderly population with a shrinking number of young people to support them as it becomes more difficult to provide the necessities for the elderly. You must consider where your parents fit in and the order of those that you desire to help. Delays in reforms, mostly due to politics, make the so-called pension time-bomb pressing for people who are worried about their own retirements and having to deal with elderly parents at the same time. Directly related to living longer are soaring costs of long-term care. At the same time, many governments are backing away from paying the total cost of some medical care. You, as an individual have no legal right to participation in any of the above programs, for title to all accounts are held by government, as guardian of the people, that they can manage in whatever manner they elect.

Bottom Line. In the Prologue, we set out in descending order the issues over which People had expressed the greatest concern. Now we match up the actions that individualists take, and the concerns that are either alleviated or eliminated. Again, the five departments that will be most active in denying you your freedom are Justice, Treasury, HHS [Health and Human Services], Labor, and Education.

INDIVIDUALISM'S NATURAL RIGHTS: *LIFE, LIBERTY & PROPERTY*

FUTURE GENERATIONS: We use this opportunity to speak directly to each of you about individuality, a life without being forced to go through other people or mediums. Individualism is the story of people who love life, of people who will not sacrifice their love or their values, regardless of the prevailing rhetoric which claims that they must sacrifice, feel other's pain and guilt. We live in a time where some people feel compelled to force their opinions onto the minds of our children, through the schools, from the pulpits and through the media. We are a society of mass production, mass consumption and mass psychology. For one to dare to defend individualism in a society dominated by the fashionable ideas of communalization [*it takes a village to raise a child*] is to subject one to ridicule and intimidation, and to be labeled eccentric or even radical.

WHO STOLE MY LIFE?

Modern society cannot fail to be impressed with the strength of the worldwide pressure working against freedom for the individualist. Yet, we are constantly reminded that individualism has been one of the historic characteristics of human nature in general, and of the American personality in particular. Each reference to the ideas and actions of our founding fathers gives credence to the role individualism played in the formation and development of our country. It is obvious that individualism is a product of our inheritance and environment, passed on to each of us from our founding fathers. American individualism or laissez-faire is rooted in the philosophy of natural rights, and expressed in the concepts of limited government and religious tolerance. We need further examination of the causes, for the type of life we encounter, in our country as we enter the 21st century.

The communist threat of the 20th century, under Soviet leadership in the WWII postwar era, was without doubt unique in modern history. Here was an ideology that claimed to transcend all national boundaries, and insisted that there could be no lasting peace in the world until socialism was victorious on every continent on the globe. The messengers of this Marxist message had no moral scruples about the means and methods they used. Human life had little or no value to them other than as tools for the achievement of their collectivized utopia.

In choosing political alliances and military intervention as the method for combating this ideological evil, the United States radically transformed itself from everything it had been before WWII and became that which they fought and hated. Respected classical-liberal historian Arthur A. Ekrich, in his book The Decline of American Liberalism, explained the nature of this transformation:

> *"As a part of the struggle against communism, the American people were won over to the necessity of military preparedness on a virtual wartime basis. In America as well as in Europe, the individual citizen accordingly continued to live in a near-war atmosphere, in which his own aspirations were subordinated to the demands of the state. Tremendous expenditures, largely for military needs, mounting national debts, military conscription, a vast bureaucracy of civil servants, and the growing official nature of thought and culture were some of the evidences of the growth of statism and the decline of individualism."*

The result, therefore, was that in the name of opposing the threat of aggressive socialism, the United States increasingly adopted in its domestic and foreign policy a defensive form of socialism. The state increasingly gained control over the lives of the American people and their property. This method was selected to fight foreign socialism because most people in the

American intellectual, political circles and East Coast universities believed in socialism, whether or not they were willing to assign that label to their beliefs. The Great Depression had convinced them that capitalism did not work and that to a greater or lesser degree, the government had a responsibility to oversee and manage the economic affairs of the citizenry. Their dispute with the Marxists, ultimately, was not over the issue of *"big government,"* but over their abhorrence to the *"undemocratic"* methods employed by Marx's followers. In line with their socialist premises, America's political leaders attempted to use socialist methods to combat socialism in those countries on the *"battle line"* of the communist threat. Statism became the means of combating statism. As a consequence, the United States has probably been the most successful exporter of socialist idea in the world. This export was cloaked in the rhetoric of *"democracy"* and *"free enterprise."* The cumulative effect of America's example and prodding is that there is now not one country in the entire world that actually practices the principles of limited government and an unhampered market economy. Worst of all, most Americans no longer have a vision nor understanding of what a free America should and can look like, nor do they even conceive of what a noninterventionist policy in foreign affairs would mean.

FUTURE GENERATIONS: Washington warned us about becoming involved in the idiocies of Europe. France, a long standing socialist country, and Germany, a long standing conservative – militaristic, country, repeatedly fought among themselves for that for which there was little if any long-term value. Today, America's socialist and fascist ideologies are fighting the same stupid wars with each other. Their radical goals have no place in the America that we all love and cherish.

J. B. MacMaster wrote about the philosophy of the Declaration of Independence;

> *"The state is presented as created by the people, and existing solely for the good of the individual. Its sole duty is stated to be to protect him in full enjoyment of his natural and inalienable rights. Public officials are declared to be trustees of the people; the right of revolution is inherent in society.*

*In no instance is the state presented as the provider
of office, the creator of monopolies."*

When government becomes unlimited in its scope, professes
to know what is best for all, and then proceeds using all means
at its disposal including the force necessary to coerce
compliance, individualists must again come to the defense of
the Constitution.

FUTURE GENERATIONS: Individualism is the antithesis of
socialization and collectivization. As the world moves
toward the complete collectivization of various aspects of
society, economy and governments, freedom and liberty for
individuals will only be found in those instances where the
individual has taken it upon him/herself to provide it for
themselves and for their family. We delve deeply into the
truths of this issue.

Individualism in America is the natural right to life, liberty
and property. These rights were guaranteed under the
Declaration, that all men are created equal. This equality
specifically consists of endowment by our Creator with certain
unalienable Rights. These rights were further expanded and
explained under the *"Bill of Rights,"* the first ten amendments
that emphatically *"tell government what it may never do,"* and
the Fourteenth *[equal protection]* amendment sets forth the
right of people to be free of government interference and
manipulation. Government was established to ensure that no
individual is deprived of his or her rights by providing equal
protection to all.

The Declaration, Constitution, and Bill of Rights were
presented to *"Individual Americans"* to fulfill a radical idea of
the founding fathers. No mention was made of groups, political
parties or special interests, and this silence was intentional to
identify that individuals are supreme. So, how did America
reach the position that individualism is scorned and power
rests in government through political parties, the wealthy and
powerful special interests? The short answer is that the
Constitution was subjected to revision and selected suspension
of key sections to establish government as supreme over people
– and few raised their voice to protest the death of our
Constitution. In essence the Constitution has been consigned
to the *"exiled"* bin, also known as file 13.

After factoring out *"Blame America First"* special interests, we find a substantial majority remaining who express an undying love for America and what it stands for – and – serious concern approaching outright distrust of American government. Many believe that government; i.e., its leaders and shakers, takes positions that it is its right to filter information and determine what people should hear and see, and to hold as state secrets information and knowledge that people are entitled to know if the people are to control governments behavior through the peoples responsibility of *'oversight.'* Elected, appointed and selected leaders and bureaucrats, supported by their apologists, loyalists, and activists, have further refined this style by exercising questionable integrity, accuracy and truthfulness. They have an intoxicating way with words and could sway opinion with just their pens. Some believe that a silver tongue and lucid prose alone can convert multitudes. These activists contribute to the corruption of government and the addiction of the people to a co-dependency system. When all else fails, they are not afraid to apply pressures of all sorts. Dream at times of what would be the state of our country if everyone refused to vote!

Some in government use extralegal methods to facilitate an agenda carried out by those who lust greatest for personal power or favor and to whom ends justify means. They investigate those who oppose their agenda in search of human weakness, be it young boys, vulnerable women or some other passion or lust that needs to be satisfied. This work requires specialists with unusual credentials and talents and there is no dirge of unqualified people willing to do it.

The alleged above behavior is common among the *"Elite 537."* If any are found guilty, by the people they must be severely punished for their failure to fulfill their oath of office. The penalty for this should be twenty years to life and banned forever from any political or other position of influence. Why so severe? The penalty must fit the crime. If the crime is a deliberate act to not fulfill their oath to the people and the Constitution the perpetrators are still getting off easy.

ARISTOTLE

Aristotle, in Book VII, defined akrasia as *"incontinence or weakness of will."* Why does a person do something he knows he shouldn't do? Why does he engage in behavior when past experience tells him there will be a heavy price to pay for doing it? Why do people do what they have been taught is wrong?

At one time or another, each of us has fallen victim to saying or doing something that we knew, when we said or did it, that it was wrong. Individuals, collectives and especially countries, also fall victim to akrasia. Winners and losers are separated by the extent to which they discipline themselves, make the fewest mistakes and misstatements. Discipline is the control of the mouth and body by the wise use of the mind. Those who succeed are known as Successful Entrepreneurs. Those who fail, if they knew that they didn't know, are stupid. You can master and control temptations and weaknesses.

Individualism can be described as the act of living *"free."* A free individualist is a person who grew up in a sufficiently free environment, free of undue pressure from peers and personalities or political pressure and restraints that would cause the formation of values inconsistent with values the individual would have made in the privacy of his mind and from his personal experiences. Individualism does indeed appear to have its own distinct personality. There seems to be a center in those individuals where everything that is seen and experienced is analyzed and then integrated. The Creator seems to have given each of us different ways of understanding and digesting reality. The founding fathers probably considered this when deciding to set forth the unalienable rights given to the individual and made them off limits to the state. If the state violates these rights, it then treats the individual as only an instrument of its will. When the state treats them thus, it is to treat them as though they had no vision of their own of the good life to express through their personal ideas, stances and actions. If we have a right to personality, along with other unalienable rights, we must have an area of freedom to express our acknowledgement of the good. Our personality should be a moral-oriented energy force with the responsibility to maintain itself against various forms of social coercion inconsistent with moral behavior. Personality, as defined above, is today on the defensive. It can be alleged that in many cases, this is the object of deliberate and directed assault from those who fear a return to individualism by the masses.

Pressures against individual human personality are visible to all who take the time to examine. Joseph Jastrow wrote,

> *"disorders of personality involve more or less disorganization of the memory continuum and the group of elements which enter into normal consciousness of personal identity."*

If personality is, in part, a product of memory of things we have experienced, choices we have made, and resulting consequences experienced, then personality cannot be the creation of a moment. Our memory is valuable to each of us and should never be viewed as an impediment in the way of progress. To surrender our memory is to deny our past and the values we believe in. Without memory there can be no conscience. Without conscience there can be no determination between right and wrong or good and evil. Since personality means depth and uniqueness, and even mystery, it does not flourish on a field of sameness. The abolition of privacy does away with the very regions where personal configuration must form. The decline of privacy is traceable to a belief man is or should be one-dimensional. But man is multi-dimensional and is more that just a thing to be manipulated. Man has a thought process that can be anathema to the parties attempting to manipulate society and government.

Self-knowledge is difficult to come by in a society that practices self-denial. Only when faced with crises do we call upon truth and wisdom to guide us. Unless we are of a thoughtful nature, even a crisis becomes but yet another opportunity to embrace sophistry as a means to rationalize away the truth. Collectivism likes to embrace the dictates of government while individualists are constantly asking why.

FUTURE GENERATIONS: No two individuals are alike any more than two snowflakes are identical. All individuals develop either under a free environment or conditions of servitude and coercion or a combination of the two. Even under the pressures of political correctness of social teachings and values, each is still different in their own unique way.

In 1776, a number of great minds came together and focused on creating the institutions that would allow Americans enough elbow room to grow into individualists. Protection of the individual's right to happiness, control of his individual life and liberty, provide them the space individuals need to develop the People who made the republic so great. This was the primary reason for the existence of America, the nation state. For individual freedom to exist and thrive, it is necessary that economic activity be organized in a free market form, as described by Milton Friedman, and referred to as *"Competitive Capitalism."* If Capitalism alone is not sufficient for individual freedom to flourish, then *"Competitive Capitalism,"* free of unnecessary government intervention, is essential. Economic freedom of the individual fosters the political and civil freedom of individualism. With the increase of authoritarian governments capitalism is itself threatened. When the state attempts to set itself up as the supreme business of the land, with the President as the chief executive officer [CEO] and the Congress as the board of directors, capitalism ceases to exist and its place is taken over by socialism or fascism. At this point, the People are disenfranchised and returned to the status of serfdom. Then, the self-interest of the individualist is submerged in favor of the more politically powerful and their version of central planning. Centralized planning ultimately brings with it the central control of individuals, their occupations and decisions on how all forms of resources will be allocated. There are but two ways of coordinating the economic activities of our populace. One is central direction involving the use of coercion, the technique of the unlimited state, and the other is voluntary cooperation of individuals, the technique of the market place. When the freedom of individuals is protected the individual has two choices. It can produce only for itself or, through voluntary cooperation, produce for all the people.

Today a change has occurred in the direction that government wants people to go while continuing the use of the words and phrases of our individualist origin in politics. This change in direction has been so subtle through the 20th century that most of us are not conscious of the fact that many of these words no longer apply to the condition that they are allegedly describing. A case in point is the word *"liberal"* – its original meaning and its usage in Europe is one who advocates change. Its usage in American politics is more closely aligned with the definition of the word socialist. Other words that do not fit their original use are fairness, equity, equality, and compassion. With this change in definition, we find it difficult to project traditional notions of individuality as we enter the 21st century. Also today, in our rapidly changing society and workplace, we find people have been segregated according to what they do and where they perform their work. We concentrate so hard on what we are doing that we create walls between us. We seldom look over that wall or inquire of others what they are doing. Do we remember that each of us has a duty to give some of our time and energy to the general good – and if we do – do we know how to go about it? Many are confused because we find ourselves living under an accumulation of conflicting jurisdictions.

Say that you work for a large manufacturer. You are subject to the rules and regulations of the corporation for whom you work. It in turn, is subject to numerous governmental jurisdictions and their agencies. You are subject to the arbitrary authority of your union, the traffic police on the road to work, taxes and regulation of the city and the state you live in. Each of these sovereignties has the power to make lives extremely disagreeable if you cross its bureaucratic will. To stand up to the pressure of abusive disciplinary powers, you have the right to hold up your hand at the union or town hall meeting and to mark your ballot, opposite the name of some politician you know little about, nor even whether you can trust or believe him. Always, we are overwhelmed with the confusion of political spin and other forms of sophistry. It is fortunate that the Constitution was written by men of courage and intellectual capacity to transcend limits of their respective professions and were thus able to consider problems of society as a whole, particularly those relating to individual privacy, individual responsibility, and individual freedom of thought and action.

If we could contribute to a generation of young men and women who feel it is important to restore elbow room, we would point them at the storehouse of records of our founding fathers. The words written and spoken on the art of politics and the concepts of families and their role, written during the period 1775 and 1801, could instill the birth of new urgency. What an irony of history! Today's zealots for total bureaucratic rule justify themselves with the same political phraseology used by men of Jefferson's day. The practices of demagogic leaders are not so far from that of dictatorships abroad. The redeeming advantage that we have is that the machinery still exists for popular will to redirect the path America should be taking.

Conformity is now more prized than individuality. It begins when our children are first sent to public school. Soon they come home with strange ideas about how to dress, hairstyles, homework, drugs, smoking, sex – and this list is not complete. These ideas are based upon the need to conform. After all, what will the other students or gang members say? Beyond school, we tend to continue the conformity in dress, attitudes, behavior; and if you don't believe that, just look around. How many children in your school have the courage to be an individual and go against the pressure from their peers? Only a small minority of our children believe in the privacy or the propriety of their own consciences, and have the courage to act upon those personal desires.

Has the day come, or is it close, when a multitude of people, most filled with envy and a desire for the good life, will choose the Congress? On one side is a statesman preaching ethics and respect for the rights of others, another is engaged in demagogic ranting about the wealth of the few and asking why the majority shouldn't be entitled to the same lifestyle: we know which candidate will be preferred by persons with envy and the desire for affluence in their hearts. Will America be at risk to the barbarians from within? Will a strong hand emerge to seize the reins of government? Somewhere between the Revolutionary War and the American Civil War, we seem to have lost our conviction that the best government was self-government. In our enthusiasm for turning over every social problem to the administrative bureaucracy for solution, we forgot that democracy is based on the maxim that the solution of the problems of social life is the business of the people themselves.

In Jefferson's day, the average citizens had a fair understanding of the workings of the society they lived in. When Jefferson scanned the horizon for dangers threatening

American democracy, he did not foresee the prodigious growth of a bureaucracy driven by intent to become a dominant vested interest in its own right. This whole subject has been confused, of course, by the spin of the zealots for total bureaucratic rule, a sophistry where the old vocabulary of democratic liberties is made to mean something wholly different from what was originally intended. The fact remains that we [Americans] are finding it harder and harder to apply the words and phrases that fit so well the society that Jefferson and Madison lived in to the pyramidal social structures of today. Society has become a collection of collectives, having as their purpose the expression of needs, desires, and inclinations found in collectives harboring special interests. The special interests do not share a consciousness of common interest with those that do not belong. An example is materializing in that leaders of the new Congress have decreed that they will take the country in a different direction. In the 2006 campaign the issue of the Left was the presidents handling of the war in Iraq. The vagueness of *"going in a new direction – without consulting with the peoples wishes – is no better than what they are replacing."* This alone can lead to totalitarianism. This doctrine holds that there is no such thing as oppression of individuals. If individuals stand in the way of something willed by government any means of compulsion may be used against them. Having said that the individual has the best chance in society by drawing more sharply the line between government and its People. When government forgets that it is the protector of the society it is tempted to dissolve society and make everything government. This dissolution of society and the abandonment of its role as protector of the People exposed society to harm from external forces. It then creates a situation of government's malfeasance and the very survival of government from this threat of forcing the People to sacrifice their own lives and fortunes to save the government from itself.

Man as an individual must have the latitude to choose for himself among the many fruits of a civilization in which he is an active participant. It is not possible for the individual to cut himself off from everything that he disagrees with. Man is a political animal who needs contact with his fellow men. Man the individual must also have the discretion of choice to determine which of his fellow men he chooses to associate with. That social contract carries with it the implication Roseau placed such great emphasis on. Roseau's theory was:

"It is the composite, at any given moment, of the presumably rational judgment of all mature and competent members of the group. The general will is therefore the whole of which the individual will, are parts. Without individuality, in other words, there could be no general will, not even theoretically."

Society is essentially the voluntary cooperative action of individuals in areas where the state is not concerned. But those areas are always subject to contraction if the state moves in to make cooperation compulsory. The price of compulsory cooperation is loss of both liberty and freedom. It is around this issue that morality finds different opinions. It is agreed, however, that rules of society are primarily voluntary agreements and can be described as conventions. He who violates a social convention is likely to be ostracized. But he who violates a state law or edict is subject to imprisonment or even death. In this area, we see an inconsistency in attempting to rationalize behavior of the state in context with the Constitutionally guaranteed unalienable rights. We must be ever vigilant that the *'social contract'* and the *'general will'* cease to be a self-denying ordinance and become instead a deceptively disguised instrument of oppression. The protection of minorities from the majority is the inspiring and historically unique objective of the Founding Fathers. If anyone had suggested the desirability of a unified *'general will,'* to be defined and exercised throughout the states from the seat of government, he would have been denounced more roundly than was poor bumbling George III. We must never forget that the first governmental authority that the colonists faced turned its guns and muskets upon these very same People. We must never forget that governments, when their very own positions of authority are threatened, will invariably turn against the People to save their own skins.

The fundamental threat from the individualist viewpoint is the theory of the general will. This absurdly named *"general will,"* as it becomes more generalized at the expense of individuals, reveals itself as the true enemy of individualism. Advocates of general will must first succeed in making People believe that such an entity as the *"general will"* does, in fact, exist within a society. Having accomplished this, they can then graft their own wishes for social controls on that anonymous and faceless body. This grafted wish translates into economic and social activities that should be undertaken for the sake of the whole society and then economic and social power will be under the control of the whole society. The problem remains that the minority does not desire to go there and the minority is prevented from majority dictatorship by the Constitution.

Men really are created equal in the sense that all have much the same basic needs, albeit, different character and in the sense that all are to be considered as parties to whatever social contracts their communities see fit to adopt. But at that point the line is drawn. To then say that each deserves equal opportunity is to tacitly admit that with this opportunity, they will become unequal. Some will push ahead, while others will go along for the ride.

Aristotle said, *"from the hour of their birth some are marked out for subjection, others for rule."* That biological fact can be obscured by sophistries, but it cannot be denied. Moreover, no system of government, least of all these alleged democracies, can prevent those who set and collect the taxes from dominating those who pay the taxes. The most that the ideal system of government can do is to insure that those who have the taxing power possess it only provisionally and within clear-cut limits. Under such a system, true individuality can flourish because it is protected from the tyranny of the general will.

Where political power is concentrated and unlimited, as it is under the theory of the general will, the unscrupulous will always rise to the top. Occasionally, a philosopher-king such as Marcus Aurelius may emerge; but the odds are enormously against that. The odds always favor the rise of a Caligula or a Nero. It is bitterly ironic that starting from the assumption of human equality we move so easily to the conclusion of the one indispensable man. But that is merely another way of saying that with Plato the constant tendency of democracy is to slide into dictatorship. Man, to be free, must create his own sphere or sanctuary, in which his knowledge and courage will preserve him his freedoms and liberties, [we name this our Principality] because...

A political system in which the *"majority or general will"* is so carefully hemmed about and circumscribed cannot with any accuracy be called a democracy and never be called a

democracy by those who take the oath of allegiance to defend
the Constitution. Those who wish to destroy the republic, and
build a unified totalitarian dictatorship on its ruins, will
naturally want first to spread confusion as to what our form of
government really is.

E. L. Godkin in 1882, called the effort to attain civil service
reform, *"The danger of an office-holding aristocracy."* Max
Weber, who later was to compose a classic study of
bureaucracy, was energized in his thinking by a visit to the
United States in 1904. Weber believed the outlook for
individualist democracy was dark. He said:

> *"...Everywhere the house is ready-made for a
> new servitude. It only waits for the tempo of
> technical economic "progress" to slow down and for
> rent to triumph over profit. The latter victory, joined
> with the exhaustion of the remaining free soil and
> free market, will make the masses "docile."*

Americans excel at institution building. The shape of our
institutions is continually remolding our lives. Careers are
tailored to fit each new process. Our lives became enmeshed
with the complicated structure of vested interests. Every
institutional change demands adaptation that is slow, difficult,
and painful. The [total] bureaucratic social structure [career
bureaucrats and politicians] that has grown up within the
present industrial/technological age has developed so fast that
we find it difficult to operate the system of checks and balances
necessary to use against inordinate political power.

Jefferson had a sarcastic young friend from Orange County
named James Madison, who set down in his federalist 51, the
basic hardheaded rule on which all the men of the generation
of 1776, radical and conservative alike, based their theories:

> *"In framing a government which is to be
> administered by men over men, the great difficulty
> lies in this; you must first enable the government to
> control the governed and in the next place oblige it
> to control itself."*

Bureaucracy has become dominant in government, in
industry, and in organizations of labor and religion. The first

interest of these bureaucracies, as of all human institutions, is in their own survival. These bureaucratic hierarchies, which seem unavoidable in a mass society, must be harnessed to the needs of self-government. The task of reversing the current trend toward individual serfdom into a trend toward individual liberty can succeed. Individual liberty, however, cannot be regained without the existence of the solitary individual. It is the solitary individual that has by their self-sufficiency found the room needed to look around objectively when observing the world. Viewing life and our relationship with our government objectively requires purging all pre-conceived notions, questioning all current conventional wisdoms, and facing each new event with a clean slate, as if you had never heard of it before.

FUTURE GENERATIONS: Our ignorance is by its very nature the most difficult for us to grasp. To talk intelligently about something, we must first possess some knowledge about that which we are concerned with. Man asserts that he has created our civilization and has the ability to change it. We also understand that early man had no conception of what our civilization is today. While it is true that man made this civilization, it must also be recognized that it was the contributions of hundreds of generations. We must thus ask ourselves, does this mean that civilization is the product of human design, man has aimed at what he produced? Even knowing how it came to be, man must understand its functioning and continued existence and what it depends upon for its continuation. The concept that man, endowed with a mind capable of conceiving the building of a civilization, set out to create that civilization as if it was already a completed concept in his mind is a leap of faith that defies reason. One would have to accept that man has the ability to simply impose a preformed mental pattern upon all of nature. It is equally misleading to think that to achieve a specific society, we have only to put into effect the ideas now guiding us. The growth of the human mind is part of the growth of civilization. It is the state of civilization that determines the scope of human values. We have no way to predict the nature of our society in the next millennium. Governments may attempt to create visions of a society of the future, and may even attempt to force the issue with coercion, but they will fail. We believe though that if individuals follow truth and morals, using free will to best advantage, the civilization of the 21st century will grow in freedom and liberty. Therefore, it is important that individuals seize the initiative and again take charge of the development of future societies.

When governments chose to endow *"collectives"* with rights that were originally given individuals as an unalienable right, they altered the nature of people's relationship with government. With the substitution of collectives for individuals, individual rights were diminished. As we continue into the new millennium, we observe what can be described as life and death struggles between these groups. While it matters which group wins, one outcome is not altered. All individuals, whether they agree or not, are forced, many against their will, to accept the outcome of the group that wins. With very few exceptions human history has seen individuals labor under the controlling myth of a *"whole society."* So, we tend to forget that mankind's rise above stagnating ways of life has exclusively depended on the emergence of independent and enterprising minds. These minds operating in opportunistic fields of endeavor have enough resistance to escape from oppressive social controls, were imposed in the name and interest of *"the whole society"* or nation. This must be accomplished without using the *Vietnam Solution* of destroying the people to save their society.

The individual is faced with a dilemma. View the planet as one sphere. Or, sub-divide the planet into separate countries [spheres]. Take the USA and sub-divide it into cities, towns, counties and states [separate spheres]. These spheres all have in common the legal authority to tax and regulate individuals and groups within their jurisdiction. Can the individual create a *"sanctuary within a sphere?"* Of course the individual can!

FUTURE GENERATIONS: Do not confuse individualism, as we describe and define in this book, with another version described as *"individualist anarchy."* We do not propose anarchy in any form. We understand clearly the corruptive faults and malfeasance of our government. We understand that representative government has long ago ceased to exist and that it is today categorized with the other lies that create the delusion of real freedom. There are but two basic descriptions to identify people. They are either pawns or players. We were once pawns but we are now players for we have discovered and learned the rules of the game that government plays.

Principality as sanctuary becomes important as we enter the 21st century still debating the question of *"is the Constitution a set of values for all time or is it a document begging constant change to satisfy the wants of successive societies?"* Inalienable rights features the individual and the *"common welfare"* clause, when implemented as it currently is, featuring preference to groups over individuals, creates a conflict of interpretation that has never been resolved.

PRINCIPALITY: JURISDICTION OVER YOUR LIFE

We offer you answers to who, what, why, when, where and how ideas for developing your personal skills, so that you may function successfully in activities as directed by your *'self,'* the Prince/Princess. Your principality will reside in your mind or the minds of you and your spouse through the love bond that you two create. Your mind has the full security of the Constitution and is yours and only yours. It is your most precious possession. So, treat your mind properly and reveal it only to those that you trust.

We have a dream. That one may early in life choose individualism as their right, and by wise and judicious use of knowledge, as set forth in the *"No Left Turn"* series, become invisible to the general population. That cloaked in wisdom and courage you move safely throughout the world, physically, intellectually, and economically, with the confidence and satisfaction that others do not know who you are or what you do.

Today there remains a window of opportunity. You may elect to remain on the socialist/fascist alternating pathways or withdraw and return to the freedom and liberty pathway. As is usual with all windows, the day will come when this window of opportunity will close. There are two choices, stay or return. A *no* choice is, of course, a choice to stay on the socialist/fascist alternating pathways. The true purpose of socialism is destruction of capitalism by substituting labor and government control over free enterprise *and* the true purpose of fascism is an unholy alliance with business leaders to accomplish the goals of government via free enterprise. If not that, then they jointly capture government and thus control over capitalism through regulation and mandates. It does appear that the New World Order is to become code for New World Socialism/Fascism and a new breed of dictators.

On this pathway, you must recognize that you are dealing with a government infatuated with self-importance, arrogant sense of unlimited power, out of control and out of bounds in matters of truth and morals, contemptible of the people who so eagerly seek to believe their lies. Government acts as if it sees itself as possessing the infallibility of a God when in reality they are a false idol. They will offer to buy your freedom, and will pay you with government benefits that can't be sustained, and are paid for with your own money. They reserve the right to withhold information from you as you are denied your Constitutional obligation for oversight of government behavior.

Government retains the right to lie to you as they have over the past centuries, in pursuit of a fantasy of political, economic and social imperialistic ascendancy. They retain the right to plunder and loot your individual wealth, while refusing to provide *"equal protection"* to you. You will fear and despise them as you would any other totalitarian government. Yet, they will provide for your every need, as determined by them, with you having little or no say about your life.

FUTURE GENERATIONS: Your task as citizen/patriot, if you decide to accept this responsibility, is to defend the Constitution against all threats foreign and domestic. The major threat today is domestic, and this threat is from your government and the middle-class [confused] majority that keeps it in power. This only makes your task more formidable. It is imperative that you do not surrender your freedom and liberty to those who seek to rewrite and revise the Constitution.

BEWARE THE BOOBY-TRAP

No matter how gloriously the *'threat'* is gift-wrapped, their ideology still offers serfdom in lieu of freedom and liberty. Never have so many lied to so many, and so many believed those lies. Political, social and economic ideology is a complex web of lies built upon a fragile foundation of a few truths. Ask and answer this question to your self. Who really controls your life, your body, your liberty and freedom, and your pursuit of your own happiness?

Politicians and activists will cease their lusting, greed and lying no more than Pavlov could make a dog stop salivating when the bell rang. When the bugle of power, wealth and control is blowing, it gains their attention and they immediately begin pawing the ground of socialist/fascist ideology.

To understand the times that we are living in, we best create another word picture. If government, especially its leaders, supported by its defenders, believes that lying to the people does not rise to the level of *"crime,"* then do they risk the argument they are guilty of behavior best described as pathological? If these same leaders practice serial adultery and argue that this matter is personal and private, therefore it does not rise to the level of *"sin,"* can this behavior be described as psychopathic? If this is the state of our government and of those willing victims who idolize, emulate and imitate those on whom they have bestowed celebrity status, has the country then made the complete transition to postmodernism? Do we now live in a state of foul ethics and gross immorality? Every minute of every day we are bombarded with the grossest forms of sex, violence and criminal behavior presented to us on television, Internet, music, magazines and newspapers. What further justification must a sane and sensible person have to withdraw their presence and their support from such behavior? We must look at one additional form of behavior.

Wise men of the past have passed on to us that those who were not born to great wealth must during their lifetime make financial and personal sacrifices to build security for their lives. We were told that we could either do it when we are young and strong, or we can do it when we are old and weak.

Some, but not nearly a majority, chose to do it when they were young and strong. The majority chose immediate gratification when they were young and tell us that they will cross this bridge when they get to it. Well, they are at that bridge. Now, old and weak, instead of making financial sacrifices, they plead for compassion from those who made their sacrifice when they were young and strong. Is it then proper for government to enforce positive response to their begging through *socialist* programs? To punish those who did right and reward those who did far less than they were capable of seems inconsistent with free choice. If people embrace *socialist/fascist* programs, then they also embrace America as a *socialist/fascist* country. People's choice is then simply to choose socialism or choose fascism, but neither embraces *freedom* and *liberty*? Each of us may have one or the other, but never both. We have made our choice. What choice have you made?

The dominant ideology and culture has reached down through the government education system to indoctrinate and create disorder in the minds of your children. Their culture spills forth from our TV screen and the Internet and completely seize the child's mind. You will have socialized schools and healthcare and buy, as a stockholder, into Socialism or Fascism Inc. You will not be required to function at a level higher than one with a room temperature IQ. Having chosen to dance with these devils, you must obediently follow wherever government decides to lead. *Socialism* or *Fascism* will offer middle-class people a seemingly compassionate form of serfdom that you will view as wage slavery in support of the good of all mankind. You will be told that the defenders of individualism, under the rights of the Constitution, are the enemy. The truth is that people have abandoned the Constitution as a condition of their choice to gain favor with popular *socialist/fascist* ideology. If you join in this choice you are now the enemy of free people; it is you who will advocate taking away the freedom granted to all individuals. It is your abandonment of the people that is criminal, no less than the father who abandons his wife and children. On the other hand, if your choice is to withdraw from the *socialist/fascist* pathway and return to the Constitutional pathway set out for all individuals, there will be responsibilities as well as freedom and liberty.

Having seen the darkness at the end of the *socialist/fascist* tunnel that America is being led down, you have returned to the pathway of the Constitution, as set out by the founding fathers. The culture that you leave behind is dying and something else is being born to replace it. You should take only what is needed to suffice your needs – leaving the bulk of the economy for others to take what they deem to be their cultural right – but they will not take it from you. You will not offend those you leave behind, as you will never be a greedy employer. You will find that your source of help will be to contract with other free individuals. Even though you know that society will never leave you alone, you need not interfere with the lives of others as long as they behave in a legal manner. Their argument is the argument of *"original guilt"* – each of us is born with the responsibility to sacrifice ourselves for the *"general welfare."*

You will accept that which you as an individual can't change. You will avoid the mesmerizing rhetoric that is constantly attempting to consume your mind as nothing more than a distraction – and proceed immediately to change that which you can change as it applies to you as an individual. To do this, you will steer clear of government's onerous web of taxes and regulation whose death grip will continue to grow tighter around those who choose the socialist/fascist pathway. You will play by the rules, but you will decide which rules apply to you.

Never again will government be able to tell that one greater lie that makes everyone forget all previous lies. You are through attempting to trade with those who think that lying is clever and the honest person a fool. Facts are real, truth will conform to those facts, you will discover the facts, and you will know the truth. You have learned the hard way that even though you follow the Golden Rule, neither government nor society will reciprocate in kind. In the past, you attempted to conceal the fear in yourself with anger. You are no longer angry, for you no longer fear. Government is not relevant. They are to be only pitied for their contemptible weakness, which shall haunt them forever.

FUTURE GENERATIONS: You will be tempted by the seductive promises of *"cradle-to-grave"* security. What is obscured is that *"cradle-to-grave"* working for wages, payment of taxes, web of growing regulations will engulf every aspect of your personal and private life. The alternative is a lifestyle in which you assert your independence and your right to manage your life as you choose. Many of you will find this comparison exciting and enticing, but you must be aware of ...

Among those who fail, the primary cause will be the following: wavering of self responsibility, erosion of discipline, infatuation with their own early success, and not understanding that when you are free you are the original 24/7 business activity. This means that at no time during any moment of any day are you prohibited from working, mentally or physically, at whatever legal activity you choose to engage. Those who succeed will be the ones who have the balls to do things the others won't - they won't let the system crap on them.

There are three types of wealth or currency: 1) physical, including stocks, bonds, real estate; 2) intellectual, one's superior knowledge; and 3) emotional currency, the objective reasoning that stops irrational action by you. It is true that wealth is difficult to come by in substantially large amounts. What is less understood is that once any or all of these forms of wealth are accumulated, the task of protecting this wealth confronts one with a huge problem that has never been experienced. The most successful will be those who develop a combined wealth strategy for the creation, protection and utilization of wealth.

PETER AND PAUL

We all know the story of Peter and Paul. That is, when you take from Peter to pay Paul, Peter becomes angry and Paul believes in the tooth fairy. So, what do Peter and Paul have to do with freedom and liberty? Thank you for asking! We have said repeatedly that people who know that they are free know this because neither their government nor society totally controls or dictates to them how they must behave. Government is in fact, irrelevant in their life, and is limited to your life. On the other hand, those who hang on every dictate of government, how it will affect them, find government relevant and themselves dependent. They do not experience freedom and liberty. The story of Peter and Paul is the story of *"taking from people according to their means – and giving to people according to their needs."* Through a series of government-sponsored programs, bankrolled by a progressive tax system, and managed by the government as the intermediary between the people's money, the benefits are distributed to the selected or favored. All the while it is holding back for itself a usurious commission for providing this perception of benevolent service. Government believes that it is the modern day Robin Hood. We should not be surprised. After all, government is nothing more than a reflection of the people it serves. In time, the people imitate government, or at least they try. It is an endless cycle. Time is of the essence – say your good-byes – begin your journey. As your knowledge increases, your imagination will be energized and that will increase both your skill level and your self-confidence. We all know that as self-confidence increases, so does courage. Courage is a function of knowledge and the ability to visualize a detailed concept from beginning to finish.

FUTURE GENERATIONS: We offer a short summary of the items that we hope you will accept as your values.

When writing the Constitution, Jefferson, Madison, Adams, Franklin, et al, deliberately left with us the idea that it was created to be harmonious with a very high level of natural morality and ethical conduct. Understand that they were as human as others and therefore did not always live up to the lofty goals of morality that they professed and strived for. The lofty goals thus were more challenges for the people to try to live up to than a statement of their own conduct. The country today is afloat with varying ideologies or *"isms."* Of those *"isms,"* the ones that encourage people to be of a lesser morality or to accept immorality as excuse to defend a leader of questionable personal and professional character fall into the category of evil.

The human environment consists of three factors; political, economic and societal. They are often referred to as the three legs of a stool. Remove one and the remaining two will not support the stool. We suspect that there is a relationship, and maybe a causal relationship, between the three legs. For example, during the '90s an economic *"bubble"* emerged in the stock markets that ended in the year 2000. The fed chairman once described it as *"irrational exuberance."* The question before us is: During the '90s, was there also a political or social bubble, marked by irrational something or other, and if there was, is there a connection or causal relationship between them? It is important that you make the correct interpretation; so it is thus essential that you acquire the most pertinent knowledge available to you.

FUTURE GENERATIONS: Those who seek and attain positions of power in government, especially the federal government, see themselves as Great Men and Women. Their human flaws are visible, but are put aside believing that it is a price of success. Their success convinces them that they are entitled to certain privilege; those that enhance relaxation, the best in food and drink because they labor through long hours under difficult conditions, and they know that they deserve that their bodies and minds be nourished from time to time from the fountain of privilege. They really believe that they are entitled to live better than the people because they have earned it, and, by golly, they will see that they get it. They differ from the rest of us in matter of principle. While people usually act on the basis of their principles, leaders tend to act more on the purpose that they have assigned to their lives. Knowing your opponent and their true or real purpose will give better insight into how to anticipate their moves and thus avoiding or even checkmating those moves.

Purpose vs. principle can best be understood by looking at America's century of Imperialism. McKinley, Wilson and Roosevelt each took America into a war that two-thirds of Americans wanted no part of. When we seized the Philippines and Puerto Rico, regardless of what name they gave them, they were still colonies of America. Eventually we gave the Philippines their independence, but for reasons not quite clear, Puerto Rico was retained as a colony with right of citizenship. Once presidents had acted against the people's principles to satisfy their own purposes and took us into war, the citizens rallied behind the flag. Governments start wars, people fight wars, people convert their rage against the enemy into a *"will to do combat"*. When the war is over, the people have saved both the country and the government. The government then takes the lion's share of the credit, builds monuments to those who died, and lives in the knowledge that their legacy is firm in fame and glory.

The growing *socialist/fascist* threat to individuals, especially small businesses, is the rapid increase in lawsuit liability. Business fears this liability that emerges from employees, customers, product, workplace, and federal and state government intervention. Individuals fear this liability from accidents, errors, enemies, governments and the frivolous. You should consider this threat when you choose a lifestyle or career. We have presented to you that the best [and safest] product is knowledge, and the best service is how to use that knowledge. We named it free labor. But the choice is yours to make.

If you prepare for a career in wage labor, you must consider that there are at least two levels of wage labor where you can be a player. First, everyone that works, even the largest corporations and/or the highest levels of government is technically wage labor. Second, because wage labor can be separated, we can label these levels as either the major league or the minor league. The major league is the upper echelons of management, and they control the power of the purse and the career of the minor leaguers. The same situation exists in government; everyone is wage labor and those at the top control the purse, justice, promotions, programs and ideology. We pointed out that individualism, the acts of a principal, is neither employer nor employee, but rather a niche somewhat forgotten by others. Principals are examples of free labor, and enjoy immensely more freedom and liberty than any wage labor. What is the future of Free Labor?

As mentioned elsewhere, there is immediate room for 20,000,000 or more of wage labor to quickly reinvent them selves as free labor. Later is this book we set forth specific examples of how this can occur. A recent Department of Commerce report states that there is a continuing increase in the number of businesses that do not have employees; Nevada being the leader with a six percent increase. Small businesses will be the first to favor contractors over employees. What are the advantages? For the small business owner it means that the entire package of hiring, supervising, and firing, plus the administrative mandates of government disappear. For the former workers, if they set up their own limited partnerships, they also, somewhat, escape that package. Now, both parties to the contract manage their own affairs with all of the benefits described throughout this book. Both can become wealthy, which we indicated was not the objective, but the means to reach freedom and liberty. Can you possibly imagine what America would look like if within the next two generations 50 million wage labor became free labor?

FUTURE GENERATIONS: We are well into what is known as the information revolution. Information in itself has little value until it has been evaluated, the source verified, and its credibility established with additional sources identified supporting that valuation. When that has been completed, it becomes *"intelligence"* and is ready to be considered for entry into your business plan. Beware of dis-information and misinformation, as well as information deliberately withheld. Propaganda and illusions fall into this category. Speaking of illusions, democracy falls into this category as it gives people the illusion that they are free and enjoy liberty. This illusion is masterminded by skilled slight of hand and mastery of words uttered constantly by *"talking-heads."* Accept that which you cannot change, change that which you can change, and strive for the wisdom to tell the two apart. To be wrong will subject you to a distractive waste of time on the first item, and subject you to unintended consequences and labeling as a do-gooder on the second. We review Bush 43 mistakes.

We draw our thoughts from two books, Carl von Clauswitz *"Principles of War"* and Sun Tzu *"The Art of War."* Mistake #1, the commander-in-chief must stand for the virtues of wisdom, sincerity, benevolence, courage and strictness. Mistake #2, know the enemies intent but more so their capabilities. Mistake #3, victory must come quickly and completely, for if it becomes drawn out, the resources of the State will not be equal to the strain. Mistake #4, it is better to capture an army in its entirety than to destroy it. Mistake #5, do not become engaged in a siege for the outcome will be in doubt and the cost will be horrific. Mistake #6, to commit additional assets to a cause that cannot be accomplished will lead to greater losses and defeat. Conclusion: Iraq, as with the wars that proceeded, never achieve the intended result. Wars beget more wars – and leaders cast their frustrations upon lost causes. The people must never know the truth about the futility of our wars for then they would round up their leaders and deal with them in a quick and just manner.

One question that is frequently asked is, *"where in America is the greatest opportunity to achieve freedom and liberty?"* We have found that the best answer is to refer the questioner to the 2000 post election map, which shows by color the counties carried by Gore [blue] and the counties carried by Bush [red]. Even in the red counties, Socialism is alive and well, growing slowly but surely. There is still time for opportunity in those areas. Study that map closely and carefully, considering what you have already read, and the answer should jump right out at you. Then you will understand the difference between the two sectors is ideology. Every two years you will be furnished an updated red and blue map of the country revealing the extent of any increase or decrease in the areas of each political ideology. This is like having your personal spy satellite looking down 24/7 at the landscape in which you are forced to play the game. The intelligence that can be gleaned from this information will give you an advantage over the opponent – you know where they are – but they can only guess where you are and who you are.

When a country with voter approval bestows overly generous privilege upon leaders – treating and worshipping them as virtual Royalty, the voters can only expect that leaders will play the role of Monarchs for all it is worth. When leaders succumb to the Royalty Syndrome, they also believe that leaders then seem more valuable than people [pawns] who fight the wars. They then fall to the *"success-disease"* believing in their own infallibility. Having chosen to pursue a course of military, economic and cultural imperialism, they have ascended to the position of King-of-the-Hill. Our enemies wish us the worst, and those with the means will attempt to push us off that hill and take our place. They lack the military means to do this, so they will be guided by their belief that America is the Satan. How? The means of terrorism are currently on display and being practiced and developed in the Middle East, as we watch Palestinians and Israelis wage war on each other. And, so they are and we are – until the shooting starts – then Royalty is about as useful as a gun without bullets.

Compassion and charity continue to be individual choices. You must decide who, what, when, where, how and why you distribute your compassion and charity to individuals that you find worthy and in need of that which you may share with them. Within what is described as the *"general population"* is the votes/voters that determine the degree and speed of ideological expansion. People select the area they prefer to live in based upon their personal values. It is not unusual that people will choose to live either among others of similar values or avoid living where the proportion of people with values they find abhorrent, is the greatest. When people act in a discriminate manner in where and how to live their lives, they are exercising several of their Constitutional rights. There is a portion of the general population you will disagree with, and you will find them in government, schools, and all other sections of society. When you act in this manner, without infringing on the rights of another, you are simply exercising your rights to freedom and liberty.

In the course of researching and writing this book, the extent to which the unknown government lies hiden within the mass of rhetoric and spin is, as a ratio to the lies that are exposed and become known to the people, grown so large that it is impossible for us to quantify within any reasonable perspective. It is possible that the ratio will exceed 1,000 or 1,000,000 x 1. Therefore, we simply turn the table and say that the onus of establishing the truth of any statement or fact rests squarely upon the politician, bureaucrat or spin master, and please furnish a second or verifying opinion. You must take responsibility in your life for your decision on this matter.

Many of us have refused to vote for the reason that government, elected leaders, and too many of the general population have accepted bad behavior, sinning, and immorality causing the general character of America to continue a slide, started many decades earlier, into a swamp of disgusting and deplorable behavior topped off *"institutional arrogance."* There is no way that those of us that left would seriously consider living among and within such a swamp. Yet America remains the greatest country in the world – not as free and independent as it once was – and maybe not as free and independent as it may later be. We love our country with a passion of pride, but we do not trust the fools who run it.

EPILOGUE TO INDIVIDUALISM

Power – the accumulation of – has always been the ultimate and greatest desire of many. Everything else – fame, fortune and authority – is just a means of attaining the real goal, which is power over others. And the ultimate power is the power to make each and every human being obey without questioning what they want and immediate obedience. We experience the same learning practices from government that we in turn use to train obedience in our dogs. Individuals can never live the life they dream of living unless they can free themselves from fear. We've tried to ignore government's evil and reconcile life by pretending it did not exist, but it does exist. It lives and it breathes, and we must put a stop to it. A government that is evil has something fundamentally wrong at the core.

> "...the micro-social laws control the individual. They define human interaction on the small scale. They tend to restrain, to inhibit, to control. The macro-social laws control the masses. They define human interaction on the large scale. They tend to liberate, to unchain, to unleash. The same person who would cry at the pathetic sight of a wounded animal might chant loudly for war, for death, for the indiscriminate destruction of men, women and children by bomb and bullet. Civilization has tamed the individual. But in the collective heart of the mob there courses the blood of primitive man. Both the micro and macro-social laws must be understood for the effective manipulation of human beings."

The Laws of Human History

FUTURE GENERATIONS: We as a nation have entered the 21st century. We are being tested and will be challenged for leadership of the free world. This is a continuation of the age-old game that even children play called King-of-the-Mountain. Of course, the idea is to push the current king off and take his place. In chess, the checkmate means literally the KING has fallen. America has been the glue that held the free world together since WWII. America became great because of its character; the character of its leaders and the character of its people. The people are the true force of the most powerful country in history. We must not allow the weakness and absence of character of our present leaders to put this country at risk. Remember *"The Tree of Liberty,"* as spoken by Thomas Jefferson. *"The tree of liberty must be refreshed from time to time with the blood of patriots and tyrants."* If we fail we will deserve our fate:

> *"Power over one's fellow man is the root of all human activity. For what better way to control one's destiny than to bend others to your plans and your will? The urge to amass that power is both irresistible and subliminal. Whether that power is gained by wealth, by beauty, by office, by the muzzle of a gun, or by the moral suasion of one's ideas, its accumulation is the end, in and of itself, of every human alive."*

The Laws of Human History

Empires never leave peacefully. We should anticipate that as our cultural excesses combined with declining character and morality of both government and People, the ultimate end will come, and it will surprise most. Individual rights will reach the level where they are deemed to be excessive and out of control. Society will demand that government do something. This fertile opportunity will incubate and hatch a *"strong-man."* Such an individual or party could come from either the Left or the Right of the political spectrum. This individual or party will seize power under emergency conditions. Laws and emergency regulations, similar to martial law, will be implemented and strictly enforced. Because we know not when this will occur, it behooves individualists to take the time remaining to position themselves and their activities globally, so that they are not sucked up in a broad and general lockdown upon the populace. This will be accomplished by vacating what will become known as *"killing fields."* We must prepare in advance positions and locations that are most likely to be overlooked, bypassed or unassailable by government.

From King George III to President George 43. When government is believed to be corrupt it is known to lie without a conscience, is observed to be immoral, is judged to be without character by most of the People, then government loses its authority to govern. The beginning of anarchy is set into motion. There can be no government if the People do not trust or believe in it, refuse to follow it, consider it no longer relevant, and prepare to take their single life out from under the grasp of the filthy, lying, cheating leaders that have stolen freedom and future from the people.

FUTURE GENERATIONS: It is this conflict that gives rise to *Principality* as an alternative for individuals who believe that their inalienable rights are being denied them. We have named ours **"Free Labor."** Our principality is patterned after "Atlantis" that is described in *"Atlas Shrugged"* by Ayn Rand. This book is a highly recommended read.

"Atlantis" was a remote mountain valley in Colorado that was essentially invisible from the air. Today's sanctuary is hiding in the open and appears invisible when the product and service are knowledge and its use. In such a sanctuary, it is possible to withhold food from and starve the mighty beast. We are not the enemy of the people or the enemy of the Constitution – we are that voice in the dark calling out for citizens/patriots to help save the Constitution.

Socialism/fascism is like an eye cataract, it slooooowly and progressively clouds the clearness of intellectual vision, leaving people in darkness of reasoning and understanding. Free-Labor remains above and beyond this obfuscation of reason and logic and from its vantage point the war of rhetoric and spin being waged by the two great selfish special interests can clearly be observed. These race-based and faith-based ideologies, which have contributed to not only the demise of the Constitution but also the unwarranted destruction of rights that free people formerly enjoyed, also exist, as they too were granted by their Creator.

Sanctuaries, by their very nature, place those individuals that have sought them out, in a location safe from the ideological/theological wars of American special interests. From this vantage point, the Blue and the Red are observed attempting to destroy each other in a manner reminiscent of the Catholic/Protestant wars of the 16th and 17th centuries, the Jewish/Arab wars of the Middle East, and the ideological wars of socialism/human rights of China or Cuba. There are no winners or losers between the extreme ideologies as their struggles for power never cease. The losers will be those willing victims who selfishly surrendered their liberty and freedom for the deceptive and treacherous promises of the psychopaths.

This bitter struggle of opposing values will lay waste to America as each ideology in turn seizes control over the levers of power and conducts its own *"slash and burn"* programs. There will come a time of *"enlightenment,"* and people will again be free to pursue their happiness. Going forward, it is difficult to assess right from wrong or good from bad or constitutional from unconstitutional in how the elite-controlled government manages people. The one liberty that must not be taken is the right to choose what it is that we believe and how it plays into our lives. Most people seek a safe harbor from the fear they have regarding government by acting in a passive manner that does not attract government's attention. Some will seek to remedy a perceived injustice by becoming a zealous activist. Others will seem to disappear from the radar of government and quietly go about their lives. We are indeed a mixed bag when our mores, morals, character and intelligence are used to achieve a change in how our government functions and affects our lives.

Modern technology has placed into the individual's hands the means and capacity to create a lifestyle which, while not totally free of government's fiscal and regulatory policy, can be made sufficiently free that government moves very close to irrelevance in that individual's life. The sphere of these individuals will differ from others in that it will be exclusively the individual voluntarily cooperating with each other as opposed to the traditional sphere where cooperation is mandated by laws. What will distinguish an individual from groups is the behavior and the way views are shared. The group derives its power from the number of members in the group; therefore, they will approach you in a manner of an evangelizer, claiming to save you through membership in their group. On the other hand, the individual would be happy to freely share his thoughts and values with you. If you choose to enter you are welcome, if you choose to not enter they wish you well and forever leave you unfettered by their acts or deeds.

FUTURE GENERATIONS: Throughout this book, information, ideas and reasons have been set out for the reader identifying the means and the methods to control the impact of fiscal, regulatory and redistribution policies of the government. It is the essence of the skills to play THE GAME. Skill and courage will permit you to checkmate that which you detest and render irrelevant that which threatens you.

The US Government [USG], having taken unto itself a perceived right to be the sole judge of what is the *"good life,"* has by their own actions violated the Constitutional rights of the individual. When one looks into the mirror, and asks oneself, *"Today, do I enjoy the unalienable rights bestowed upon me by the Creator, guaranteed by the Constitution, by prohibiting the government from infringing upon them, or are they diminished by the actions of government?",* many will answer that question by affirming that they do not enjoy all of their inalienable rights. The action that must be taken is to demonstrate the success of individualism in America. It seems appropriate that, when one or more individuals conspire to change the Constitution by means not provided in said Constitution, such a crime should rise to the level of a capital crime. If we are to be governed not by the arbitrary dictates of a nation state but by the rule of law, then it becomes incumbent on the individual to understand these rules. The individual also has two types of responsibilities. The first is to defend his country against foreign threat. The second is to defend the Constitution against domestic threat. Defending the Constitution has two principle responsibilities. The first is to be a *"well-informed electorate"* for the purpose of selecting the best among us to represent us. The second is *"oversight responsibility"* of those whom we elect. We fulfill the second responsibility by demanding from our elected that they make complete disclosure of their activities. The business of the people is the selection and oversight of the elected. The business of the people is both nonnegotiable and cannot be delegated back to the elected. When people abdicate their oversight responsibility, loss of their freedom quickly follows. This was the great fear of Washington, Jefferson, Madison, Hamilton, et al.

It is more than a coincidence that Roman jurisprudence developed the theory of persona, or personal and individual rights, which the state must carefully respect and protect. It was believed that the *"highest good"* was to be found not in any form of communal life, but rather in each man seeking for himself the type of life that fulfilled him. The barbarian invasions and the collapse of the Roman Empire put an end to abstract discussion regarding the relative merits of collectivism and individualism. When order was restored during the latter part of the Middle Ages, there developed a sort of compromise between collectivism and individualism. The extremes of both were rejected.

> **FUTURE GENERATIONS:** We have learned that people tend to form collectives to protect themselves from each other. The collective then designates who will be in charge to protect everyone, do so with fairness and equality, do no harm to any member, and provide for the peace and tranquility of the collective. Of course, the Constitution that the people created, and the people in turn establishing the federal government, is the first and best example of an American collective. Today, something has gone wrong with this concept.

COLLECTIVISM IN SHEEP'S CLOTHING

Those hired to 'protect and serve' are viewed with a skeptical eye. With each passing year, we find numerous instances where those hired to protect us are, in some cases, themselves perpetrators of acts that may or may not rise to the level of crime. Imagine the stress of being stopped by policemen, knowing that a certain percent [?] of them are themselves practicing criminals. You can only wonder at what are the true odds or probability that the one stopping you is a threat to your property and life. All you really know is that he/she is armed, dangerous and highly trained in control. This breakdown in trust and confidence in government impacts other aspects of people's lives in the collective.

If the government fails or appears overwhelmed by the degree and amount of crime, leaving fear and doubt in the minds of the people, the people then view their neighbors and others in the same manner as they view a questionable police force. Is or isn't my neighbor a threat?

When society is unable or unwilling to trust the politician, police, neighbors and strangers, they continue to withdraw into smaller groups living in a fear that continues to grow within their minds. Now, they are both skeptical and fearful. They lose more of whatever trust and confidence they had. They begin to say, *"what happened to our society?"* or *"I think society is going in the wrong direction as there is so much rage and complaining."* So many people exhibit a lack of conscience and an unwillingness to accept responsibility for their actions. A growing body of people are moving toward the idea that they are entitled to everything new that comes along, and that they should not have to work for it.

When you make a personal judgment of what you believe is wrong and what should be avoided, it becomes possible for you to identify the problem. Once you determine the nature of the problem, you can then begin to take that action that will compensate, in your life only, for the breakdown in society that you have observed. If the majority of the middle-class is, in your opinion, going in the wrong direction, then it behooves you to find a new road for the journey through your life. The lesson here is that if you understand that there is nothing that you as an individual can do to change society, than you must...

ACCEPT THAT WHICH YOU CANNOT CHANGE. In January 2001, USA TODAY published a poll they took with CNN and GALLOP, under the heading of percentage of those polled listing various issues as *"top"* or *"high"* priority. The published results are:

       1. improving education [94%],
       2. prosperity [91%],
       3. Social Security [89%],
       4. prescription drugs [88%],
       5. balanced federal budget [88%],
       6. Medicare [88%],
       7. improving health care [87%],
       8. military security [85%],
       9. minorities, poor [80%],
       10.combating illegal drugs [78%],
       11.environment [78%],
       12.race relations [75%],
       13.cutting federal taxes [65%]

You can do all these things or you can accept that which you cannot change, but you cannot do both simultaneously. You victimize yourself with the greatest distraction there is.

Now hear this! Fully 95% of the words and pictures that enter your senses via the radio or TV [network and cable news] are supposition, innuendo, speculation, spin, and out-right deception tainted by the occasional deliberate lie. The only value this has is that it alerts you to what mischievous ideas the elite are harboring. Interestingly, this bombardment of useless information serves the purpose of those serving it up only when the receptor reacts to this disinformation.

There exist those who believe that they can change anything. Those who refuse to accept that which is beyond their ability to change – who press forward for change with high emotional hopes that tend to obscure rational reality – are unaware of the trap of *unintended consequences'* lurking in wait that their actions will trigger and produce huge amounts of dislocation, distress and damage. Their noble plan does not permit them to acknowledge the failure and faults of their plan and they never repudiate their failures.

When disinformation is not reacted to or ignored, the source or server is not relevant to the individual. How do you control this invasion of your mind? You substitute another activity or source of information so that instead of always turning on the news, you read a good magazine or listen to a fine educational tape. Bad habits are overcome by supplanting them with good habits. It is a way of life – learn it because...

FUTURE GENERATIONS: The greatest pitfall waiting to assure that you fail is distraction. Distraction is an event or condition, usually mental or emotional, which compels attention or distracts, especially such as sports, amusement, violence, terrorism, death or injury, politics, corruption, scandal, gangs, sex, drugs, or just hanging out. They become an obsession that turns aside doing and thinking the things that are really important in life. This list includes education, family, career, character, morality, and conscience. We are what we think about!

FOCUS, FOCUS AND THEN FOCUS AGAIN

You have viewed polls of people's concerns that are published in daily papers. For each concern, the government is alleging itself to be an honest broker or intermediary acting in the best interest of all the people. Your attention has been distracted by the spin put on each of these issues so that the people express their concern by saying, *"why doesn't government do something about this?"* Government will never repudiate its secret agenda. The only way to correct the problems of these issues is to eliminate the government as intermediary. Take government out of the equation.

However, lacking the qualities, you will not succeed. You will be condemned for the rest of your life to raging. *"I never had the chance or opportunity; it isn't my fault."* When distraction is recognized and dealt with, then proceed to change that which you can change in your life. Items in the preceding section, and as defined in the preceding paragraph, are examples of distraction. The clever manipulator will always distract you before making a foray into taking from you that which is coveted, albeit, without your knowing. Learn to exercise due-diligence to protect yourself from shysters, con artists and politicians by...

CHANGING THAT WHICH YOU CAN CHANGE. Each of the above items you must learn to accept as they affect society in general. They are also the items that you can and must change insofar as they impact your personal/individual life. However, if you are engrossed in complaining about the above, you cannot focus on changing them in your life.

FUTURE GENERATIONS: Taxation is called progressive because it takes from people according to their means and gives to others according to their needs. Here the currency is usually measured in dollars, yet, for the average middle-class worker, it is also measured in labor – hours of labor. Up to fifty percent of the hours you work are to pay taxes that the government collects because of:

      a)Government's irresistible urge to scratch their *"do-gooder"* itch, even if it harms others.

b)demand of others upon you as an illegitimate claim to your labor and money.

What do you wish to do about this, if anything?

Education is defined as free and equal to everyone without exception. Free and equal is defined as the same amount of dollars spent on each school or pupil. The socialization of public education, which began in the mid-nineteenth century was completed in 1976 with the creation of the Department of Education. Since that date, student achievement has been flat or declined, leaving America near the bottom of the developed countries when measured by the AIM's test. It is clear that a subtle effort has been made to confiscate [take] from achievers and crudely attempted to be redistributed to those labeled as disadvantaged. Education of your children is the best example of *"if you want it done right, then do it yourself."* Your home is the best school as it is free of crime, gangs, drugs, alcohol, promiscuous sex, and all of those other new morality falsehoods. You must take charge of the education of your children, help them develop a conscience, learn right from wrong, recognize the real values in life, and to be wary of closet psychopaths. Schools indoctrinate your child's mind – parents educate their children with the knowledge necessary for survival and success.

REGULATION must follow the first rule of *"do no harm"* to either the many or the few by deviation from the intent of the Constitution and the *"equal protection"* Fourteenth Amendment. When government violates this rule, the result is similar to the handicap systems found in horse racing and amateur golf. The intellectually challenged are legislated a handicap from government to allegedly:

a)   level the playing field,
b)   place a handicap upon achievers to slow them down,
c)   permit the challenged a head start, and
d)   equalize the potential results.

This handicap consists of the achievers carrying a greater share of the burden, just like adding weight to the jockey who rides a swift horse; or the amateur golfer who must give strokes to the other to balance the different level of skill. The problem with handicaps is that the person receiving the benefit of the handicap can and does manipulate the future handicap by deliberately performing below their standard for the purpose of receiving a greater future handicap. These forms of harm are ideologically defined as fairne$$, compa$$ion and $ociali$m.

When people are free to act as they see fit without pressure, coercion or compulsion, and choose to help another out of the goodness of their heart, it is an act of compassion. When people are not free to act as they see fit, are coerced or pressured to help another, then the act of helping is compulsion, not compassion. It is the sense of guilt created by the coercion for reasons such as the fact that some, by their own effort, became more successful than others. The problem with compassion is, how do you tell the truly needy from the illegitimate needy? It is the same problem that you have when you attempt to tell the lying elected official from the honest one. Just as there are honest politicians, there are truly needy people. Just as there are illegitimate needy who hide among the truly needy, there are illegitimate leaders who hide among the honest leaders and pretend to be what they can never be.

Regulation costs the taxpayers money – the greater the amount of regulation, the greater the cost to the people. You play this game automatically unless you opt out! If you want an education on this subject, direct a letter to your senator and Congressman telling them that you do not believe that you enjoy the life, liberty and pursuit of happiness guaranteed by the Constitution. Of course, give them a few examples of why you believe this, and ask them what they plan to do about it. You will not believe the answer that you will receive! Learn that politicians are just like you and me, with the same strengths and weaknesses. The only difference is that they prey upon others, while we always leave others to their own destinies.

According to John Locke, primitive men came together, and by means of a social contract, created the political unit known as the state. The government was granted certain limited authorities with the balance being retained or reserved by the individual. This artificial government was never, under any circumstances, to interfere. The history of the struggle between collectivism and individualism has existed for as long as man has had the artificial state. This struggle flowed and ebbed like a tide. As we enter the 21st century, the tide is flowing strongly in favor of collectivism. History teaches us that this too will ebb, and that the flow of individualism will again prevail. The question that must then be posed is what does an individual do in the interim in a country dominated by the theory of collectivism?

We live in a world of *"feel good; be happy."* We must be aware that while we are having a good time, others are working behind the scenes to shape government and society into their vision. The blueprint by which today's government and society function was conceived in the minds of a few men and women in prior years. They are the individualists who created their own sanctuary separate from that of government.

Individualists insist that the source of property rights is the law of causality. All property and all forms of wealth are produced by man's use of his mind and his labor. We cannot have effects without causes; therefore, we cannot have wealth without its source, intelligence. You cannot force intelligence to work. Those who are able to think will not work under compulsion; those who will, won't produce much more than the price of the chains needed to keep them enslaved. You cannot obtain the products of a mind except on the individual's terms, by trade and by volitional consent. Any other policy of men toward man's property is the policy of criminals, no matter what their rank, even if it is government. Criminals are immoral savages who play it short range and starve when their prey says NO. You who believe that crime could be *"justified"* if government decreed that certain forms of robbery were legal and resistance to robbery illegal, will perish by the sword that you lived by.

THE PRICE OF FREEDOM

FUTURE GENERATIONS: We have talked a great deal about taxation under King George and the years up to 1913. The year 1913 brought us the beginning of the downside of taxation and regulation "with" representation. The temptation to tax and spend was an addiction of such proportions that all elected, at least most, have failed to stand the test of what has become our countries greatest evil. They truly believe that our money is their money and that they know better how to spend our money than we do. Yes, we call this evil.

AMENDMENT XVI

The Congress shall have the power to lay and collect taxes on incomes, from whatever source derived, without apportionment among the several States, and without regard to any census or enumeration. Ratified February 3, 1913

FUTURE GENERATIONS: John Marshall, Chief Justice of the Supreme Court in 1819, had this to say about taxing the individual. *"The power to tax is the power to destroy."* We know about the Sixteenth Amendment to the Constitution, ratified in 1913, and we all have separate opinions about whether the warning was correct. If it was correct, what are today's ramifications? That tax genie is out of the bottle, and it would be an unrealistic expectation to believe that it could be returned. A world without income taxes would indeed be a world of greater individual freedoms and responsibilities. Therefore, in this book, we will examine the income tax for both individuals and business and decide how best to manage our affairs in view of this new information.

We have commented in an earlier part of the book about the cost of government, but must repeat ourselves here. All forms of taxes take, on average, 45 to 55% of the Peoples gross income. Statistically over 40% of households pay no income tax and some of these, the (alleged) needy, get a tax subsidy. This of course means that part of our people are net taxpayers, and the others are net tax subsidized, or also expressed as those who pull the wagon and those just along for the ride. If you are at the tax payer median, say 50%, you spend one-half of the total hours that you and your spouse work each year for the purpose of providing government(s) with the money they say that they need to fund all the programs they want and approve. On April 16, 2007, The Christian Science Monitor published results of a study that showed that 52.6% of Americans receive significant income from government programs. This is money that doesn't belong to them. At the same time, the percentage of the working population, **not employed in a government reliant job,** has **fallen below 29%.**

FUTURE GENERATIONS: Governments steal from the people and spend it foolishly. The people steal from governments by claiming illegitimate and sometimes fraudulent need. For FY 2006 the difference in the two thefts, the government's claim on our taxpayers and the exorbitant claims of the needy, will run about $825b, in budget overrun. All of this asinine waste incurred by government is preventing tens of millions of average citizens from being affluent and self-sufficient.

The redistribution-of-wealth ideology began as voluntary help by people for people and grew into full-fledged welfare. It masquerades under different names for different groups. The Sixteenth Amendment clearly states that government may tax income from all sources. Government has taken a literal interpretation of it as it taxes income of Americans from any source throughout the world. You should not be surprised if, when the time comes that we go there, income will be taxed anywhere throughout the universe, moon, Mars, you name it. This is neither tongue-in-cheek nor a facetious remark, it is a reasonable projection of today's tax code.

The Constitution speaks to the issue of socialist assistance only in the preamble, which states that government should *"promote the general welfare."* Our college dictionary defines promote as *'to contribute to progress or growth, to advocate, to move forward'*. This is very vague and open to argument. For the purpose of our discussion, we take the position that there is little if anything that a citizen can do that would have any impact on the tax system or generate any beneficial change. Further truth of this matter is that to use time, energy and other resources to debate this issue is nothing more than a distraction and waste of the energy and those resources. Energy and resources scheduled can be saved for use at a specific time. Time on the other hand has no shelf life, it is here now and then gone. We make better use of these resources by studying the code and learning what the code says we may and may not do. With that having been said, let us move onward to managing our respective tax code affairs. Remember, you hesitate, you lose the value of time.

Income taxes are intended to provide the funds necessary for government to carry out its mandates under the Constitution and fund the additional programs that have been established to *"promote the general welfare."* Karl Marx, in his manifesto, spoke to the issue of taxes, and in his words said, *"Socialism is taking from people according to their means and giving to people according to their needs."* The progressive tax system continues to be hotly debated with very emotionally persuasive arguments offered by both sides. Actually, all of the *"promote the general welfare"* programs have their proponents and opponents, so the question is not which side is right but rather which ideology is in control of the levers of government. The 2006 election has reversed the fascist move to the Right and will now take America further into the socialist Left. Our tax code is an example of insanity used by people driven by a lust for power, who are truly idiots of great magnitude. Those who choose wage labor, such as is defined in the Dominant Ideology section, should not be surprised to learn that wage labor, as a percentage of income and time, carries an extremely heavy portion of the tax burden. Should we be surprised? No! That burden falls on wage labor for the same reason people rob banks – that's where government finds the money, and best of all, this portion of our population is completely without security to create and protect any assets they may have from government confiscation.

The 2001 tax relief act has brought the tax code to an unprecedented 95,000 pages. Fortunately, you need to understand less than 200 pages. For a brief period during the Civil War, and again commencing in 1913 with the passage of the Sixteenth Amendment, we have lived under the fear of the tax collector. Allegedly, tax collections are to fund the operations of government. This seems to be one of the many reasons that government continues to grow and grow. The more activities that government takes unto itself justifies ever bigger and bigger taxes it collects. The tax code can also be seen as the means by which government offers incentives, bribes, to those who will do as Big Daddy wants, and disincentives, punishment, to those who want to do it their own way. Your tax consequences are determined by how you take your income, known as the character of the income, as defined by government. If you are an employee, your taxes, as a percentage of income are among the higher. So if you desire to rid yourself of this burden, you must change how you conduct your affairs. Where do you find information on how to do this? Well, would you believe that that information is set forth in the tax code? Or, if you want it written in plain English, pick up J. K. Lasser's tax guide.

Keep in mind our earlier discussions on wage labor and free labor and before-tax dollars and after-tax dollars. Free labor pays their normal, necessary and reasonable costs out of before-tax dollars. In the discussion on taxes, you learned that free labor actually earns a tax refund of tax paid on that product or service. Follow closely how tax collection goes around in a circle and when it reaches the end it is wage labor, buying and paying for normal, necessary and reasonable items from after-tax dollars.

It can be said *"everyone can be lied to by their politician some of the time, some can be lied to all the time, but not all politicians can lie to all the people all of the time."* Having said that, it then becomes apparent that the probability that your politician is lying to you are between 90% and 100%. People lie because it serves their purpose, helps them achieve their goals, and provides them with plausible denial.

THE UNITED STATES INCOME TAX

FORM 1040 – U.S. INDIVIDUAL INCOME TAX RETURN. The most important issue to learn pertaining to gaining freedom in your life are the basics of the individual income tax form 1040 and associated schedules and forms. It is this form that will provide you with the tax knowledge you need.

FORM 1040
Lines 7 through 22 are provided for the different types of income to be reported, by character. Character refers to the nature of income and how the income is taken. Of those lines on page one, for entering your income, be advised that all but three lines require either a positive number or a zero. The other three lines may be either positive or negative or zero.

Schedule [A] to form 1040 – itemized deductions
Medical and dental expenses are deductible to the extent they exceed 7.5% of your adjusted gross income [AGI]. For example, if your AGI is $25,000, you multiply that number by 7.5% [$1,875] then subtract that amount from your total medical expenses to determine the allowed deduction. Businesses generally have a medical plan for their employees and themselves.

A primary tax paid by homeowners is the property tax. In addition, homeowners may deduct mortgage interest. If real estate is held for trade or business, expenses associated with its operation are, if they meet the test of normal, necessary and reasonable, deductible to the business.

Miscellaneous expenses are deductible to the extent that they exceed 2% of your AGI. In the example above [$25,000 AGI], the non-deductible amount is $500. The typical miscellaneous deductions of individuals are generally for business type expenses.

If you do not have expenses to report on schedule [A] because they are reported on   another return, such as a corporate return, you should determine if the standard deduction is greater than the itemized deduction, and take the larger of the two. Schedule A is primarily for wage labor workers' use.

Schedule [C] to form 1040 – Profit or loss from business

Income and expenses are posted according to the line item descriptions on the form. If line 31 shows a profit, enter that amount on form 1040 and schedule SE. If you have a loss and have checked that all investment is at risk, also enter the loss on both forms.

Schedule [E] to form 1040 – supplemental income and loss

If you are claiming the *"up to"* $25,000 real estate offset as an individual, complete page one. Total rental and royalty income or loss is entered on line 17, form 1040.

If you are a *'real estate professional'* operating as a business enter income or loss from all businesses in part II, page two, schedule [E] and net on line 31 part 2, and carry that amount to line 40 and then to line 17. Example: Husband is real estate professional [partnership] and has losses totaling $40,000. Wife has a for-profit activity [partnership] and has a net profit of $45,000. The amounts are reported in part 2, schedule [E] and netted leaving $5,000 net income on line 31 and line 40. Enter on line 17, form 1040 to be netted with other income and deductions to determine AGI. This introduction only scratches the surface of the code but if you make an effort you will strike gold.

A FEW CAVEATS ABOUT TAXES AND TARGETING

TAX EVASION occurs when people deliberately or knowingly withhold the reporting of income from their tax return. Most who work in the cash underground are aware of what they are doing. Many others are ignorant or not fully aware that what they are doing is fraud.

TAX AVOIDANCE is principally an attempt to operate as a *for profit* business where tax rules are favorable. This is not a crime. Be prepared to be audited and face possible disallowance of deductions, and get hit with back taxes, penalty and interest.

TAX MANAGEMENT begins with individuals taking stock of their activities. The next step is to associate each activity with a business endeavor. Then conduct affairs in a business-like manner, maintain complete and accurate records, and pursue a legitimate profit motive.

TAX MANIPULATION is the injection into the formulation of tax legislation by the government. It is mostly done for the purpose of creating what government calls incentives/disincentives. There are two processes involved that, when combined, create an incentive. These two processes are 1] the aggressive ideological lobbying by members and activist supporters for its constituency [proper name is special interest collective], combined with 2] the ideological politicizing of tax law by politicians for the purpose of satisfying the demands of a selected interest group, in exchange for their support. This technique is an eBay type auction. Before you jump to criticize, remember that the above anomalies in tax law are there for every taxpayer to use and exploit even though they are a direct result of this collusion with lobbyists or, to be candid, corruption.

WHAT TAX LAW SAYS THAT YOU MAY DO. Tax law isn't limited to telling taxpayers what they can't do. The law also spells out clearly what you may do and how it must be done. This is called government regulation; so let's take a look at what the IRS regulators say.

1) You may choose to take your share of the GDP by whatever lawful means you wish. This determines the character of income and ultimately how it will be taxed.

2) If you choose to take your income through business activities, you may have whatever number and types of businesses that you deem appropriate and are able to properly manage.

3) All businesses you choose must be conducted in a business-like manner, for a profit motive, following the required accounting procedures and generally comply with the guidelines shown under the section for businesses.

4) REMEMBER that honesty and integrity reign supreme. If you cannot live by these criteria, do not attempt to go into business.

WHO IS THE IRS AND WHAT DO THEY DO? The Sixteenth Amendment established the right of government to lay and collect taxes of any sort. The IRS was created and made a part of the Treasury Department to regulate this program.

1) Congress enacts the legislation and the IRS promulgates the regulations.

2) Tax legislation has several purposes including;
    a] raise money to support government operations,
    b] redistribute overall tax collections to those constituencies favored by the sitting party, and
    c] finance the cost of wars.

3) Tax law was originally opposite to traditional law. Now, when IRS alleges guilt, the IRS must prove guilt – sort of.

4) If the taxpayer initiates a frivolous lawsuit, the IRS can assess a fine.

5) If the IRS initiates a frivolous claim, the taxpayer must take the IRS to court. If the taxpayer is upheld, the court gives the IRS a slap on the wrist.

6) In any court challenge of an IRS claim, the IRS has access to the full economic and legal power of the government. The taxpayer is on his own and therefore should seek professional help.

7) The IRS may change its interpretation on similar issues regardless of whether it has sound reason to do so, and the taxpayer must defend himself.

8) The IRS has the power of subpoena, the taxpayer doesn't.

9) Do not divulge any information to your tax preparer that you do not want later divulged to the IRS, as the tax preparer does not have client confidentiality privilege.

10) The IRS uses a number of computer editing programs to determine which returns they should consider for audit. Among these are: Schedules A, B, and C plus form 2106. You should avoid using these "killing fields" in your economic life.

This can usually be accomplished by restructuring how you conduct your personal and business life.

11) Tax returns can be used as excellent tax planning tools. Study lines 7 through 22 on the front of form 1040. Notice that some lines can only be positive numbers, but that there are a number of lines that can be either positive or negative. Research these latter lines because your AGI is determined by netting these lines.

12) In March 1995, as reported by the National Taxpayer Union, the government for the first time in history now takes over 50% of the average income leaving less than 50% for the taxpayer. The actual numbers are 50.3% to government and 49.7% retained by the taxpayer.

Tax management has as its primary purpose the maximization of profitability of your business efforts. Reducing taxes thus becomes a positive byproduct of that effort. By increasing your profitability, you increase business and employment for others. Business planning that ignores tax implications is likely to fail. Businessmen who run their businesses without tax management knowledge are sailing blindly through uncharted business waters and, inevitably, they will hit or be struck by a hidden IRS iceberg. Businesses that make decisions based only upon tax considerations also tend to fail.

AUDITS: Suppose the IRS notifies you that your return is going to be examined to determine whether you correctly reported your income and expenses, especially if you show a business loss. Here are some factors that would tend to prove that you are actually conducting a business and not merely pursuing a hobby that produces income. Remember, the burden of proof rests with you.

1) You contacted the agency that issues business licenses in your state to get a license, if required.

2) You opened a separate checking account with your business name on the checks and kept it strictly for self-employed income and business related check writing. While there is nothing to stop you from running your activities out of your personal checking account, it smacks of amateur.

Besides, an auditor will probably scrutinize your records much closer to make sure you did not deduct personal expenses as business expenses.

3) You promoted your trade to the general public through the use of business letterhead stationery, business cards, flyers, handouts and paid advertising.

4) You maintained a complete and accurate system of record keeping and used those records in a business-like way to analyze how to increase your income and reduce expenses.

5) You prepared a schedule of charges for the various types of work that you do. When billing customers, you always billed for the job and not the time spent doing the job.

6) You periodically took out a classified ad in the newspaper stating that you are engaged in certain type activities.

7) You always think of yourself as a self-employed entrepreneur. You always act like one and talk like one [the duck test].

8) You never allowed the customer to require that you follow specific instructions in accomplishing the task they requested of you.

9) You never allow the customer to provide you with training unless the nature of the work was unique and not normally available elsewhere.

10) You always retained the right to hire subcontractors in the accomplishing of the task.

11) You set your own work hours.

12) You maintained a professional relationship at arm's length to the extent that circumstances permitted with your customers.

13) When utilizing assistants, you hired, supervised and paid them independent of their employers.

14) You retained time to permit yourself to pursue other work and for other customers.

15) You decide when and where the work is to be done, free of customer control.

16) You control the sequence of tasks that lead to finishing the job.

17) You do not submit interim reports unless the job is phased and such reports would be necessary to permit the customer to plan, etc.

18) You pay your own expenses involved in the job.

19) You furnish your own tools. You either own them or make prior arrangements to lease.

20) Your investment in the operation is sufficient to maintain independence from any one customer.

21) You are at risk through your liability for any expenses encountered in performing a job.

22) You understand that as long as you produce a result specified in your agreements, your work cannot be terminated; however, you cannot be paid for partial completion of a job unless it is provided for in the original agreement.

CAUTION: IF YOU ARE AUDITED AND IRS DETERMINES THAT IN A GIVEN YEAR YOU WERE NOT IN A *"FOR PROFIT"* ACTIVITY, THE BUSINESS DEDUCTIONS COULD BE DISALLOWED, THE TAX RECALCULATED AND YOU MIGHT FIND YOURSELF OWING BACK TAXES. DO NOT TAKE SHORT CUTS OR THINK IT COULDN'T HAPPEN TO YOU.

1) THE MANNER IN WHICH THE TAXPAYER CONDUCTS THE ACTIVITY. We should keep track of our income and expenses in a businesslike manner. Get a license. Professional advice from accountants or tax professionals will help show a businesslike approach to the activity.

2) EXPERTISE OF THE TAXPAYER OR ADVISORS. Courses, seminars, and professional advice from others in the

field will help show you are gaining expertise in your profession.

3) TIME AND EFFORT THE TAXPAYER SPENDS ON THE ACTIVITY. This is in relation to other activities, such as a full-time job. Regular and steady hours will help show you are spending as much time as you have reasonably available to produce results. A few isolated sales do not make an activity a business.

4) EXPECTATION THAT ASSETS USED IN THE ACTIVITY MAY APPRECIATE IN VALUE. A profit motive can exist even if the SELF-EMPLOYED knows there may not be a profit from current activities, but believes that an overall profit may occur later that will exceed overall expenses.

5) TAXPAYER'S SUCCESS IN SIMILAR ACTIVITIES. If the SELF-EMPLOYED had success and profits in prior years similar activities, there is evidence that the current activity is for profit.

6) TAXPAYERS HISTORY OF INCOME OR LOSSES WITH RESPECT TO THE ACTIVITY. Due to the nature of SELF-EMPLOYMENT, it may take a considerable effort over a period of time before making a profit. It is reasonable to assume, however, that as a SELF-EMPLOYED ability grows and as others become more aware of that ability, losses will eventually give way to profits.

7) THE AMOUNT OF PROFITS. Tax years that show an upward trend of profits are more likely to show a profit motive than those that stay about the same.

8) TAXPAYER FINANCES. Large outside income, such as from a job, will tend to reduce the claim of "for profit" if the activity has a high recreational value.

9) ELEMENTS OF PERSONAL PLEASURE OR RECREATION. There is nothing in the Regulations to say you shouldn't enjoy or derive pleasure from the "agony" of your SELF-EMPLOYMENT. But it could tend to have a negative impact when we try to show a "for profit" motive. Imagine the pale, chalk-faced auditor stuck behind a desk reviewing your Hawaii expenses incurred to write the article entitled "Surfing

Techniques in Maui." How impressed will the auditor be if you sit there bronzed and healthy?

SOLE-PROPRIETORSHIPS [either employer or non-employer]. We talked earlier about them and how to use the schedule C. These are the simplest to set up and discontinue. There is really no limit to the number that you can have provided that you can manage them all in a businesslike manner. Income or losses from proprietorship is netted for both income tax purposes and self-employment tax. Any losses from them are used to offset any other income reported on page one of form 1040. There is no maximum or minimum that has to be met as far as losses or profits are concerned. All of the business entities that we teach here include meeting the criteria of the "HOBBY RULE." This rule states that a business must be profitable three out of the last five years. If it does, it is deemed to be a "for profit activity." All business people must live by this rule.

What are the activities that you can consider doing as a business and where do you find a list of them? There are several resources available.

1) Page two of schedule C gives a partial list and assigns codes to them.

2) One excellent source is the yellow pages. About every five years, take time to scan through the headings and study the ads. This is a stimulating exercise and a great source of ideas.

3) Many businesses are successful because someone found a new or better way to do something that the public was willing to pay for, or they became experts at doing that which others didn't like to or were unwilling to do. The most common objection we hear to self-employment is that they do not want to set up and keep detailed and accurate records. It is amazing how many taxpayers will pay thousands of dollars each year in taxes (and complain about taxes) before they will learn to manage detail.

Following are some of the records to meticulously and contemporaneously maintain:

1) A daily activity diary.

2) A daily automobile(s) travel log.

3) A daily planning schedule.

4) Monthly and annual income and expense sheets.

5) Quarterly analysis of the above to determine if changes are needed.

6) Pre-tax estimates and worksheets.

7) Five year tracking of performance.

PARTNERSHIPS: [may be either employer or non-employer] From the moment of birth governments create a partnership with each and every one of us. In this matter we have no choice, but we do have the choice of managing our affairs. Earlier we introduced the existence of the *"800-pound Gorilla."* While that reference is somewhat *"facetious,"* it unfortunately does ring with considerable truth. From birth, we have to live with government's laws telling us what to do, how to do it, etc., etc. They tell us what their share of our income they will take leaving us with crumbs. They literally connect their fiscal umbilical cord to each of us from the very first moment that we are beginning to earn money and all the way through our senior years, when they siphon away our pensions and any little income we try to create. They have tapped into the very muscle of our energy, effort and freedom. The program we are defining will allow you to minimize the adverse impact of this relationship. Remember, if we do nothing regarding the choices we must make in managing our lives, income, investments, behavior, etc., then our partner, aka *"The Big Gorilla,"* will choose them for us. And we know from bitter experience what those choices will not be with first considerations for all the little apes that toil for survival.

GENERAL PARTNERSHIPS: Approved by the State, partnership papers and federal ID number required, must submit separate tax Form 1065 with K-1's. This is an excellent entity for husband and wife or trusted and respected friends. Can be used for any business activity that is legal in the state where filed. Provides minimal protection from lawsuits. All partners may be held jointly or severally liable for the acts of

other partner. Basically the same income tax spreading
capabilities exist with the general partnership as exist with the
limited partnership. Also, the same estate tax advantages exist
as with the limited partnership. You can spread your wealth to
the children in a family general partnership and thereby lower
your estate and inheritance taxes.

LIMITED PARTNERSHIPS: Same set-up requirements as a
general partnership. As a general rule, a limited partnership
may not be broken up or dissolved simply because one limited
partner is sued. Under most limited partnership statutes, a
separate provision protects the assets of the partnership from
the individual creditors of a limited partner. Income may be
spread to individual limited partners, such as children or
grandchildren age 14 or older who are presumably in a lower
income tax bracket simply by such children holding ownership
interests in the partnership. Income is then allocated,
generally, in proportion to the ownership interests of the
various partners.

There are eight hurdles that an enemy must cross to get to
your Limited Partnership assets.

1) Take judgment against the debtor.

2) Prove the debtor has an interest in the Limited
   Partnership.

3) Obtain a charging order.

4) Obtain ancillary orders (such as an appointment of a
   receiver) to receive distributions of earnings or
   withdrawal of capital.

5) Apply for foreclosure on debtor's partnership interests -
   an option not always available.

6) Pursue forced sale of partner's interest at the
   foreclosure.

7) If the creditor is the plaintive, he can only receive the
   charged partner's cash flow with no right to

accounting.

8) Obtain judicial dissolution. The creditor can finally obtain whatever share would have come to the debtor partner after payment of all partnership creditors and claims of co-partners. As you can see, this is a very expensive procedure, especially if the partnership is in a state other than where you reside/do business. This means your enemy (creditor) needs two law firms, dramatically increasing his legal bills.

NOTE: When the creditor obtains a judgment and charging order against a limited partner, the creditor creates an immediate tax consequence for himself. They must pay tax on the amount of the judgment, in the year the judgment was obtained, even if they do not collect on the charging order. This can spoil their entire day.

"C" CORPORATIONS: Approved by the State Corporation Commission, "C" Corporations are regulated by them and require a federal ID number. Form 1120 is filed for each tax year. Excellent for operating a business activity. Considerable protection from liability if all requirements are met. Stockholders can make tax-free capital contributions in exchange for stock. Avoid being classified as a PHC [Personal Holding Company]. It's not so difficult getting your money into the corporation, but more difficult to get it out [tax free]. Provides a large array of benefits not available to the individual; medical reimbursement, life insurance, annual meetings, on-site fitness and health facilities, and on and on. Often, many of the deductions previously listed on Schedule A, fit nicely into this operation. Also, there is no limit to deductions, such as the medical limitation of only deducting expenses in excess of 7.5% of AGI.

"S" CORPORATIONS: Generally has the same type of lawsuit protection as the "C" if done properly. The difference between a "C" and an "S" corporation is very sharp in the income tax area. Generally, many more specific deductions and fringe benefits are available in a "C".

PRIVATE OR PUBLICLY TRADED BUSINESSES

Private businesses are of course not publicly traded but they can still be bought or sold to other private parties. Private business is primarily governed by and under the laws of the state in which it is filed. Publicly traded implies that the business is listed on an exchange and others can buy and sell shares or interests in those companies. Publicly traded companies are subject to oversight by the Securities and Exchange Commission [SEC] by federal as well as state law, the justice department to name a few. All publicly held companies are required by the SEC to make quarterly and annual financial filings. The quarterlies are call 10Qs and the annual 10Ks. If you desire to read these filings, log on to the SEC website. Pay special attention to the balance sheet, income statements and statement of cash flow.

Public companies often use 'mark to market' accounting. Your company makes a sale, you debit the amount in your asset column, and credit your liabilities by the same amount. The two columns are always supposed to be equal. Here it gets tricky. Your client agrees to buy a set number of what you produce over the next four years. For every dollar you debit from the asset side, you credit four times that amount on the liabilities, as that represents the transactions worth over time [four years]. At times the price of the product will be calculated for each successive year and a larger number posted. You have just inflated your revenue. Remember how Boeing executed an order for so many 737 planes to be delivered over a fixed time period? Occasionally the buyer will have to reduce or cancel part of their order. That amount must be recalculated and changes made are debited from the liabilities.

Another item is special purpose entities [SPE] a device often used for securitization of debt. At least 3% of the money invested must be independent money. You sell a part of your accounts receivable and interest payments due to your SPE. The SPE then sells shares in the SPE to investors and get their money back in installments earning a percentage on the transactions. This creates an increase in debt in lieu of a shortage in cash flow. These arrangements are to be approved by the board of directors. If a company violates these rules to keep their stock price pumped up, or maybe to sell their own stock, they have a problem. If they had a 401(k) program for their employees it is sayonara or good bye pension.

INTERNATIONAL BUSINESSES

There are various types of businesses, trusts, annuities, etc that can legally be established in other countries. You definitely need professional advice for this. Two sources are info@sovereignsociety.com and assetpro@toast.net. Do not attempt to go this route without professional advice. The purpose of offshore business is to protect your assets from confiscation by the US government and not for the purpose of avoiding taxes. Before you consider this remember that you will need a very substantial amount of money, as it will cost more than similar service for US businesses.

FUTURE GENERATIONS: The authors are not and do not hold themselves out as professionals or authorities on matters of business. Our information is only general knowledge available to anyone through normal channels.

Self-Employed Business Attitude

THE SELF-EMPLOYED ATTITUDE: Think of yourself as a business entity, conducting all of your activities in a businesslike manner and always for a profit motive. Whenever asked what you do, always respond that you are self-employed, an entrepreneur. If your self-employment becomes very profitable and you are acquiring too much money, you can always give it away to those you choose.

Networking with Other Self-Employed

Simply stated, Self-Employed doing business with Self-Employed, with people sharing similar values and understandings. Basically, we are talking about people with individualistic and entrepreneurial characteristics that are associating with others of like mind for mutual benefit, prosperity, sharing of ideas, freedom and happiness. Networking also occurs in the area of multiple business activities. You can do business with your own businesses if you do it at what is referred to as *"Arms Length."* Also, networking is used for the exchange of new ideas and the sharing of mistakes. We help others, and are in turn, helped by them.

FUTURE GENERATIONS: With the *fall* of common man democracy absolute control has flowed to the political elite who continue with their plan of a monolithic, single super power unity, dominating in totality whatever authoritarian norms necessary – the end justifies the means – the means are total authoritarian power – the end masquerades as democracy. Behind this illusion reigns an Elite *oligarchy* that will lead to the demise of *'Empire.'* This elite oligarchy is made up of connected families like Bush, Clinton, Gore, Kennedy, Roosevelt and today wannabes like Cheney or Kerry. The 2004 national election was nothing more than an ideological feud between elite oligarch families competing for control. At the last count there were about 50 elected federal officials who have or had other family members elected to federal positions. When we add the number of key staff members that accede to their bosses jobs, upon their retirement, the number stifles any optimism one would expect to have about the future of our country.   These families are essentially driven by the principle that *"too much is not enough"* and their lust for power is insatiable. It is these efforts of oligarch families that led to the common man losing control over his republic. Wars between nations are little more than feuds between oligarchies of different nations, with different values – which the common man is then forced *"not to question why – but to fight and die."* An oligarch considers itself *the* country – but they are mistaken. When the common man fights a war, he fights it for the country, not its government. That is why so many are leaving the ranks of the disillusioned. There is little prospect for any true freedom for the common man having lost democracy to oligarchs. To regain freedom and control, each individual must deconstruct government to recreate what the Constitution provided them. We speak to you in a manner of understanding the nature of our responsibility.

Your responsibility is first to self, family and country. It is not your job to make decisions regarding the duties of government, as you are not responsible for their failures. Actually, you should not even care what they do and why they do it. However, you will automatically have the thought, *"but how can I not care?"* If you have decided that you care – for example – the safety of our boys and girls fighting in Iraq, that's fine. But it is not your job to solve the problems someone else is being paid to. You are being paid for the job you have. Caring and concern, yes, but if the people responsible continue to fail the country, then get rid of them. You get out and do your job, self, family and country first, as best you can. If you see government as the problem, put yourself in a form of war footing and meet that challenge. What is the challenge? If government will not obey the people it is then time for the people to change their form of government.

DECONSTRUCTION OF BIG GOVERNMENT
FROM BAD TO WORSE

"Of all tyrannies, a tyranny exercised for the good of its victims may be the most oppressive." – C. S. Lewis

FUTURE GENERATIONS: You have greater knowledge when you first understand that you *"do-not-know,"* and you do something about that weakness. If you think learning greater knowledge is more difficult than ignorance, try or continue living in ignorance, then you will understand.

DECONSTRUCT or ELIMINATE THE MIDDLE MAN

We deliberately belabor the point that government is not an honest broker representing equally all citizens and doing no harm to anyone when doing something allegedly good for another. Every department, even those provided for in the Constitution, such as Defense, Justice, and Treasury, are politicized to the extent that government cannot be removed as intermediary. That does not mean that you are without alternatives in protecting your Constitutional interests in the absence of equal protection. Most of the departments added in the last 75 years offer you opportunity to deconstruct government as a dishonest broker. Your child does not have to attend a public school, and you can deflect the disproportional administration of justice. You may not be able to get your own *"stay out of jail card,"* but you can substantially minimize an unfavorable encounter with the police and justice system.

EVADING FRIENDLY FIRE

Individualism stands at a mid-point between the two conflicting ideologies of race-based and faith-based. The major problem with this location is that you find yourself between two antagonistic forces, each throwing its devastating shots at the other. In addition, you must always be aware of the guerrilla warfare of other opposing special interests that will not hesitate to do you harm in their selfish and greedy effort to gain an unfair advantage over you. You are literally in a sort of *"no-mans-land"* from where you are taking what is known as friendly fire. That is, you are being fired upon by your own people and government, and are taking casualties. The secret now is to locate a sanctuary where you will be safe from friendly fire.

In editing earlier portions of the book, we reviewed our comments regarding all of the stupid and unnecessary wars that government fights, and the light came on. The war against *poverty* is not a war at all. It is part of the *illusion* mentioned in book one. It is really a war against wealth. You see, if government had the choice between eliminating poverty and taking as much money from the wealthy through taxes by labeling the rich with every slanderous comment they can construct they would always choose robbing the rich and playing Robin Hood with redistribution of wealth. The same is true with the war on drugs. Given the choice of winning the war on drugs or stealing money from its citizens, the latter will always win. Here they legislated numerous currency control measures to stop money laundering by the so-called drug cartel. The truth is that these currency control measures are used more routinely in preventing Americans from using cash or investing overseas. This clearly comes to light in view of the 2006 squabble over the border with Mexico. True, a wealthy person would have a good chance of crossing the border into Mexico with a large suitcase filled with $100 bills. What is in place as border control is that the border extends upward into cyber space and creates a border that is patrolled by the National Security Agency [NSA] to prevent investment overseas and to monitor all communications using the ether wave.

FUTURE GENERATIONS: In essence, all of the phony wars that government fought, are pure illusion as to intent. It is one of the greater lies told to us.

BEST PRODUCT AND SERVICE

If we wish to identify the best product and the best service, we might first look to the qualities that they should possess. High among those qualities we would list: non-polluting, unlimited, easily transported, readily replaceable, adaptable to changing conditions, available on demand, non-taxable, simple to store, free of customs and tariffs, in great demand, beyond government regulation, available to all, not subject to product liability and class action suits; and the service would be how to best use this product. So, what is this great product? Simple – knowledge and ideas. In technology it might be computers and computer services, in finance it might be investment skills, in health better ways to extend life and improve health, or in housing how to buy, sell or build. Many learn skills in these areas as wage labor, ideas created by thinkers and visionaries, and then use these ideas as free labor with imagination and creativity. Only free labor provides the incubator from which these ideas emerge and grow. The total list is far greater than those identified. It is from these ideas that a man and woman, working together, can create their own sanctuary within which to grow their family, free of the contamination of society and government. In a later section we share ideas on creating your own business.

FUTURE GENERATIONS: Two-parent families offer the greatest opportunity for achieving your goals of freedom and liberty. In addition to double incomes, you can create matching or pairing of incomes as it takes two to form a partnership. The children grow up in the freedom of the sanctuary, free from the collectivist/socialist/fascist world of welfare and ideological/theological action. The alternative is truly not a very nice sight.

BLABBERING

THINKING OUT LOUD. A mentor, older and wiser than we, opened our eyes to the understanding of what is happening. He explained to us that the war against King George started with one person, probably unable to sleep, who realized that his freedom and liberty had been compromised. Slowly the number increased, but only with the idea that they wanted fair representation in the court of King George. It was only when

King George's government troops fired upon the colonists that the desire for representation gave way to a demand for independence. We are all aware of how that issue ended. We must be alert for a repeat of this and make plans to take the appropriate action.

Today, and for some time, voices have arisen to say that their inalienable rights granted by the creator, protected by the Constitution, and defended by all those who have sworn an oath to the United States to defend the Constitution, have systematically been taken from them. These voices have been met with constructionism - labeling, claims making, and spin masters and rhetoricians chanting a persuasive company line. This constant deceit and deception has festered doubt in many Americans about America's true nature and direction. We are all the same in that we face daily the temptations of sin, and are drawn to sin by the sense of success and pleasure that sinning will bring to us. But for politicians it is the only thing.

All sides in this struggle believe that their cause is just and honest, and that justness of God is on their side. Who is to argue successfully against that? Some argue that once we choose our paths, we are committed. We're all the same. We're true to ourselves, victims of our character. No, we are not all the same when it comes to character. While we are all the same in that we are constantly tempted, we are all different in character, which determines how we deal with temptation and immorality. Some convince themselves that their pleasure is worth the sacrifice of morals, but they are wrong. Others are honest and having to live through dishonest times rise to the challenge of character and courage. It is those who will be called upon to change our form of government and punish the wrong doer's.

Martin Luther King left us with the phrase hoping that the day would come when his children would be judged by the content of their character and not the color of their skin. Some have succeeded, such as M. J. (Michael Jordan), Tiger (Woods) or Colin (Powell). We have tried judging people by their character. First, we must say that our definition of character is a bit old-fashioned, like integrity, truthfulness, moral, kind, responsible, etc. It doesn't always work in terms of what we expect. So, like everything else, we researched this issue. We find that the tendency is for each person to define character in a manner that allows them to rate themselves as a ten, maybe a nine or eight. When we judge them according to our definition of character, we often see them as less than they see themselves. Immediately we are labeled *"racist," "anti-Semitic," "sexist," "insensitive," "bigoted," and "prejudiced."* Their claims making includes those old goodies including *"stereotyping" or "profiling."* All we ever wanted was to do business with and associate with others of character through our respective sanctuaries. We care less about labels and claims making when we focus on character.

How do we put flesh on this framework of constructionism and de-constructionism and yet feel none of the emotions that grow into so difficult a task? We would like nothing better than to put an end to this game, once and for all. One thing that is left to us is trust – it may be for many the only thing. Trust in one's self and trust in one's heart. The primary issue is and always will be *"who is supreme – the people – or – government,"* for whoever is supreme the other will fear them. Fear is a powerful emotion that can destroy a person – so never take counsel of your fear from the source of that fear. If one fears hell, one does not seek counsel from Satan. Therefore, if one fears government, one does not seek counsel from that perpetrator either. The second issue is and always will be *"what philosophy defines governments actions in governing the people – are they in consonance with the Constitution? Do those who take the oath to defend and protect the Constitution faithfully and honestly carry out their responsibilities?"* We also use de-constructionism in presenting our arguments. We label political ideologies as socialist or fascist. We make claims about how these ideologies fail to defend and protect the Constitution by revisionist methods to change the intent.

We now say to you *"The goal of everything written by the authors is focused on individual freedom and liberty as the final end. Creation of wealth is only a means to achieving this end and preserving freedom and liberty for individuals."* *"Free-Labor"* has dis-intermediated fully 70% of the Socialist/Fascist beast and more is to come. There is an old saying that goes, *"remember, anything you say or write can and will be used against you."*

It is becoming clear that the growing divergence of wealth between the haves and the have nots results primarily from their early education and indoctrination. The have nots are trained to be wage labor, and aspire to a lesser goal than the haves. The haves are trained to be free labor, and aspire to higher goals than have nots. As the country's wealth increases, it goes to each category according to their education, early indoctrination and character. This disparity is seized upon by thousands of ideological socialists, both in and out of government, to foment class hatred and envy, a legal *"hate-crime."* Concern is greatest over the loss of the rights of life, liberty and the pursuit of happiness. Think of your heart and soul as life; this is your courage, integrity and morality. Think of your mind as liberty; your knowledge and discipline form the values of truth and reason. Think of self-responsibility and the willingness to do for your self as pursuit of happiness. Remember, if one plants a fruit tree and it bears fruit, that fruit belongs to the person who nursed and nourished the tree. It is their fruit to enjoy or share with others of their choice.

When you successfully reach this height, you will see society and government as a condition, circumstance or event totally disassociated with either the Constitution or your sanctuary. You can feel and sense that you are like a sole and separate country within a country, yet no one is able to recognize it for what it is, for your personal country is within your life and your liberty. Even as you pursue your happiness, they will not know unless you tell them. Government becomes irrelevant to your person. Instead of respect for government, you feel pity, distrust and contempt. The less said to others the better. In one section we refer to *"principality"* as a metaphor. We now tell you that it is possible to breathe new life into that metaphor and produce a living viable circumstance of your life.

Always care about your country. Caring for others is a separate issue. How do you continue to care for others who willingly accept victimization by government leaders? Actually, many are standing in line begging to become a victim. Caring then becomes pity for the willing victims and contempt for our socialist/fascist leaning governments. Always be mindful of the individual that is sincere but appears lost on how to get started in becoming a free individual. Be a big brother or sister to those worthy of your consideration.

We sense a question within your mind. Why, after such total emphasis on privacy, are we now stepping out from behind the veil of privacy and revealing our self to those who will condemn us? There are several reasons for this.

First. Between us, we have over 160 years of learning experience. This has alerted us that if we do not want this knowledge lost, we must make it available to the largest possible audience so that they may exercise their freedom of choice. We do not know how many or how few years we have to complete this effort. We do however, firmly believe that fully 20% of wage labor, or approximately 25 million families, have the potential to move into free labor and become wealthy in terms of freedom and wealth.

Second. We know that those who violently disagree with us will not hesitate to label, make claims, and otherwise attack our positions. Remember, that when you have established your sanctuary and achieved freedom and liberty for your self, everything that they say or do is neither relevant to you nor does it present any threat or danger. Such reaction will only further the awareness within people of the existence of this alternative.

Third. The existence of sanctuary in your personal principality continues to remain invisible to those who do not know that they do not know, the truth. Even though they pass us on the street, if they do not understand, they do not recognize our existence.

FUTURE GENERATIONS: When all of the IDEAS are rolled into one package, we have what is labeled as *"deconstruction of government,"* which is the proper term for the actions we have to take. So, this is how it goes.

We must, of course, ask and answer the question *"why – why do I desire to deconstruct government?"* The answer, of course, is *"Freedom."* The first lesson that we learn is that even when we, as individuals, label something e.g., government is evil, and follow up with claims making [return freedom to the People], that there is no real anticipation that changes will be forthcoming. Therefore, your break from government must be as complete and total as you can make it. It must be done with thorough preparation, and all the time maintaining and enhancing your anonymity, while defending the Constitution from domestic threat.

A basic principle taught by all religions and philosophies is do not encroach on other people or their property. The religions and philosophies express this principle in different ways. Christians derive the principle from their bible and use different words than Moslems, Jews, Hindus and others, but this principle is the foundation of every culture's rules against assault, rape, kidnapping and theft. Thou shall not kill. Thou shall not steal. Do not encroach. Government is the one and only institution with the privilege and the power to violate this principle. Governments encroach, this is what they were invented to do, which is why our founding fathers believed government is an inherently evil institution.

Outside of the majority that keeps government in power, there is a growing number who desire freedom. What is it that they desire freedom from or freedom of? It is the natural rights to their bodies, their minds, and their property. Those inalienable rights, which have been forfeited by the majority to government by the exercise of their majority powers, in which they exchange freedom of all, for the questionable right to desire, pursue and obtain pleasure, entertainment and materialism.

Today, just as throughout history, those who desire freedom must extricate themselves from the conditions they find unbearable, using a means or vehicle to take them someplace. Like the early patriots who stood their ground and fought for their liberty and freedom – we can do no less. The greatest failure of government has been it's incessant effort to divorce the people from any association with government. The name of this game is, *'it is not the right of people to ask but theirs to do or die.'* When government, in a wholesale manner, severs the people from their Constitution then their only contact with government is the issue of, obey or else. Government, among other matters, denies the country the potential use and talents of the people. Talents and skill that originally made America great was the great resource of individualism in creating business and technology and in being a *trained and ready to use militia,* when needed. Government initiatives in controlling people, partly through entitlement programs but we suspect more through fear, is that people will ask too many questions, answers to which government doesn't want brought into the sunshine.

President Roosevelt, in the 30's, had a need to put large numbers of unemployed into productive activities and created the Civillan Conservation Corp [CCC] for unemployed youth and the Works Progress Administration [WPA] for unemployed adults. Today we have very high unemployment among young men and women, especially in the inner cities. Some of the non-working people are truly unemployed or unemployable. Others are disabled, unwilling to do certain jobs, not required to move to be available and so forth. The cause of a large number of Americans being non-productive, who are liabilities for taxpayers, has been government's willingness to encourage and allow this condition to exist. We have forests and sea-shores that need attention, roadways and parks, borders and security functions all in need of manning, but government continues to sit on their hands and talk, and talk, and blame, and criticize, and talk some more and make foolish legislation, spend money selfishly and, in general, diminish the quality of the lives of so many. This really needs to be changed. If it is not changed, then change the people in charge.

SORTING AND ORGANIZING KNOWLEDGE INTO PLANNING

In previous chapters we covered specific ideas and thoughts that became knowledge. The first book revealed how, in a sense, everything was an _illusion_, as if the Wizards feared that the people would find the truth and throw them out. We identified _addiction_ to be the _"opium"_ of the masses, which led to the denial of truth and the creation of co-dependency, with people the dependent and government the controller. The section on _dominant ideology_ laid open _"the plan"_ which the elite minority uses to control the middle-class majority. In the broadest of senses, it is the 21st century version of Master and Serf.

Envy is probably the most dangerous and prevalent of St. Augustine's seven deadly sins. It is the breeding ground for class hatred. Notice how socialist leaders of government and political parties pound and hammer this evil into the hearts and souls of people throughout America and the world. Envy is the core of socialism for it manifests itself through political correctness and politicians' use of it in perpetuating hate crimes of envy and wealth.

Education, along with media and government, is the prime means of disseminating the ideology and indoctrinating the dominant ideology into our children. Our leaders tend to send their children to privileged schools such as Phillips or Andover, which are like Eaton in Britain. They then matriculate from Ivy League schools like Yale and Harvard. In England it is Oxford and Cambridge. These schools teach their students the basics of socialism and how this system gains them power. As children, they are taught that they are the ones responsible, the future leaders of the country. Public schools, managed by government, offer a curriculum to the children of common-man, best described as *"wage [slave] labor."* This gives government the belief that they have the authority to declare wars, to create and fund socialist programs for help in re-elections, and is the key to what is referred to as, *"the special relationship that America has with Great Britain."* This relationship now appears to have begun years before the revolutionary war. This group is part and parcel with the group we speculated earlier was formed prior to that war with the purpose of finding ways to bypass the Constitution and the will of the people.

It is important that there be in place means of <u>compulsion</u> to control and punish those who tend to be contrarian by nature. To government, contrarians are a major threat that they must, at all cost, prevent from taking root. This leads us to the nature of threat.

<u>*Threat*</u>, as perceived by and dealt with appropriately by the common-man, is in descending order something like this. First, federal government, then state-county-city governments, corporate governance, attorneys, political parties, lobbyists, special interests, customers, employees, even homeowner associations. It is important to understand this and take whatever steps are necessary to isolate and insulate yourself from such dangers inherent in being on a lower or middle rung of the food chain.

We have always been told that America is a country of <u>equal justice</u> for all. America has a history, beginning with slavery and continuing through the present to favor the more wealthy, connected and powerful as having more justice than the common-man.

<u>*Jobs*</u>, also known as wage-labor, and by some, as a form of serfdom, are key to controlling mankind. Jobs require that there be employer businesses that govern and direct wage-

labor activities. This is done under the direction of government, that dictates, through legislation and compulsion of both business and labor, the distinction between those who rule and those who obey their rule.

RISK

Each day or night brings us a continuous stream of risk. Risk comes in several flavors including the need to understand basic math.

FINANCIAL   CALCULATORS/CALCULATIONS.   It   is necessary that you first learn to train yourself on how to use a financial calculator. So, let us look at a few basics. We use the HP 12C, which is very adequate for our needs, and retails for around $65.

There are five basic keys that we need to discuss. Beginning from the upper left hand corner they read from left to right as: n – I – PV –PMT – FV.

> n – is the symbol for TERM, such as 30 years for a typical home loan.
> i – is for INTEREST, which is expressed as an annual rate.
> PV – is for PRESENT VALUE, such as the value of a new loan.
> PMT – is for PAYMENT, the amount that you will be expected to pay on a regular schedule.
> FV – is for FUTURE VALUE, when we want to know the time value of money at a later date.

There are three other keys that you will find necessary to use.

Blue g key is used to convert annual numbers to monthly numbers. This allows you to be working in months with all the appropriate keys. For example, with a 30-year loan, you can enter 30 on the number pad, press blue g, press n and you will enter 360 under that key, which represent 360 months. If you enter 7 as the annual % rate, you need to convert it into a monthly rate before you can calculate the monthly PMT. Put 7 into the key pad, press blue g and press the [i] interest key and you will find 0.5833333333, which is the monthly rate. If the loan amount is $100,000, enter that into the keypad and press PMT. You have now loaded the term [in months], the interest rate [in months] and the loan amount. Press PMT and you read $1,883.94 that is the monthly payment of principal and interest. If taxes and insurance are impounded, that cost will be annualized and added to the payment.

Gold f key is used to activate the gold designations on certain keys. The one that you will be interested in is the gold f – gold reg. This allows you to clear all functions of any numbers presently stored in them.

1] INSUFFICIENT DECISION MAKING SKILLS: Clearly identify the task or threat at hand and the time available to reach and implement a decision. Research and develop as much pertinent information as time permits. Evaluate this information and convert it into intelligence that you will use to formulate your decision. Develop a comprehensive plan or strategy that has a high probability of success. Implement your plan aggressively, continuously evaluate the progress to your plan, and revise your plan as necessary. Supervise and manage – again and again.

2] LACK OF PATIENCE: The act of impulse, not allowing sufficient time to research the issues and evaluate information available, prevents acting in a timely manner to a sound decision.

3] FAILURE TO ANTICIPATE AND PLAN FOR OBSTACLES TO YOUR PLAN: Develop contingency plans for every anticipated obstacle with the same thoroughness as the basic plan. Do not hesitate to implement the contingency back-up plan aggressively when evidence shows that the basic plan is not working as intended.

4] EXTERNALITIES: An externality is when two parties agree to an action that affects a third party, one who was not voluntarily a part of the agreement, in either a positive or negative manner. Positive example: Government, in conjunction with a special interest, passes a tax law change reducing the lowest tax bracket from 15% to 10% for the first $12,000 of taxable income. The party intended to be benefited – low-income wage earners. Upper income wage earners also automatically benefit, but to a lesser degree. <u>Negative example</u>: Government, in conjunction with a special interest, mandates certain sized business to provide or do for employees, consumers, etc. Businesses then incur added costs, which increase their cost of doing business. If they then raise their prices to compensate, consumers become the unintended victim.

5] TRUSTING THE WRONG PARTIES: The media abounds with snake oil salespeople offering get rich schemes. You probably don't seek investment advice from your Congressperson – and for good reason. They are not on your list of those to consider as baby-sitters for your children – so why would you trust them with your money? You take with a grain of salt all free offers of friends and relatives of how and what you should do with your money. Learn to hold your own counsel, and seek advice only from those who have the experience and knowledge to advise you.

FUTURE GENERATIONS: Take a deep breath we will now continue with the answers to the question *HOW*. But first.

CONSRUCTIONISM [AGAIN]

All that exists from central government down to the smallest group was created through constructionism. It consisted of labeling [we know it also as political correctness], claim making, misuse of facts and history, abuse of scientific knowledge all pounded into our heads through government, media, schools and activist groups. Deconstructionism is the reversal of the former. We will look at the most grievous failures and show how to deconstruct them for the individual, as the individual is not only the victim of failure, it is the way out for many.

There remains the matter of character. Using St. Augustine's seven deadly sins, we offer a short synopsis of cruel and immoral behavior.

GREED is defined as a rapacious desire for more than one needs or deserves. Go back and study that part that talks about how much money you think you need. Greed quickly can become addictive, and this leads greedy people to putting their ends ahead of the means; that is, he sees the means as justifying the end. The middle and lower classes tend to see need as their right to part of the wealth of the upper class.

GLUTTONY or excess in eating and drinking – and let's throw in smoking and drugs – is a loss of self-esteem, self-respect, self-confidence and self-discipline. If one can't control gluttony, then how can we expect them to control other things that are for the benefit of all the people?

WRATH is a violent person being resentful, angry, tending to rage or fury. The driver who speeds past you and then cuts in front causing you to hit your brakes is a good example. What is more important is what does this, if anything, do to you? If it causes you to react with the *"finger"* – the horn – some form of getting even, you become the loser. Learn to control your feelings. Drop a safe distance back and ask yourself what is his problem. Try, late for work, angry, showing off, or whatever. It may be wrath or it may be one of the other deadly sins or a variation or combination of them. If you react *'in kind,'* you lose and he doesn't win; he also loses. To be a winner, you must develop the patience of Job and the understanding of Freud. It is difficult, but it is worth the sacrifice.

PRIDE is the individual's own perception of his dignity and the degree of self-respect that he believes he is entitled to. People with high, very high, egos and an ambition that drives them tend to believe so forcefully in the magnitude of their excellence that they are above and beyond the ability to understand how others feel about them and how they see them. The highest level is known as conceit or arrogance.

ENVY [We wrote an entire essay on this subject.] Bad envy is simply the powerful desire driven by discontent and resentment for something another has and refuses to acknowledge that the other is entitled to the possession.

SLOTH manages to grab each of us from time to time, usually reflected in our desire for a lazy day. This is not in itself bad. However, when one acts upon a feeling of aversion to work or making a necessary effort or exertion, we see them as indolent. Not really a good situation.

LUST being the sexual craving that it is, becomes a sin when it is unrestrained, having melted the person's discipline, at which time he or she simply says, what the hell, if someone blows the whistle on me I'll cross that bridge when I get there. People with great ego and ambition tend to convince themselves that it is OK for them to lust, either for sex or power, while the ordinary person will normally confine himself to envying the person and wishing him nothing good, also known as *schadenfreude.*

Probably the most evil by today's standard, involves the two words *"choice"* and *"racist."* Political correctness won the day with their labeling choice or selection, when it did not fit another's brand of political correctness as *racist,* by their dominating the claims making and the fixation that entered the minds of so many. Go back to MLK's speech *"I have a Dream."* He clearly established that there is a difference between judging people by their color and judging people by their character. We agree that people should be judged by their character. Therefore, when another lies, cheats, steals, or betrays the cardinal virtues in favor of the deadly sins, we learn that with each person there is a different set of values known as character. When confronted by another whose character is deficient, evil or beyond the bounds of good behavior, it isn't the person you wish to escape from or avoid, it is their wrong behavior. When you choose to not relate or associate with that behavior, another consequence occurs in that the source or perpetrator is also avoided. It then appears that what one calls discrimination is not discrimination, but rather an unintended consequence experienced by the perpetrator through his or her character and behavior. When you do not allow an evil character into your world, you also ban the source of that evil behavior, the person. You must learn to be your own person, and avoid the behavior that is generally not acceptable in society.

Can too much knowledge water down the value of that knowledge leading you into making an unsound decision? Richard J. Heuer Jr. wrote about this common phenomenon in a 1979 article entitled *"Do you Really Need More Information?"* *"Information that is consistent with our existing mindset is perceived and processed easily. However, since our mind strives instinctively for consistency, information that is inconsistent with our existing mental image tends to be overlooked, perceived in a distorted manner, or rationalized to fit existing assumptions and beliefs. Thus, new information tends to be perceived and interpreted in a way that reinforces existing beliefs."*

FUTURE GENERATIONS: Before beginning the *"Free Labor Family"* section, it is important you know WHY so many have chosen to step aside from the current culture. We can't speak directly for those that have already gone, therefore, we share with you what led us to take these actions.

Imagine that you sit at a poker table. The other players are; education, justice, treasury, Congress, Supreme Court and administration. It is dealer's choice as to what game and rules we play by. The deal moves clockwise with each hand giving all players, except us, the opportunity to deal.

Education wants to play *'dominant ideology'* – justice chooses *'unequal justice'* – treasury chooses *'taxes for better or worse'* – Congress chooses to play *'buy votes'* – supreme court wants to play *'ideological litmus test'* and the administration plays *'the debt game.'* We are denied our choice and must play their games by their rules. Obviously, we are a consistent loser for the deck is stacked against us. For a lifetime we have been lied to, cheated, deceived, stolen from, had our money devalued, our gold confiscated and treated like a numbskull. We must admit that as long as we stayed at the table and played their games, we deserved every terrible event that befell us. It was when we realized that common man democracy had fallen – no longer existed – and further realized that government had morphed into *"Elitist Oligarchy"* that we pushed our chair away from the table and refused to play their games with our hands tied. First, we sought the truth, then we thought of means available to us [legal] to mute or reduce the oppressive results of their one sided rules. The final straw that broke this camel's back was when voters described their choice as the lesser of two evils – it was then we realized that we would not associate with any form of evil. We realized that the game we were playing was actually called *"liars poker"* with a twist. Everyone at the table could lie with virtual immunity, that is, except us. If we lied, it would be in the slammer for us. That reminded us of that card in Monopoly – go to jail, if you pass go, do not collect $200. The irony? Life is imitating a silly game. What have we become?

CHARACTER

FUTURE GENERATIONS: We learned from George Washington the personal traits of good character – high morals – creative intellectual curiosity – stand alone courage. We examine now how each of these four traits will lead us to freedom and liberty.

Good character is one of the two primary antitheses of government. Government is aware of this, and to compensate, uses the tactic of creating standby laws and regulations. Good character will automatically stand you in good stead in avoiding most of government's laws. Equality of justice continues as one of the great myths of the dominant ideology. For over 200 years, those who have wealth, power and access always enjoyed greater equality than those who don't. Yet, no one person can master all of the regulations. We are all vulnerable, whenever attracting the attention of government, that, an investigation will turn up instances of our having violated a particular rule that we had no way to know existed.

High morals, when combined with good character, places the individual in a position of diametric opposition to everything that government espouses. Your high morals will permit you to see through the obfuscation and sickness of their dominant ideology. Continued due diligence will alert you early on to the nature of the foolishness, monster egos and super-socialism that they are pandering. You are, however, vulnerable to the morality police of the 21st century. Remember that their morality is yesterday's deviance. It is the Justice department that will hunt you down if they believe you have done wrong. Armed with this knowledge, it becomes much easier for you to steer away from or around this sinkhole of socialistic failure.

Creative intellectual curiosity, while shared with government, will find for you and show you the myriad ways in which you can checkmate government. Some of these ways include:

a. Your effective income tax rate is low or zero, and you invest the tax dollars yourself. This will eliminate the Treasury department as your worst nightmare.

b. You eliminate Social Security, Medicare, long-term health care, fiscal policy, and monetary policy. Having once qualified, mandatory by law, for Medicare, etc., you can turn your full attention to your personal health care savings account. Now, when government takes to the airwaves to promote their dominant ideology, you can truly say, "I don't care how you tax or how you spend."

c. When our leaders lie to us, they defraud us and they betray the country and everything good that it stands for. Lack of character and integrity of any leader is immoral, if not criminal, and the perpetrators should rot in hell.

d. When you truly do not care what government does, as it is totally irrelevant, and do not feel guilty because of it, government has been overthrown [peacefully], and you are the master of your life.

e. Your creative intellectual curiosity will ultimately lead you to emotional education, and free you and your progeny once and for all from the psycho-babble of their dominant ideology. Say good-bye to the Education department.

f. When you create your businesses, engage others by contract, and offer 'use of knowledge' as your service, then the Labor department becomes only a bad memory.

Stand-alone courage. Washington gives us the best possible example when, preparing for the Christmas attack on Trenton, he received the following message [not his exact words] from the Continental Congress. *"The Continental Congress is evacuating Philadelphia and will relocate to Boston. You are in charge of the war and must do what you feel necessary for the country."* It is hard to believe that any situation could place a leader into such a singularly stand-alone predicament.

When Eisenhower prepared for the invasion of Europe, he received the following operation order [paraphrased], *"You will enter the continent of Europe and destroy the armed forces of the Axis."* He also had the full support and cooperation of the USA and its Allied partners.

It is not difficult to be a groupie, follow the crowd, the wind or the stream, but it takes true courage to stand against that wind, even when in your heart and mind you know that you are right.

When you learn to leave others alone, accept those things that you cannot change, and change those things that you can change, you discover a truth. That truth is that others will not leave you alone, as you leave them alone; others will pursue your participation in attempting to change that which cannot be changed; and opposing you for changing those things in your life that you can and should change. When you have accomplished this, others will be frightened, just as they always are, when a few refuse to go along with the majority and leave the collective to take another path. They cannot and will not tolerate this behavior.

Many will believe that they possess these four traits of Washington, and maybe they do. The true test is: Do you succeed in becoming in heart and soul an Individualist? This test cannot be cheated on, for if you do not have the right stuff, you will fail.

The theme of Individualism is "Lassen Sie mich in Ruhe," which translates into English as "Please leave me alone." Individualists will instinctively leave others alone, but they will have to fight with all their might to preserve their own freedom and liberty from those who refuse to grant them the same rights.

People need to study the national framework within which they will operate for the purpose of first, survival with freedom and liberty and, second, wealth creation. The final plan becomes a social/economic/political model of survival in a collectivist/fascist/socialist environment. Those People willing to learn to manage risk will find opportunity and wealth necessary to undertake these risks. Those people who continue to rely on government to protect them from creative intellectual curiosity, and the changes such curiosity will bring to our environment, will continue to fall even further behind.

And third, is the ability to understand and engage in political arbitrage. Political arbitrage is the examination of the claims, rhetoric and spin that the various political parties flood the media with on a daily basis. It is important to understand that this information defines the foolishness that government is up to or wants to engage in. It is offered only for the purpose of controlling people's minds through a process known as mass psychology. What is important in political arbitrage is the analysis of what it is that government really intends to do. Once this knowledge is possessed, then people can make their move with the same confidence that the player at the crap table could, if he knew in advance what number the next role of the dice would be. For as long as governments label and make claims against others, it can only be concluded that there is no truth in the packaging of their ideological product. You can exercise total due diligence and probably will never arrive at a substantive conclusion of the truthfulness or integrity of what some say. However, if you start from the premise that all are in one way or another attempting to deceive you, that you refuse to believe them unless they can convince you that they are truthful, they become irrelevant to your life. What is needed to convince you? We suggest that you require at least two independent/impartial sources confirming what the politician/bureaucrat has said is reasonably correct. Now the monkey is on their back! You are free to go about your life.

This amalgamation of Capitalism / Collectivism / Fascism / Socialism is a mysterious economic/political system in America as we enter the 21st century. People cannot survive for long without a clear understanding of this incredibly complex ideology. We cannot say with certainty that America is either a capitalistic or socialistic nation. To be capitalistic, we need clear evidence that government exercises only the minimum of authority and operates no activities that were either not granted under the Constitution or could be managed better by the private sector. We cannot label government as socialistic in that it does not own all or most of the means of production and the majority of workers are employees of the nation state. We understand collectivization as the grouping of people into various categories, and agree that condition does exist. The real debate is over whether the control by government over business and industry has reached the level at which it can justifiably be labeled fascism. The prize to be won or lost has remained constant throughout the ages. Who shall control the mind, and thus the support, of the individual – government or People?

THE GOVERNMENT IS OUR SHEPHERD? ABSOLUTELY NOT!

Government fancies itself the "Shepherd" – the people the "flock," and the bureaucracy the "sheep-dogs," whose responsibility it is to keep the flock together. Those who escape from government's collectivist/socialist/fascist flock become the "black sheep" to be isolated, so they cannot tell the flock what they have discovered. The "black sheep" are eternally feared, as it is they who know the truth. The "shepherd" believes him self to be a "Saint," while all the time acting the role of the "sinner," and thus remains a mystery to most of the flock. Government views authority not as the most important prize, but as the only prize. Therefore, government devotes all of its time to winning, while for the people, winning is only a part-time effort. People view its responsibility as controlling government. People devote only a small portion of their time to winning. People err in wanting to believe that government can be trusted, benevolent, kind and fair. Government, as the collectivist/fascist/socialist intermediary, derives its authority by placing itself between the people and the separate parts of their lives.

PSYCHOLOGY OF WINNING

CHANCE

FUTURE GENERATIONS: What exactly is chance? It might be considered an opportunity [take a chance] or it might mean a surprising event like [by chance] or maybe it is just another name for risk. The lottery states spell it out this way, *"you can't win, if you don't play."* Of course, this is true. The other side of that coin would appear then to be, *"you can't lose, if you don't play."* They are, of course, referring to whatever amount of money you normally spend in buying lottery tickets and totally disregard risk or arbitrage. In life however, if you do not play their game of choice, by the rules set/changed by them, you automatically lose by default. It is the same as the old saying that *"no answer is a NO answer."* Therefore, life should be seen as a game that must be played. You have only the cards dealt to you at birth to start the game, so what you do with your life [taking risk on chance] will depend entirely on how you prepare to play the game from your understanding and ideas of what you want from life and where you want to take your life. So, we must first gain knowledge relative to chance and risk.

Consistent with the purpose of this book, the study of the people's relationship with their government, what was the intent of our founding fathers. For what it is today and what it likely will be tomorrow, is one of the chances as a part of the risk of your life. Knowledge is one key to individual ability to solve the puzzles concerning life, country, and government. In the following sections we share additional findings of our research to assist you in forming your solutions to the puzzles. It is everyone's responsibility to exercise due-diligence, to question and evaluate each item of information for its truth and relevance and finally to fit the pieces together to reveal your solution to the puzzle of life.

When the parts of the puzzle are identified and understood, this knowledge becomes one of the means to compete effectively in the game(s) into which we are born and required to participate. Needless to say - the greater the knowledge and skill - the greater the probability of winning. Good luck to all of you!

PUZZLES

Definition: To solve by reasoning something confusing [puzzle] in an effort to understand its nature and how solving it can be used to advantage. So, what are these? Major puzzles are described immediately below; lesser puzzles will be encountered throughout the book.

REGULATION PUZZLE. [Government use of power to control and manage economic and social behavior.] The Federal Register [where government posts new laws and regulations for public consumption] is again growing by hundreds of pages a year. How does one solve this puzzle? How does one legally reduce, avoid, and side step those regulations that the individual believes to be unnecessary, unconstitutional, or down right onerous and intrusive?

FISCAL POLICY PUZZLE. [Government taxing and spending policies.] With government taking about 50% plus of every family's income in taxes of one form or another, what strategies are available to help the individual lift some of this burden from their shoulders? The government writes tax laws, the IRS promulgates and interprets these laws, and the people must obey those that they chose to be a party to. Income and expense items tend to be treated [characterized] by the manner in which it is received for income, and allowable as a deduction [expense] according to how the income is taken.

MONETARY POLICY PUZZLE. [Federal Reserve action to maintain a strong currency.] The Fed manages monetary policy through interest rates [Fed funds and discount rate] and money supply [increasing or decreasing liquidity]. If the Fed errs, the result is usually an increase or decrease in the inflation rate causing rising prices or increase in unemployment and tight money.

ETHICAL RELATIVISM AND NARCISSISM. If, in fact, a change in cultural values emerged from the revolutionary 1960s, how does one trust what government and the media tell us, and how can we use the information to protect our own security?

EXTERNALITIES. [What occurs to a third party, that is not a party to an agreement, between two other parties? The result may be either positive/profitable or negative/unprofitable.] EXAMPLE: When government protects and rewards special interest groups, both government and the interest group are winners. Taxpayers and consumers are third parties and pay for the rewards, usually without personal benefit.

INCENTIVES/DISINCENTIVES. Any action initiated by government, business, labor or special interests and individuals that takes from Peter to pay Paul. This will usually make Peter sore. Peter immediately seeks remedy from this by finding ways to act in his own best interest so as to avoid being a loser in the game.

PRICE/SUPPLY – DEMAND/DEMAND. [Price, supply-demand and the relationship between them, demand.] Entrepreneurs possess large skills in the supply-demand area acquired through knowledge and creativity. Society has a high demand for those talents. Those talents produce new products, better products, lower priced products, all of which creates jobs and benefits for workers. The puzzle is in the price that the entrepreneur must pay to produce the product. As the size and scope of government increases through taxes and regulation, the cost of supplying this benefit also increases. This creates a disincentive for entrepreneurs to increase supply-demand. This shortage increases demand for the product in short supply.

FUTURE GENERATIONS: The following information was determined through the research efforts of the authors. This information was evaluated by the authors and believed that, while it does not necessarily represent a majority or consensus opinion, it does represent the opinion of the authors and is, in part, pieces of the puzzle that are used by us. Therefore, you must use your own due-diligence, seek other information, and form your respective opinion about life.

GAMES

A competitive activity played by a set of rules specifying the permissible action of and information available to each participant, the probabilities with which chance events may occur, and the distribution of payoffs.

EXAMPLE. Chess is a game for two players; each of who starts with 16 pieces [chessmen], which can be moved according to fixed rules across a chessboard in an attempt to trap [checkmate] the opponent's King.

    King – The most important piece. The one in whose defense the game is played.

    Queen – The most mobile piece, able to move in a straight line in any direction for any number of squares. Pawn becomes a queen when it succeeds in crossing the board.

    Bishop – A piece that can be moved any number of squares from one corner toward the opposite.

    Knight – A piece shaped like a horse's head. Its move comprises one lateral and two vertical or two lateral and one vertical squares, and it can move over an occupied square.

    Rook – A castle shaped piece having the power to move over any number of unoccupied, consecutive squares either horizontally or vertically.

Pawn – One of the men of least size and value, each player having eight. A pawn can move forward only one square at a time [two on the initial move if the player chooses], but captures only a piece that is one square diagonally in front of it.

Chess was selected as the game to relate the game of life to. In chess, the rules are all known beforehand, and cannot be changed during the game. In the game of life, the rules [known as the rule of law] can be known at the start, but your opponent may change those rules during the game, without notice, arbitrarily and to your detriment. These rules and subsequent changes are published in the Federal Register, which now reaches into the tens of thousands of pages. No one person is able to master all of the rules and changes. It is essential, therefore, that the player selects activities and learns those rules that apply to the choice.

While you may exercise choice in whether you play chess, you may not exercise choice in playing the *game of life*. If you chose to default in the game of life, the opponent must treat you as a *"pawn"* and you will be limited to the nature of the moves assigned to the pawn by the opponent. As long as you continue to choose default, you remain a pawn. You may, however, at any time choose and decide to become an active player. When you acquire the skills necessary to take control of your life, you can become the King, Queen, Bishop, Knight and Rook. You may now make all of the moves appropriate to the game of life, according to knowledge of the moves available to you. This is known as upward mobility.

Assuming that you intend to become an active player, start by visualizing an oversized chessboard. Opposing you are the chess pieces that make it difficult for you to win. Name them according to what they are and do. For example, all of the puzzles described immediately above can be given names. When you have solved each of the puzzles, you understand how those opposing pieces will be maneuvered against you. EXAMPLE: Payroll taxes [Social Security and Medicare]; you would identify two pieces that are maneuvering against you and later, after you have solved the puzzle, identify the chess pieces that you desire for your side of the board. For example, you may select to form a partnership or a corporation. If your solution is valid and you know how to identify and maneuver your pieces, you can successfully check or slow the opposition.

BLACKJACK

A game in which the dealer deals two cards face up to each player and she turns up her first card, keeping the second card dealt to herself as her hole card. All of the rules of the game favor the player with the exception of one. If the player breaks ahead of the dealer, the house automatically wins. Apply this to your personal life in which certain things that you do automatically cause the-roof-falling-in experience. Almost all players play a strategy named *'basic strategy.'* Virtually every blackjack book teaches a form of basic strategy, and most casinos provide free instruction to players about their table games. Casinos teach basic strategy, as if it was a dominant ideology, which prescribes how the player should play his cards under all circumstances. The house has only a one percent advantage over the player. To beat this game you must study the trends of the cards as you would study laws and regulations in the game of life. Cards are not always randomly consistent and neither are regulations that are imposed upon people consistently fair.

When you play, you see everyone's cards, the dealer's up card but not her hole card. If you knew what her hole card was, it would be simple to consistently beat her. Casinos go to great length to train the dealer to never allow anyone to see the hole card before it is time to turn the card up. To win at blackjack, you do not need to always know exactly what the hole card is. What many learn to do is predict whether her hole card is high [8 – ace] or low [ace – 7] and what the dealer's hand is. The general probability is 50% correct over time. When you learn to increase that probability; that is, does she have a made hand [two high cards], does she have a breaking hand, or does she have two low cards then the advantage moves to you. The player only has to overcome the one percent advantage that the house has to be a consistent winner.

VIDEO POKER

This is another game where you can alter the normal house advantage. Borrow a page from the casino business plan. The page that describes how the casino will take a percentage of all money played in a machine. This percentage will usually run between 1% – 4%. This is called the vigorish [the difference between *true* odds and *house* odds or for poker the rake]. Learn how to take a percentage of money played in a machine.

Most games lend themselves to some player manipulation. When the house discovers the gimmick, they will make changes to the rules.

FUTURE GENERATIONS: These stories are intended as analogies on how government operates as the house in everyone's life. They take a percentage called a tax, they teach in government schools a behavioral form of basic strategy, which we know as dominant ideology. In life, most people play the dominant ideology strategy when confronted by government. Many rules which government makes can be finessed by the player. That is what individualism is about.

FISCAL POLICY PUZZLE

Within the fiscal policy puzzle, we have taxation and spending. Within taxation, we have personal, partnership, corporate and trust income tax returns. In addition, we have payroll taxes that are divided between Social Security and Medicare. When you identify the opposing pieces, you proceed to solve the puzzle. When you have solved the puzzle, place a piece on your side of the board and give it the correct name. If you have correctly understood the puzzle and solved for the answer, your piece may be maneuvered successfully against the opposing piece(s). The result will range from a significant reduction, in the case of taxes, to a significant gain, again, in the case of taxes.

If and when you succeed in checkmating the opponent [in chess it is referred to as *"the king has fallen"*], government becomes irrelevant and is recognized as *"the emperor has no clothes."* In the game of life, it is known as having seized your Constitutionally guaranteed unalienable rights to life, liberty and the pursuit of happiness.

RULE # 1 – Rules are constantly changing in both their nature and interpretation; thus, constant due-diligence is essential. It is this factor that changes the puzzle, which one must always keep their eye on. Anticipate changes, prepare contingencies to permit quick reaction, check and double-check your concept and plan, and always enjoy the fruit of your victories. Contingency planning must include the moves that you will make when conditions and circumstances change. The most obvious contingency is having selected the limited partnership or limited liability company. You must also understand the advantages and disadvantages of a "C" corporation, trust, schedule "C", etc., so that you may substitute when the need arises.

RULE # 2 – Successful players have the persistence to stay with their ideas day after day, month after month, year after year, which is hard to work. It is called discipline.

RULE # 3 – Just as the queen in a chess game can move in any direction, and the pawn can move only one space forward, the skilled player [queen] can move in any direction while the unskilled [pawn] player moves only forward. Each player moves to their own drum beat.

RULE # 4 – Without core values, you're not going to be able to hold onto your beliefs or hold on to your strategies during really difficult times. You must fully understand, strongly believe in, and be totally committed to your plans. In order to achieve that mental state, you have to do a great deal of independent research.

RULE # 5 – It's important to have a blend between a creative side and a scientific side. You need the creative side to imagine, discover, and create gaming strategies. You need the scientific side to translate those ideas into firm rules and to execute those rules.

RULE # 6 – Remember, a successful player is someone who does his own work, has his own game plan, and makes his own decisions. Only by acting and thinking independently can a player hope to know when a move isn't working. If you ever find yourself tempted to seek out someone else's opinion on a move, that's usually a sure sign that you should reconsider your strategy.

RULE # 7 – Follow all of the above rules.

FUTURE GENERATIONS: The plan is your thoughts and feelings; the game is reality. We respond to our thoughts and feelings about reality; we don't respond instinctively to reality.

PSYCHOLOGY OF GAMESMANSHIP

Experience has a structure. In other words, the way in which memories are arranged in our minds determines what they will mean and how they will affect us. If we can change the structure of our memories, we will experience those events in our lives differently.

If one person can do it, others can learn to do it, for it is a learned trait. Excellence and achievement have a structure that can be copied. If we can learn to use our brains in the same way as the exceptionally talented person, we can possess the essence of that talent.

The mind and body are part of the same system. If you change your mind about something, your abilities will change. If you change your posture, breathing, or other parts of your physiology, your thoughts will change.

People have all of the resources they need. An image, a sound, or a feeling is a resource. Our brain has the ability to see inner pictures. Whether those pictures begin as fuzzy or clear, they can be built into great motivating visions. Inner voices can criticize us or they can encourage us.

FUTURE GENERATIONS: If you don't live true to your values and fulfill them, you experience disappointment and emptiness. You must recognize that through your experiences you adapt yourself to the conditions of your life. You are taught to submit to the demands of government and fear government; if you do otherwise – you become a passive partner of co-dependency, subservient to your government. Yet you are undergoing an internal change of dissatisfaction. You will initially repress this feeling against government fearing its wrath. You are at a crises point in your life. Do you surrender to the almighty force of government or do you begin to focus on how and when you will make your move to be that free person that you so intensely desire?

PREPARE FOR THE FUTURE

Imagine that there are two futures; the future of desire and the future of fate. Man has always had difficulty separating the two. Desire, the strongest of emotional and mental influences, is itself the future. So, how do we reconcile desire and fate? The future can yield to our minds an objective analysis only if we can put aside all desire of one future over another. At first, this seems like an unattainable desire, but it does appear that by some mutual influence our desires and the events emitting from those desires do grow more into harmony. If future observation is not possible as an experiment, what is left to us?

The sheer fact that you must provide your self with food, shelter, clothing and a means of protection from a variety of dangers will force you to look for work as a means to satisfy these needs. Usually society has within its dominant ideology requirements that predetermine for you the conditions under which you find work. Therefore, it is essential that before you submit to the conditions of the economy that you live in that you have and take the opportunity to identify and evaluate alternatives for the work you will do. Thus this new personality will become dominant in your mind and not the dominant ideology the government and society have planned for you. You will create in your principality the sense of belonging, direction and meaning to your life and to those whom you have been joined with in this venture. Your actions will literally breathe life into your principality and it will become real.

FUTURE GENERATIONS: Never forget that the future is an extension of the present. What we as a society do in the present will combine with the axiomatic bases of the universe to determine the future. Our greatest importance lies with the near future and less importance with the distant future. What ideas can we find to take the place of naïve anticipation that the future will be like the present, only hopefully more pleasant?

First, exclude illusion and fantasy, as the future is the compensation and fulfillment of the present and the future. The future being unknown and incontrovertible has always been, and because of its elusiveness and our inability to foresee it, it cannot be a ground to place our hopes and desires. Add to this the opposite danger that is even more insidious. Here we take the present for granted to an extent far greater than we realize, failing to grasp the impact of this act unfolding into our future.

Second, what are the disciplines that we can use to understand the nature of the present and the forces operating in it, and how interpreting the present can help us to understand the future? History tells us how things have changed and suggest causal relationships between the past and the present. The physical sciences present information to us suggesting how the future is created and the manner of that creation. The knowledge that your future according to your desires, is itself an illusion or dream of what it is that your life desires. The actual change from the present into the future is rarely the desired change for we are susceptible to choosing the easy path and becoming content with half a loaf when a full loaf of freedom is within our grasp.

The difficulty in predicting the future is its enormous complexity and the interdependence of all its parts. Our cause is not desperate or hopeless. We can always attack it by considering it as a function of chance and determinism; chance, where we cannot see causal relationships and determinism where we can. This is a convenient simplification. The future unfolds according to its own rules, but these rules always include the statistical chance interaction of a lower order than the human mind can comprehend. Hold these thoughts. In the next subsection, we offer a more indepth discussion of the mind.

FUTURE GENERATIONS: You, the reader, will be able to act – pro-act – upon the opportunities presented by our 20 years of study and research into the relationship of *"We-the–People"* and their government [USG]. Economically, you will be aware of hidden pitfalls and pending windfalls. Socially, you will be able to position yourself and your family advantageously as familiar social structures disappear/change/emerge. Emotionally and intellectually, you will be able to anticipate the exhilaration of the impending opportunities available to you and your family to achieve and enjoy those unalienable rights given each of us by the Creator. Spiritually, you will be in a position to experience the renewal of your sense of existence and purpose, express your creativity and personal freedom that will distinguish the new century from the late Nation State and the industrial/corporate age it replaces. It was the Creator, not government, that gave us the right to life, liberty and the pursuit of happiness. It is the government, and not the Creator, who wishes to take them away. Life includes our own and those that we create. This includes the right and responsibility to raise and train these new lives in matters of conscience and education, and to lead them into a maturity with free will, and prepared to take their rightful place in this country. Liberty is the right to speak what is on our mind. It carries with it the responsibility of understanding the truth and facts of that to which we speak. Pursuit of happiness is the right to pursue, without hindrance from government, what makes us happy, but not infringing upon the rights of others.

YET TO COME

> *"The only way in which a human being can make some approach to knowing the whole of a subject is by hearing what can be said about it by persons of every variety of opinion and studying all modes in which it can be looked at by every character of mind. No wise man ever acquired his wisdom in any mode but this."*
>
> John Stuart Mill

In our media-intensive culture, it is not difficult to find differing opinion. Thousands of newspapers and magazines and dozens of radio and television talk shows resound with differing points of view. The difficulty lies in deciding which opinion to agree with and which *"experts"* seem most credible. The more inundated we become with differing opinions and claims, the more essential it is to hone critical reading and thinking skills to evaluate these ideas. In "CHANCE", we attempt to offer you a contrarian opinion that you normally cannot find in the public media, because it is by today's conventional wisdom labeled radical. It is, however, the opinion of our founding fathers. We hope to bring it back into vogue.

Research into the Peoples relationship with their government reviews the actions by government that have led to the general distrust of government and a skeptical view of government by its citizens. It is limited and does not cover every possible perception of the people's relationship with USG. The findings are not hard and fast, as no one really knows for certain what is going on in the minds of others or what the future truly holds for us, both individually and collectively.

We outline significant events during the life of our country that played a role in determining why we are what we are, how we think and, our expectations and fears. We discuss issues in America today and offer an insight and understanding into why what happens is happening. We analyze the relative impact upon workers, entrepreneurs and individualists that the major concerns of voters and citizens have. We look prospectively at the future and some of the issues that may or may not emerge as significant in people's lives. It is intended to tantalize your imagination and look closely at who you think you are, and what you need to consider for your future. We look into the way things used to be and how those same values can be pertinent to today's life.

Throughout the book, you will be presented with discussions on how to better play CHANCE. You will have an insight into the reality of the world in which you live, a world that you did not have a choice of entering. A world in which opportunities truly are unlimited. An opportunity to choose what YOU want your life to be, not a life that is assigned to you. With knowledge comes confidence. With confidence, you will become an expert at playing CHANCE.

PLAYERS CREED

As you look back over the previous years, you can inventory both the many good things that came your way and also, the many unwanted events that crossed your path. You can now see everything [good or bad] that became a part of your life and memory you gave to yourself, and it was exactly what you deserved. We each have a passport into the 21st century; but do you also have a first-class ticket?

PLAYING GAMES AND WINNING

FUTURE GENERATIONS: At the beginning of this story were listed the concerns that Americans expressed, and we shared with you a detailed insight into GAMES AND PUZZLES. Games consist of a series of puzzles, which when solved, breaks the code of constructionism. It is like removing the key apple in a supermarket pyramid of apples, and all the apples come tumbling down. Just like Humpty Dumpty.

The number one puzzle is wealth, the need for an income stream and the discipline to divert that income stream into positive wealth-creating investments. This is the old saw of transition from working for money, to money working for you. How much wealth? Pick your own number! We believe that several million dollars accumulated over time, protected from a confiscatory government, is adequate. If you want $2 million in 30 years, and accept a 10% compounded rate, you must have an investment stream of $885 per month or approximately $10,620 per year. Then, if you simply leave that $2 million invested not adding to it, that amount will double in seven years, plus a few months. Do you know how to do this?

FUTURE GENERATIONS: When the task is over, you wonder where it is exactly that you will find yourself living. We also went through that uncertainty, and we now share with you our findings.

FREEDOM AND TRUTH

"The world is filled with men and women seeking pleasure, excitement, novelty; seeking ever to be moved to laughter or tears; not seeking strength, stability, and power; but courting weakness, and eagerly engaged in dispersing what power they have."

"Men and women of real power and influence are few, because few are prepared to make the sacrifice necessary to the acquirement of power and fewer still are ready to patiently build up character."

These are the words of James Allen, author of As a Man Thinketh, and the first words written in his book Freedom and Truth, published in 1971.

We have the opportunity of choices, alternatives and options in the conduct of our lives. We may choose between those expressed by James Allen above. We must acknowledge to ourselves that when we confront choice, there is a trade-off. If we choose that our character be guided by paragraph one, the trade-off is that we cannot have the character of paragraph two. Whichever one we choose, we shall never truly know the other.

The majority of Americans have and are choosing paragraph one. Likely, you are also pointed in that direction. We think that only a small fraction of one percent of our population will pursue the choices we define. Are you curious about your choices? In the following pages, we will define and delineate the nature of the choices available to you to seek a better understanding of them.

We believe our choices are a model for individual life, liberty and the pursuit of happiness for the 21st century. We accomplish this by recognizing that our society is like passengers in a bus driven by government. However, our destination is not the same as government's. We do not always play according to a given set of rules or guidelines. Some rules we simply avoid by not playing in those areas. For example, we do not hire employees; this permits us to avoid rules regarding labor-management, facilities, labor contract, benefit packages and the ever increasing adoption of responsibility for the lives of others that government is so fond of. We look for changes in the rules and act according to them. Every time that Congress changes tax law, they effectively discriminate against one group and favor another. By understanding what ideological mischief the government is up to, it becomes a simple matter to adjust. We can literally use the rules for our benefit. We proceed in our plans with a healthy sense of insecurity. We recognize that from time to time we will be wrong. This sense of insecurity keeps us on our toes. We conduct multiple and repeated analysis to assure us of our correctness; always being alert to correct any errors or identify new changes that enter our world of interest. Recognizing our mistakes gives us pride and confidence. We have a confidence that we understand our own fallibility and that we can move quickly to correct course direction. We will not be a follower as in a herd. We see the trend as our friend. However, we will buck the trend when convinced that it is not in our best interests to follow it, always taking care to avoid being trampled by the herd.

Who are you to judge another? How many times have we heard that? Character is the ultimate in individual distinction. Each of us critically judges oneself and then adjusts behavior and personality accordingly. If you observe behavior in others, hear their conversation and note their personality, it is not necessary to judge the individual. Just take note of the individual self-judgment, which is the best of all judgments. Individual productivity is a person's value as determined by the market. Investments in people begin with what the individual thinks of himself and his willingness to invest his own capital, in himself. Our behavior as a society grows in arrogance, ignorance and stupidity. Be alert for evidence of the following undesirable traits: Refusal to grant the truth of a statement or allegation that is supported by fact, a feeling of discontent and resentment aroused by contemplation of another's desirable possessions or qualities with a strong desire to have them for oneself, a rapacious desire for more than one needs or deserves, as of food, wealth or power, and a strong demand that distribution of wealth be done over again in a different way.

Stereotype is often a media creation using government statistics. They combine negative news with a parade across our TV screens of members of groups that behave in a similar negative pattern. Viewers accept the obvious conclusions presented to them and tend to act accordingly. In your face is not an acceptable character trait.

Dependency goes far beyond selling one's soul to government in exchange for something referred to as government-provided economic security. Another form of dependency [private sector] permeates our life through our willingness to passively accept the premise that we must depend upon fee-for-service providers for certain types of alleged difficult or involved needs.

It has become faulty conventional wisdom that we must buy stocks and bonds through a stockbroker, or that we can only buy and sell real estate through the professional guidance of a real estate broker, or that only a mortgage lender can prepare loan documents, or that all real estate closings must be handled by an escrow company.

Each of us can minister to our medical needs to the extent of our medical knowledge and the immediacy of individual needs, each of us daily acts as our own attorney for routine matters, and we are free to do this without a license, which also frees us from the regulation of the licensee.

Where the line is drawn between when we do for ourselves and when we hire professional help, is individualized for each person and circumstance. That line is now drawn as a circle around us too close to be comfortable. Each of us must push it out from our personal space. This is done by the acquisition of superior knowledge. We must possess knowledge if only to avoid being deceived by fee-for-service providers.

Dependency is unnecessary, except for those individuals who fit the description expressed in James Allen's opening paragraph. If each young person, instead of buying that first car invested that money in a well-managed mutual fund and then added $50 per month, by the time they reached retirement they would have little or no worry regarding the basic needs for survival such as poverty and homelessness. Too many of us, as described in that opening paragraph, are ignorant, spoiled and lack self-discipline, leaving our real value to society in question!

The greater our dependency on government, the more relevant government is in our life. Conversely, the less dependency we have on government, the less relevant they become to our own life.

CO-DEPENDENCY: A second opinion. Governments have spent upwards of $5 trillion on social/welfare programs since 1960. These programs were aimed at reducing poverty. Now, more Americans depend on welfare than ever before. America is rapidly approaching the crises that helped precipitate the fall of the Roman Empire, that there are more people receiving payments from the treasury than there are people paying money into it. In reality it is government tax policy that drives people into poverty, creates a category know as *"working poor."* Then government turns around and gives money to these people that it impoverished. Taxpayers have worried about this spiraling cost and now government itself is showing signs of panic. The question taxpayers ask is, *"Are we just subsidizing what we want to eliminate?"*

There is what we refer to as mysteries of existence. We frequently hear that a particular action of government falls heaviest upon the poor. They are correct in saying that. However, they are remiss in not carrying the thought to its conclusion. Which is - that everything in life falls heaviest upon the poor - beginning with conception and extending to death. The mystery of existence is that whatever power created mankind, created the existence that everything would fall heaviest upon the poor. Why can we say this? Since before the civilization of man, the natural act of poverty bearing the greatest burden was in place. It could be called a law of nature. It has existed from the beginning, exists today, and will surely be with us tomorrow. Again, how can we say that? For centuries man has attempted, through man's laws, to change or alter this law of nature, but with no success it only makes matters worse. We truly hope that at some point in time this will occur. We do not believe that it will in our lifetime though. As Socrates said, *"What ever something is it will always be, and no amount of rhetoric or sophism will cause it to change its given nature."*

In 1950, government(s) took about 4.5% of income; a family could raise the children and buy a house with one spouse working. Today, the state takes about 50% of income, provides housing for the poor, and supports the jobless while single-parent benefits make the father unnecessary. Do you believe that families are breaking apart, or that today's children are confused, rootless and easily tempted into drugs and petty crime?

The welfare state tries to help the sick, the old, and the jobless by taking resources from the healthy, the young and the employed. Does this polarize the issue between the groups, separated by an impersonal bureaucracy?

If government behaves as if all wealth is the property of the state, the state to decide on how to spend it, otherwise honest citizens will avoid the taxes and join in the milking of government money that they believe belongs to no one.

In the former Soviet Union, citizens did not consider stealing from the state as a crime. Their rationale was that the state owned all wealth; therefore, they were only taking what was theirs. And we know what happened to them.

Approximately 100 years ago, we had briefly experimented with social Darwinism and quickly put it behind us. Today, we have reached the excesses of social universalism. We wonder where the social ideologues will attempt to lead us next. Maybe we should not follow them anymore.

Politicians take great pleasure in using the analogy of *"those who ride in the wagon versus those who pull the wagon."* This argument is intended to advance their ideological values and gain support to seize power over others. Notice how the argument presents limited choice of alternatives. You are riding, pulling, or possibly doing a bit of both.

We can identify their political agenda by examining the power factor. The Left advocates the power to highly regulate economic matters combined with granting limited individual social freedom. The Right advocates the power to highly regulate social matters with limited economic regulation. And, the moderates advocate power to highly regulate both economic and social matters. Moderates are easy to recognize. They are the ones saying, *"there ought to be a law against...."*

The ATTITUDE and BEHAVIOR of Americans is interesting. We offer two examples.

Upon his election, JFK said, *"ask not what your country can do for you, but what you can do for your country."* So what happened? America embarked upon its greatest period of human dependency on government in its history. Need became the code word and entitlement became the battle cry. Five trillion dollars later we are faced with a major debacle of family, taxes, spending, responsibility and debt.

Martin Luther King Jr., in his dream speech, said and we paraphrase, I dream that when my children grow up they will be judged NOT by the color of their skin, but by the content of their character. So what happened? Every time an issue arises, the code word is *"racism."*

Affirmative action, gender, and alternative lifestyles have all become battle cries of special interest groups. Welcome to a liberal democracy.

Americans love their country, yet many have come to hate the government that rules the country. America is disgusted with the deteriorating behavior of its people, the lack of consideration, and the demands to accept values that betray failed ideology. We now have so many separate special interest groups that are each pulling America in their direction that we risk being literally pulled apart. That is the bus that many are no longer willing to ride in.

Try to understand the causal relationships of taxes; that a tax obligation is the result of a tax consequence, which is itself a result of a taxable event. You control the event; therefore, you control the tax consequence and obligation.

Informal studies of taxpayer attitudes reveal startling insight into the real world. The following categories represent only absolute numbers. The majority of people accept taxes as a necessary evil and limit their actions to complaining; the next largest group simply doesn't work and goes on welfare; the third group withholds reporting of income through such evasions as the underground economy; the fourth group makes a serious attempt to manage the event, usually relying upon professional advice; the fifth group doesn't file; and the final group [contrarians] stop creating taxable events, live the entrepreneurial lifestyle, and live off the wealth that they have earned. They refuse to fuel the corrupt machines that identify so many governments.

In the beginning, taxes were necessary to fund the national defense and other operational functions of government. In addition, the code was structured to make it easier for the lower classes to participate in government. It was never intended that government should redistribute income to favored groups and thus determine who shall be winners and who shall be losers.

Individuals are permitted to deduct certain expenses from taxable income. When they pay taxes on taxable income, the income becomes free of future taxes. Most people freely spend income that is free of taxes for consumption instead of investing. When they finally reach the time when they decide that they must begin saving, they must again first pay tax on taxable income before investing. A truly stupid series of events.

If you control the event, the IRS becomes irrelevant, and you become the relevant factor in your life.

The SOCIAL CONTRACT that each of us has with our Republic provides that we agree to voluntarily give up certain selected freedoms in exchange for the Republic providing laws and regulations governing certain aspects of behavior. Examples of these are traffic regulations, social behavior of a cooperative nature, and laws patterned after the nature and intent of the Ten Commandments. These form the basic framework of our collective conscience that makes it possible for us to live in peace.

Beyond the social contract, we have great latitude in which laws and regulations we want to function under. EXAMPLE: When we feel that laws and regulations governing the hiring and utilization of employees is excessive, we may at our discretion refuse to hire full-time employees. We may also encourage others to act as independent contractors for the purpose of our doing business with each other and accepting responsibility for ourselves. Each of us has the right of choice as to which areas we wish to participate in and which we wish to avoid. Our life belongs to each of us, and if we take control of our life, government is then truly irrelevant.

To walk away from society is a terribly difficult action to take. It flies in the face of all we have been taught. Walking away begins with the knowledge that governments and societies are like lemmings heading for the water and a cold, silent, wet death. When we talked to many of you, we always asked if you would seek and act on advice of elected representatives or the federal bureaucrats in the matters of your personal investments, personal behavior, retirements, family matters and your beliefs. The answer is always, NO! Yet, most of you are doing it just the same.

Emotional intelligence permits us to evaluate; various political, social and economic rhetoric, and understand the truth of its spin, thus embracing the good and throwing out the false. Knowing that emotion is confusing our mind, and drawing upon our training, we hope to avoid the rash decisions and acts that live to haunt us. It is the reason why we always take the time to sleep on it until logic and reason have the opportunity to rise to the surface. At which time, we will alertly recognize it and act accordingly. We hope.

Superior knowledge frees us from the yoke of government. That is why we do not have to either ride in the wagon or pull it. An examination of superior knowledge compared with government's sophistic rhetoric reveals some interesting truths. Superior knowledge is not taxable, does not pollute or harm the environment, cannot be seized or confiscated, is beyond regulation, is transferable to our progeny through parental guidance, can be used or stored, is taken everywhere we go, and finally, is the mortal enemy of big government and special interest as it stands as the truthful example of what the exercising of the intent of liberty, as expressed in the Constitution and the Declaration of Rights, was intended to be.

If, as many think, the government believes that all wealth belongs to government, that government has the responsibility to determine its nature, use and who is to benefit, then, the various agencies, like the IRS, ATF and FBI, become instruments of government to control the behavior and thoughts of people. It is superior (truthful) knowledge that permits each of us to evaluate and judge this matter and to take individual action as we each see fit. Those who disregard knowledge become the sheep that make up the flock. We must be alert that we do not slide into a government where taxation with representation is allowed to be more abusive than the taxation without representation that precipitated the American Revolution.

Here's another example of superior knowledge. The tragedy of ill-defined conventional retirement. Conventional wisdom is *"work hard and save your money."* Government says, *"invest in a IRA, the contribution and interest is tax deferred."* What does unconventional wisdom say? Big Government survives by attaching its life support system into people's wages, investments and retirements. If you follow conventional wisdom, you have government(s) as a parasitic financial burden for your entire life, death, and the life of your heirs.

Entrepreneurs create a laissez faire culture with its own lifestyle. Substitute control for ownership, and begin the process of severing the umbilical cord to government that finances their profligate [recklessly wasteful; wildly extravagant] ways. Wealth is safe, secure and generally beyond the reach of those that would confiscate it. You worked hard for what you have, so you are entitled to enjoy it in your particular manner. Increasing wealth brings with it increasing responsibility. Money requires management, which requires knowledge. Opportunities are created when large amounts of capital suddenly flow from one area into another. The cause of these flows is generally caused by government(s) action or consumer fads.

The tax changes of 1981 and 1983 created incentives for investing in real estate creating huge capital flows into that sector. Coincidentally, Congress changed the insured limits of accounts from $10,000 to $40,000 and then $100,000 per account. Banks and savings and loans were tempted to loan without adequate consideration of risk. In 1986, the tax law was changed again, pulling out from under investors the generous depreciation schedules, and the opportunity to offset ordinary income with real estate losses. Real estate tanked. Borrowers defaulted. Banks and savings and loans went bankrupt. Government was forced to bail them out at great cost to the taxpayer.

As capital flowed into real estate in the 80's, there was an opportunity to benefit, if one saw it coming. When real estate tanked in 1989 through 1993, there were opportunities to benefit. Government created the circumstances that created this bubble, and then burst it.

If we understand how governments behave and the crises that they will cause, we can anticipate where large changes in capital flows will occur. If we believe that certain major countries will experience civil wars, we should own good defense stocks. If we believe that there will ultimately be a shortage of oil due to war, embargos, etc., we would own some good oil and gas stocks. I'm sure you see the point. If we want to plan for opportunity, know where the money is next going to go. Areas to watch are crime, fiscal policy, monetary policy, trade policy; be alert for any forthcoming inflation, deflation, recession and yes, a possible depression.

Historical personal memory and experience is a great teacher. Having been born during the final year of the Coolidge administration, we had the opportunity to personally experience the social, political and economic conditions that followed. With one exception, there is great similarity between that period and the most recent two decades that most of us have shared. That difference is that the 20's and 30's were driven by the excesses of conservative ideology, and the most recent period by excesses of liberal ideology more than a political ideology. When ideology becomes excessive it tends to appear as a theology. This occurs because of the zealous drive of its supporters. To an outsider it resembles more a mythology. Intellectual entrepreneurs have no real desire to be a part of anything that lacks truth, logic and reason.

The MIND as our principal means of survival is a truism, but one that is mouthed by many and understood by few. At birth, our mother is the most relevant person in our life. She nurtured us and gave us, with dad's help, the values that make up our conscience. As we grew up, the church, school and government all became relevant. As we developed our mind and grew to the point where our mind was, or should have been developed to provide for our own survival, we became the most relevant to ourselves. Everything else became less relevant, especially if and when their input was deemed not in our best interest. At least that was the way it has been for ages.

Did you know that you could use your conscious mind to program your subconscious? That your subconscious mind will work continuously to solve issues that you task it with? That you are what you think? That your thinking must be controlled for it will absorb what it is exposed to? That the mind can work as efficiently to create evil plans as it can work to create positive results? That if you are unwilling to use your mind correctly, you have doomed yourself to the world of ignorance? That the world of ignorance is the worst of all worlds? Your mind is your computer; garbage in-garbage out. What are you going to use your mind for? Truth? Fiction? Success? Failure?

Each of us may from time to time, continue to prefer certain political actions over others as being more favorable for the country. However, when we view politics in the large perspective, politics is irrelevant. It is irrelevant because while we may recognize the good or bad in various issues, because we have taken control of our lives, we have also prepared to protect ourselves from government mischief, mistakes and mismanagement. Life is always subject to random chance, uncertainty, and human error. We view government in the same manner Warren Buffet (the world's greatest investor) views companies he plans to invest in. The company should be so sound of value that even if an idiot became its CEO it would still survive, and sooner or later an idiot will be in charge. When one understands the irrelevance of government(s), it does not matter which politician or party seizes control of the levers of government. We will survive and create wealth regardless. If we understand their true agenda, we can anticipate the events that will ultimately occur and the nature and extent of the capital flows resulting from them.

YOUR MIND IS YOUR COMPUTER

FUTURE GENERATIONS: This you must understand. Your brain is the best computer you will ever have – better even than the best that MIT has, capable of sorting through vast amounts of data, stored on your neurons via your synapses, and coming up with the answers you are searching for.

MANAGING OUR MIND

The complexity that we are primarily concerned with is the human mind. Assume that the rest of the universe goes on its way determined by its physical, chemical and biological laws, except in as so far man intervenes with the use of his mind. In our society, the immediate future reveals itself in the following observed tendencies visible in the present. This is the minimal basis for prediction, which is the basis of rules by which to play CHANCE for life. When we consider applications or developments of knowledge in society and government, we have already introduced the element of chance. We can predict the development in the field of government relationship with the people, but we cannot predict the rate of change. It is our inability to predict change rates that react on each other; thus, the future becomes more uncertain the farther we look out. We can deal with this complexity by separating the variable as best we can.

Man has always been occupied with the struggles of life. His first struggle is with the massive, unintelligent forces of nature; heat and cold, winds, rivers, matter and energy. Concurrently he struggles with things closer to him; animals and plants, his own body, and health and disease. Finally, with his desires and fears, and his imaginations and stupidities created to implement prevailing philosophy.

Everyone understands the significance of the mind; but very few understand how to manage the mind to focus its strength and increase knowledge. The basic functions of minds operate similar for each of us. It is when knowledge [either fact or fiction] is introduced that each mind acts in its unique way. Each mind will produce a result somewhat dissimilar from any other mind. This occurs because each mind, while the basic function is identical, will calculate an answer based upon the other information that the mind has introduced or allowed to enter. It is when a person is in a mindless mode, not editing or evaluating the information floating around, that unintended or invalid information enters. The mind is not programmed to distinguish between good and bad; right or wrong; or fact or fiction. That is why some people appear out of touch with reality. They have convinced themselves that something is true and then like an actor saying his lines presents the thought as fact. That is why certain liars are so convincing; they block out that they are lying.

The mind has a conscious and subconscious part. The conscious mind receives information. Its responsibility is to sort this information and accept that which is correct, truthful and useful in the individuals plan and reject that which isn't. The absence of a conscience disrupts this process. The subconscious mind processes that information assigned it by the conscious mind. Napoleon Hill said, *"we are what we think about."* It is the conscious mind with which we think, daydream and fantasize. This function of our conscience was to have been developed through the nurturing of parents assisted by the extended family. The nature of our thoughts, time spent on them, intensity, their morality, the truthfulness of them, etc., is the act of programming our subconscious mind. The subconscious mind, unlike the conscious mind, works constantly even when we sleep. Its function is to seek answers to whatever the conscious mind requests. If the conscious mind desires answers of how to be successful as a sexual predator, so be it; on the other hand, if the conscious mind desires answers to how to build a better mouse trap, that is what it will produce. Therefore Hill was right, we are what we think about.

WHERE HAVE ALL THE 'SURVIVAL COURSES' GONE?

FUTURE GENERATIONS: Did you or do your children learn about *"Basic Survival 101"* in your government school? Probably not, as this subject is not routinely taught in wage labor schools. Welcome to the world of reality.

This section is devoted to the mind – so let us stimulate your mind and offer it a few easy challenges designed to develop in your mind *"problem solving"* techniques.

Today [circa 2006] the value of the dollar stands at 10% of its post WWII value and is continuing its downward trend. The common theory is that government is deliberately on this trend line, into the near future. Government being the world's largest debtor, $53 *trillion* dollars and counting, benefits the most as it rolls over its debt and makes interest payment with devalued dollars. Inflation benefits debtors that have fixed interest rates and punishes the creditor holding that debt. Of course, when deflation occurs then it is the creditor who receives dollars of greater value than those loaned to the debtor, who is punished severely. Because we can't judge with any accuracy when inflation or deflation will ascend or descend, we face a quandary. There are two types of debt; investment debt that creates something of value other than momentary happiness and consumer debt that gives a great happy tug to the heart when the new TV screen is delivered. These two types of debt are also referred to as *appreciating* or *depreciating.* Of course, the first one is the best as that makes you wealthier and the second is bad because it only makes you feel wealthier, thus when you pay the piper, the piper's name is your creditor. Each transaction must have a buyer and a seller, a borrower and a lender, a spend thrift and a saver, and one who ends up in old age defeated and the one living comfortable as the winner, and being blamed for the bad luck of the first.

Inflation is well known as the world's most insidious tax. It is almost invisible, can be blamed on anyone, but in the end it is simply the government embezzling the peoples wealth. Yes! Some people become wealthier, some feel the wealth effect without the wealth, and others are falling through the cracks. Do you have the courage to look in the mirror and honestly say which you see?

The Federal Reserve is attempting to find a balance between inflation vs. deflation, with a bias to over inflating rather than deflating and throwing the economy into recession/depression. The fed funds rate today stands at 5.25%. Both increases and decreases in the fed funds rate take many months to work their way through the economy, so at best, timing becomes a guess subject to unintended consequences.

Erich Fromm, in his book *'Escape from Freedom'* spoke to the love / hate and other needs of people. He said, *"Although there are certain needs, such as hunger, thirst, sex, which are common to man, those drives which make for the differences in men's characters, like love and hatred, the lust for power and the yearning for submission, the enjoyment of sensuous pleasure and the fear of it, are all products of the social process. The most beautiful as well as the most ugly inclinations of man are not part of a fixed and biologically given human nature, but result from the social process which creates man. In other words, society has not only a suppressing function – although it has that too – but it has a creative function. Man's nature, his passions, and anxieties are a cultural product; as a matter of fact, man himself is the most important creation and achievement of the continuous human effort, the record of which we call history."*

From which part of society do you see the greatest impact in developing both suppressive and creative functions in man?

FUTURE GENERATIONS: We see now that the socialization processes to which young people are exposed and indoctrinated in, have life-long lasting effects on each person. The socialization of your children will, or should, reflect the parent's values of their understanding of the nature of the general population so that exposure to those of an unsatisfactory nature can be avoided. We have talked about the many threats to our freedom. There is one specific threat, which is so threatening that it scares us just to write about. We are not predicting this threat for we do not know that it will occur. What we do know is that if *'we-the-people'* do nothing to take back our government, it is likely that all freedoms and liberty will wash overboard and America will become a tyranny.

BASIC SURVIVAL 101

Information is now beginning to creep into the arena of awareness of the future, of the struggle between the mommies [leftist] and the daddies [rightist] that regardless of which wins America takes a huge stride toward dictatorship. We can use the following descriptive terms regarding the ideologies of the two parties interchangeable. Leftist or liberals are also the mommies and radical leftists are communists masquerading under the banner of *'democracy.'* Rightist or conservatives are also the daddies and radical rightists are fascists masquerading under the banner of *'democracy.'*

The people will win who take up this struggle individually by withholding the sanction of their vote, by their demonstration of their demands, and their refusal to continue the charade or illusion of honest government. If we reach this state of disorder, then the novel by Vince Flynn, mentioned earlier, will probably come true. People must take action now to protect themselves and their families from both evils described above. Our leaders and leadership wannabes are over inflated with personal greed, lust and power over people. This is our warning to our future generations. Act now or perish. Act now or enter serfdom. Act now or surrender your rights.

FUTURE GENERATIONS: Your survival will depend upon the use of your mind in understanding the basic threats to freedom, understanding the means and ideas available to counter these threats and the will and courage to take up this challenge.

Again, the two categories of threats are government(s) and the tyranny of the middle class. The company line espoused by public schools, media, special interest, etc., is essentially federal propaganda. Specific threats are ideology, withholding of information so that you can't evaluate both sides of political, economic and social issues, the pure greed, stupidity and lies of our leaders, their unfettered lust for power over all others and this silly dream of Empire.

May 2006, Barney Frank (D), House of Representatives, spoke out about the greed of corporate salaries. He stated that salaries should not be set by just the Board of Directors, but that the stockholders should have a voice. Basically he was promoting direct participation by the stockholders in critical areas of corporate governance. As we listened to him, we became furious at the duplicity and hypocritical nature of his demagoguery. He was speaking out of both sides of his mouth saying; don't do as the Congress does do as the Congress says. Congress sets their own salaries, retirement plans, health benefit plans, without any consulting with the people who must pay for them. The people are, as Barney said, the stockholders of the country. In addition, they consistently exclude laws from applying to the Congress – to us that comes across as unfair, greedy, selfish, cowardly and down right wrong. The people have the right to vote on salaries and benefits for their Congress. They have within this right to lower the salaries of Congress when Congress lies and cheats the people. This is known as direct democracy, without it we can't limit or prevent the out of control politicians from waging wars throughout the world for the purpose of Empire of influence. For they are more concerned about their history and legacy. They want their names in the history books of the world, their faces carved onto mountains, airports-buildings-highways, bridges, etc. named after them. We should really be naming public restrooms and outhouses after them to express the shame they have brought down upon we-the people.

The tyranny of the majority is directly related to the freedom and the will of people. Every American is born free yet the majority feel freedom a threat and they, therefore, fear freedom. Among the elite minority there is a will to power over another. The elite minority truly understands the majority. They seek and need *security – safety – survival.* The minority is quick to present plausible answers to the majority. The elite majority dislike their having to make critical thought and to move against the tide of conventional wisdoms that the minority offers to take over this fearful burden. Knowing that the majority really wants to be told what to do by a person who appears as a strong leader with wisdoms beyond their comprehensions, they propose initiatives [entitlements]. Matthew tells us that when Jesus was tempted to turn stone into bread he answered, men do not live by bread alone. The politician does otherwise when offering to turn welfare into bread telling people they can live by bread [entitlements] alone. The elite minority turns the phrase that America is a land of laws by then making laws that harm people, while they profit from their knowledge of the fear people have at making their own choices and their desire to tie themselves to someone they can worship for the security they seek. Will people sell their soul for cash? You better believe they will – eagerly!

Recently, we came across an article titled *"Conation as an Important Factor of Mind,"* by Huitt, W. "Educational Psychology Interactive," Valdosta State University in GA. We quote directly from his download the following:

Psychology has traditionally identified and studied three components of mind: cognition, affect, and conation.

Cognition *refers to the process of coming to know and understand; the process of encoding, storing, processing and retrieving information. It is generally associated with the question of "what" [e.g. what happened, what is going on now, what is the meaning of information?]*

Affect *refers to the emotional interpretation of perceptions, information, or knowledge. It is generally associated with one's attachment (positive or negative) to people, objects, ideas, etc. and asks the question "How do I feel about this knowledge or information?"*

Conation *refers to the connection of knowledge and affect to behavior and is associated with the issue of "why." It is the personal, intentional, planful, deliberate, goal-oriented, or striving component of motivation, the proactive (as opposed to reactive or habitual) aspect of behavior. It is closely associated with the concept of volition, defined as the use of will, or the freedom to make choices about what to do. It is absolutely critical if an individual is successfully engaged in self-direction and self-regulation.*

Conative issues speak directly to the question that too many high school graduates can't answer except to say, *"I don't* know." These are "what" questions dealing with what the child has set forth as the goal of life, what the child is going to do, and what plans and commitments has the child made up to this time in their life. Conative issues are precisely the primary goal of the "Free Labor Family" and its development of individualism within the child.

When we stand at the altar of government and government tells us that if we kneel down and worship government we shall for all eternity have peace and a fulfilled life of happiness! Will people sell their future, and we each only have one future, for that promise? You better believe they will – eagerly!

The lust for political power to create one great world state is the goal of all those who seek power over people. Never surrender your mind for the false promises of false gods.

FUTURE GENERATIONS: Throughout book one, BETRAYERS, all that has preceded in this book, SURVIVAL, are to outline the high crimes and misdemeanors of our leaders. Before you proceed be absolutely sure that your MIND is totally focused on the threats and that you understand your assets and ideas for here we will go in this next section.

SURVIVAL: FREE LABOR FAMILY

Every great public proclamation must start with a great and plausible lie.

Anonymous

You question that? Polk and his war with Mexico, occupying Mexico City and coercing a treaty giving USA what we know as the Southwest. Lincoln and his Civil War between the states, allegedly to *"preserve the Union."* McKinley went to war with Spain against the will of the people. The battle for the Philippines with the assistance of the rebels and then telling them *"no thanks,"* delaying their freedom for another half century. Wilson's going to war in WWI to *"save the world for democracy"* when actually he went to war to pull the British chestnuts out of the fire. FDR sandbagged the Japanese into an attack because the vast majority of us did not want war. Was December 7, 1941 a day of infamy or is it more appropriate to be known as the day of *deceit*. LBJ's deceit that our fleet off Vietnam had been attacked by an enemy boat – so small it resembled the likeness to the fly biting the ass of the elephant. Nixon and Ford claiming the Paris treaty, bringing an end to the Vietnam debacle, was an honorable pact. Reagan's Grenada. Bush One's Iraq. Clintons Mogadishu. Bush Two's preemptive wars with Afghanistan and Iraq. And, we have only begun what will yet prove to be an even deadlier and more

violent century than the last. World leaders are like young boys
on the playground spoiling for a good fight. The difference is
that these are not boys. Our best young men and women must
go forth, fight those wars, many die or get injured. All we gain
is that our leaders are in the history books, glorified as the
great defenders and protectors of our country. Parents do not
raise their children to go forth and fight wars for those idiots
that start them. They raise children who will love their country
and work to make it a better place to live. They are our
supposedly grown, mature leaders and they are making war
not play.

Aldous Huxley, author of the dystopian classic 'Brave New
World', said it this way.

*"There is, of course, no reason why the new totalitarians
should resemble the old. Government by clubs and firing squads,
by artificial famine, mass imprisonment and mass deportation, is
not only inhumane (nobody cares much about that nowadays), it
is demonstrably inefficient and in an age of advanced
technology, inefficiency is the sin against the Holy Ghost. A
really efficient totalitarian state would be one in which the all-
powerful executive of political bosses and their army of
managers control a population of slaves who do not have to be
coerced, because they love their servitude. To make them love it
is the task assigned, in present-day totalitarian states, to
ministries of propaganda, newspaper editors and
schoolteachers... The most important Manhattan projects of the
future will be vast government-sponsored enquiries into what the
politicians and the participating scientists will call 'the problem of
happiness' – in other words, the problem of making people love
their servitude.*

FUTURE GENERATIONS: Carved into the porch lintel
above the entrance to the castle, The Chateau de
Blanchefort, in the Languedoc, is the Latin phrase, "*Veritas
vos Liberabit.*" This translates to read, "*The truth will set you
free.*" Ironically it is but a half-truth. Yes, truth will set your
mind free, but only your acts will set both your mind and
your body free. We all know the truth that government lies
to us, that they cheat us out of our opportunities, and
regularly reduce and remove from us our Constitutional
freedoms. Those truths have not set us free. Those truths

have succumbed to political correctness. We ignore those truths until time convinces us that they are not truths. This is your challenge to be or not to be. Are you up to it?

We live in a world where things seem to be relative, but we lack a solid point of reference. People act in a manner that seems to lead into their bumping into or crashing with other people's action. We call this chaos. Truthfully it is not possible to persuade government(s) to reform their corrupt and disastrous ways. We appear to be in a cycle, at the point at which the momentum of the world can't be stopped, until the cycle returns to its mean. Winners and losers will be determined by those who observe and study what is happening and why it is happening. You must be adaptive and have the intellectual courage and confidence to act. That is why survival is so important, more important than trying to change government.

We remember former president Gerald Ford who served out the final year(s) of disgraced president Nixon's term. The media referred to him as one who has trouble chewing gum and walking at the same time. Yet, in his inauguration speech he had this to say, "*I must say to you that the state of the Union is not good. Millions of Americans are out of work. Recession and inflation are eroding the money of millions more. Prices are too high, and sales are too slow. This year's Federal deficit will be about $30 billion: next year's probably $45 billion. The national debt will rise to over $500 billion. Our plant capacity and productivity are not increasing fast enough. We depend on others for essential energy.*" The government knew three decades ago that a crisis in energy availability was engulfing us and yet government failed in its Constitutional responsibility and oath by placing greed and irrational judgment ahead of the countries true need. That is unacceptable. We and our children now pay the price for their stupidity.

Forget government, it is on a death march; a struggle between the warfare and welfare parties and that will not change. It is run by a passel of over-paid *whores* pandering us over TV and radio, looking to do a *trick*, something that will refill their bag of *power-over-people*. They have sold their body to groups and now they want to buy our bodies at a discount to true value. We have elected a passel of fools and idiots to run our government and we are the guilty party, for we elected people in our image, the image of a fool or idiot. Both parties have wandered off the reservation and are traveling a course no man has traveled before. We, as a country, are orbiting within a galaxy of egos, greed, lust, ambition and to hell with the people, full speed ahead. It is only a matter of time. Here is an example of what we see. Congress will not deal with Social Security and Medicare until it is about to blow up in our faces. The president [?] will appoint a bi-partisan panel to study the matter and recommend a solution. It's like selecting red foxes and blue foxes to study the security of the hen house and recommend a solution. Why do they do this? First, they want to spread the blame over everyone in the country; second, they want to make sure that no one can point a finger at them as individuals; third, when payroll taxes are raised much of the money will be reinvested in expanding an already bloated and disgusting government. But, the fools we all are, we will buy into their bull-crap and go along, partly from fear and greed. But, not all of us are fools. Many have secured a safe haven.

Imagine you are driving down a main road. You see a fork in the road ahead. There are two signs. One points to the LEFT and tells us that Communistville is but a short drive in that direction. The other points to the Right and announces that Fascistville is but a short drive down that road. What are your choices? Left leads to communism and Right leads to fascism. The road does not continue straight ahead. You may turn around but that will take you back from whence you came. You can just sit there. Or you can seek safe haven and find your private principality.

FUTURE GENERATIONS: For simplicity of speech we will substitute the noun 'red' for fascism and the noun 'blue' for socialism. Each color has that end to justify their means.

Alan Greenspan coined the phrase *"Irrational Exuberance"* to describe the action of investors when markets seemed to be going straight up, forever. The phrase is also appropriate to government spending and regulation of the people. It is amazing that with the Declaration of Independence we overthrew the British, a foreign power, and with the Constitution created a powerful government that defies us now far worse than good old King George. Talk about an irony! Have you wondered about the phrase, *"America and Great Britain have a special relationship."* It is amazing, when researching one subject you uncover the perceived truth about another. Earlier we said that there is a perception that there were those, even before the Constitution was ratified, that were developing plans on how to get around changing the intent of the Constitution and deceiving the people in the process. It goes back to the early days of colonialism, let us say 371 years ago from 2007, with the establishment of the University of Harvard at Cambridge, Massachusetts. The alumni and professors of Harvard developed ties and relationships with, you guessed it, Oxford and Cambridge in England. Bonds and personal family alliances were obviously formed and carried on to other Ivy League universities, such as Yale, Princeton, etc. We now know, or maybe we should say believe, that these alliances of common thought and purpose are part of or affiliated with those who planned for the anarchism of the Constitution. Remember that Wilson was a zealous anglophile and that FDR had a love/hate relationship with other leaders. He loved both Winston and Uncle Joe and he hated Hitler and all Germans. We will continue our research on this matter.

FUTURE GENERATIONS: Recall that earlier we said that without survival nothing else is possible. Therefore the free labor family will never exist for you unless you first learn how to survive. Our government has declared war not only on Iraq and the Taliban, but also on Bin Laden, terrorists in general and the American people. Think. We have a war against poverty, a war against drugs, a war against education, a war against the Constitution and yes, a war against the people and their freedom. Therefore – having had war declared against us, *"we the people,"* are fighting for survival and will best be accomplished if we place our self on a *"war like footing."*

DECONSTRUCTION PLAN

A war-like footing requires vision, strategy, tactics and above all information that we can convert to intelligence. To accomplish this, we visualize five separate but integrated categories. These include, and we will discuss later each in detail, [l] leadership – [pa] personnel/administration – [ii] intelligence/information – [po] planning/operations – [ss] supply/service.

Leadership within the family will usually begin with the father and includes the mother as a leadership team. To succeed, the leaders must always be the most capable family members available to lead this operation.

Personnel/Administration will include identification of available human resources and the potential skills of each. It also includes having an efficient record section and detailed responsibility for administrative tasks, policies, correspondence, tax management, etc.

Intelligence/Information is the gathering of information both educational and about the enemies, their plans, methods strengths and weaknesses.

Plans/Operations utilizes the intelligence furnished and develops plans for the operations based upon latest knowledge of techniques and the best way to either defeat or thwart the enemy.

Supply/Service will be responsible for office space, housing, equipment, supplies and repairs.

In summary, we quote from Carl Von Clauswitz's famous book, *"Principles of War."* The following are extracts that have survived the passing of time.

PRINCIPLES FOR WAR IN GENERAL

The theory of warfare tries to discover how we may gain a preponderance of physical forces and material advantages at the decisive point. As this is not always possible, theory also teaches us to calculate moral factors: the likely mistakes of the enemy, the impression created by a daring action,...yes, even our own desperation. None of these things lie outside the realm of the theory and art of war, which is nothing but the result of reasonable reflection on all the possible situations encountered during a war. We should think very frequently of the most dangerous of these situations and familiarize ourselves with it. Only thus shall we reach heroic decisions based on reason, which no critic can ever shake.

In the decisive moments of your life, in the turmoil of battle, you will some day feel that this view alone can help where help is needed most, and where a dry pedantry of figures will forsake you.

Whether counting on physical or moral advantages, we should always try, in time of war, to have the probability of victory on our side. But this is not always possible. Often we must act against this probability, SHOULD THERE BE NOTHING BETTER TO DO. [emphasis is ours] Were we to despair here, we would abandon the use of reason just when it becomes most necessary, when everything seems to be conspiring against us.

Therefore, even when the likelihood of success is against us, we must not think of our undertaking as unreasonable or impossible: for it is always reasonable, if we do not know of anything better to do, and if we make the best use of the few means at our disposal.

We must never lack the calmness and firmness, which are so hard to preserve in time of war. Without them the most brilliant qualities of mind are wasted. We must therefore familiarize ourselves with the thought of an honorable defeat. We must always nourish this thought within ourselves, and we must get completely used to it. Without this firm resolution, no great results can be achieved in the most successful war, let alone in the most unsuccessful war.

In any specific action, in any measure we may undertake, we always have the choice between audacious and the most careful solution. Some people think that the theory of war always advise the latter. That assumption is false. If the theory does advise anything, it is the nature of war to advise the most decisive, that is, the most audacious. Theory leaves it to the military leader, however, to act according to his own courage, according to his spirit of enterprise, and his self-confidence. Make your choice, therefore, according to this inner force; but never forget that no military leader has ever become great without audacity.

Remember, the war you are in is not of your making. It was thrust upon you by continuous treason that is knowingly violating the Constitution, by leaders driven by improper ideology that places a wall around itself to prevent truth and facts to enter into and change it. An example of audacity is that you never tell anyone in advance what you plan to do or not to do. This is audacious for you are now engaged in a form of guerrilla warfare. Think of your struggle to succeed in reaching the goals you have set as a war with the powers that be, and you can see the above principles apply to it and will help you achieve success.

!!!HOW IT CAN WORK FOR YOU!!!

FUTURE GENERATIONS: We know that people of all ages will read this book. To give continuity we select two young people and follow their actions creating their personal *"Principality."* Those older or younger can pick their entry point, utilize what will work for them, and if too old for the early part, look for the section on grandparenting. Make certain you pass this opportunity on to your progeny so they will not suffer what you may have. Each of you, including your family, is an integral part of a larger group. In this discussion it could easily be the war in Iraq, or it could be the war against poverty, the war against drugs or any of the many other wars. Or war like moral and physical efforts that our country wages against something or just phantoms. What, is not as important as the why and how. A struggle is lost, or to be lost, when both the moral and physical strength are expended in an effort that is not moving forward. To continue the struggle under such conditions usually results in lost effort. America finds itself enmeshed in a struggle that more resembles quicksand than a field of battle. Break down the struggle of America into its basic fighting elements, the individual. Say that individual is you. For you to continue your participation in the struggle after your moral and physical strength has been sapped is to face your destruction. To avoid your destruction you must withdraw, taking with you your remaining moral and physical strength until the balance of power is reestablished. Your efforts can be resumed only when new and favorable factors indicate that your chance of success is probable. For a war to continue in the face of serious depletion of moral and political strength, consideration of total depletion of energy, momentum of effort, and ability to carry national cost of this must be given. In Vietnam, the call came from our leaders that they needed more men, more equipment, more time, more money, more everything; then the final disaster washed over us like a tidal wave and all was lost. An example is the *"surge"* being executed today in Iraq. There are two items we know for sure, first, that the cost will escalate proportionally, and second, that KIA and MIA will also increase, probably greater than proportionately. *[See Clauswitz's 'Principles of War.'"]* There is not much that you as an individual can do to influence government leadership in the course of a wrongheaded war. You can, however, apply the teaching points of the above to your life and your family and move to save yourself.

CASE STUDY

We find two young people fresh out of high school and beginning their college work. They each will identify questions for which answers must be found. Each will discover truths that will seem earth shattering. Each will make mistakes but learn from them, each will find the other and become like one. Together they will plan and carry out their lives to reach their goals and purpose and leave their children the greatest gift possible.

FREEDOM without fear.

FUTURE GENERATIONS: The bonds to dependency that tied us to parents and family in our early years slowly fade as we find that we have a mind and desires of our own. We can't return to that old comfort but must seek a way to find relationships with all of mankind, including our intellectual and emotional needs. In our society this task falls directly on the public educational system. Therein lies the seed for failure to succeed. Public schools do not invite dialogue into economic, social and political conditions on which individualization can be realized. This denies us full information to make choices. It is like a mini Dark Ages. For people, having lost the early security of their youth and then fail to find security ties to individualism, the perception of individual freedom seem beyond reach, scary, fearful and lacking any meaningful direction. The dominant ideology, taught in the public schools, promises a form of false relief from these fears and tantalizing persuasion to submit to the false promises and lock-step conformity. Thus, the individual is denied any perception of available pathways to individualism and servitude appears very desirable. This explains the popularity of wage labor to the masses, as taught in our public schools.

CHOOSING A PARTNER

Obviously the first question to ask yourselves is how do I know that the other loves me and that it isn't lust only? If we had children together what will they look like, what traits will they possess based upon the gene pools that we bring together? What personal characteristics does the other have that will or will not mesh with mine? If each is one half of a whole, will the other complete the whole in a manner that will allow us to work closely together as full partners in all aspects of our life?

Having passed that point, we question how to define a desired lifestyle, goals and purpose. Are our goals and purpose better satisfied by wage labor or by free labor; or will we need to consider phasing into and out of one or the other. We must attain the pathway to our goals and purpose by including the rearing and education of the children. If we choose wage labor for the purpose of acquiring an income stream, what type of work shall we choose that will permit us to take home with us knowledge that we can in turn put to use for our benefit? If one works temporarily at wage labor and the other creates a home-based business, what type of business would be best for allowing the other to later join and permit easy and early assimilation of the children into the businesses?

What if conditions of freedom and opportunity are stifled, that the current trend continues to render the Constitution to *"just a piece of paper,"* as Bush described. Where would we consider living if moving to another country was deemed correct for us? Are we faced with considering only *"fight or flight?"*

As soon as the previous question is answered, you should research a destination and determine, if their children are born there, will they be entitled to dual citizenship and can they obtain a second passport? ALERT: September 2006, Anna Nicole Smith, an American citizen, gave birth to a baby girl in the Bahamas. This child is an automatic citizen of the Bahamas. The Bahamian government has extended to Ms. Smith permanent residency. Anna is a former playmate featured in Playboy magazine. She married a multi millionaire who was decades older than she. He died leaving a very substantial fortune. After years of civil action a previous legal decision denying Anna a share of her deceased husband's estate was overturned and she stands to inherit millions of US dollars. Obviously, a very knowledgeable individual advised her wisely on where her daughter should be born. You should also, if your grandparents came from another country, check out if you are entitled to dual citizenship on that basis or any other basis.

FUTURE GENERATIONS: When selecting a country for the birth of your child do not overlook Mexico. Here is how I reached that point. Mexico is an emerging country that has been stalled in poverty for over 70 years. Drive through Mexico and you see abject poverty among people for whom an education was not in the cards. Millions have fled to America to work for substandard wages in agriculture, construction, landscaping or processing plants. Success for Mexicans is limited to the small minority that is educated, wealthy and connected. Americans often can't own property or businesses in their own name in Mexico. Imagine an educated American with some wealth and ideas being permitted, because of Mexican citizenship, to participate in an economy in which the majority is excluded. Those odds look pretty good to us.

Having decided upon the business activity, what type of business model - corporation – partnership - sole proprietor best supports the business plan? One of the trick decisions in business accounting is to understand the difference between 'cash' and 'accrual.' Which accounting system you select is a basic need for a successful business. We explore this through the use of analogies. Posting and balancing your checkbook is an example of 'cash accounting.' All income is deposited and all expenses are drawn from this account, the remainder, either +

or - is your balance. You also have credit card debt, mortgage debt and who knows what else. These are not always used in balancing your checking account. To account for these items you must use the *'accrual accounting method.'* Publicly traded companies are required to use *'accrual accounting.'* Small privately held businesses often use the *'cash accounting'* method. This option is selected by indicating in a box at the top of your IRS form 1065 for partnership or IRS form 1120 for corporations. These businesses, depending upon their total assets, are required to complete schedule "L" which brings to bear your other business incomes and debt. Thus you have a sort of *'accrual accounting'* system. Small private businesses whose assets are worth less than $600,000 are often permitted to not complete either this schedule or schedule M-1. The balance sheet is where many businesses play games. The government exempts itself from using the *'accrual accounting'* system. The reason for this is that they can then produce a headline number that is a lie to the people. We look at their true balance sheet.

After government has accounted for expenses and income [lets refer to this as their checkbook] that is, of course, the number they broadcast as the deficit. It is then necessary to add in all appropriations that were declared emergency and were posted to the *"off-budget"* deficit to know the true total deficit for any year. But first we must go back to government accounting and its comparison with publicly traded accounting. Businesses have long-term obligations to employees such as retirement and health. Businesses must account for their cost in their obligations extending into future accounting. Government also has long-term obligations to employees. It collects taxes from employees for Social Security and Medicare and promises to pay future health and retirement cost. These promises do not show up in governments *'cash basis'* budget figures. The total accumulated cash basis deficits comprise the $9+ trillion debt that is only the beginning. If federal law required Congress to fund Social Security in the same manner as businesses fund retirement programs, the annual federal deficit would be increased each year by over $700 billion. Unfunded federal employee pension accounting would further increase the annual deficit to over $900 billion. Add in Medicare and it would rise to more than US$ 1 trillion per year. When all other accountings are added in, the true federal debt could go as high as $55 trillion. All of this *'cooking of the books'* will have to be paid, and you and we are going to be among those called upon to pay this debt. This is why taxes, because of this monster threat, must be included in your family planning. Government does not intend to pay this debt. It does, however, plan to tax all of us and raise the money with which they could pay the debt, but they won't – and that you can take to the bank.

Which states are most friendly to businesses in terms of regulations and taxes? Is your business one that can be best operated with the help of technology or do you need to provide for a location for customers to come to? In other words, is your business one that needs a brick and mortar location or is it more into the intellectual area that allows most of the work to be done alone at home with technology? If you decide to operate out of your residence you have two choices; 1) office in home or 2) home in office. There is a major difference between them.

Our *'case-study'* couple in discussions, regarding savings, investment and planning for retirement, with a smirk and a smile, toss on the table $2,000,000.00 by age 60. If they are now age 20 and they anticipate an 8% annual compounded return - you do the calculation - how many years would it take to reach that goal? This task is to increase your knowledge regarding investments.

This last discussion raised the question that there are many things that they were not taught in school and that a high school graduate needs to know to survive in the 21st century. We call these omissions *'survival courses.'* Don't leave home without them! Realize that the majority does not want to feel that they are swimming against the tide of conformity. This fear is monumentalized in the minds of their children through indoctrination and propaganda in the public schools. There they are taught to be aware of the conformity of society and the punishments that will be dealt them if they fail to follow this rule. This teaching is the exact opposite of what parents want for their children. It will be easier to understand if we refer to the current traditional system as *"Public 'Politically Correct' Schools"* that are favored by parents who do not want the responsibility for their children's education. The other system that we favor, is *"Private 'Parental Alternative Schooling"* designed for those parents who will accept responsibility for the education of their children. It is a generally accepted wisdom that today's public schools are no better than they were in 1976 when Carter socialized them. Public schools will always be with us to pander their mediocrity to the poor and misinformed [less fortunate]. That does not mean that you should deny your children their future in exchange for the easy way out, the irresponsible politically incorrect public education.

FUTURE GENERATIONS: Robert attended public school in a conservative county in Minnesota. His graduation class numbered 55. There were no minorities that he was aware of. Most children could read before they entered first grade. When we refer to the failed public schools we must factor in that these comments are aimed at the totality of the public education system. Robert considered his public school education to be good. It would have been better if he had tried harder. He has no knowledge of the quality of the education in that school today as it has incorporated other schools from many miles away from where the children are bussed. Maybe it is still good or maybe it is better or maybe it is worse – we don't know.

BACK TO THE SCENARIO:

Time, as it always does, has passed quickly. The children have arrived, being born in other countries of their choice. So their thoughts turn to the children's education and development. Many children from middle-class families learn to read well before the age of entering school. Actually, some kids even teach themselves. The traditional schools - leave no child behind - operate like a wartime convoy at the speed of the slowest minds. These schools also omit the survival courses that you have previously determined necessary but not available in traditional schools. In fact, most of those schools do a poor job of teaching reading, writing and arithmetic. They offset this by claiming that the child needs to learn the socializing process. Now to you or us that would mean teaching children the social graces, manners and how to behave in public by adhering to generally accepted public mores. We would all be wrong. The school teaches socialist behavior from feeling the pain of the poor to hatred of the wealthy. This teaching is an assembly line to manufacture clones of good little socialist children. So, they have decided that they will teach their children themselves to include the survival courses and take advantage of one or both of them being home regularly.

As the children reach the age of eight, they are introduced into the parents businesses as paid employees performing those tasks that they can do adequately. Start with emptying wastebasket, running errands, filing, etc. Their employment is integrated into their overall education. As quickly as they learn *"Dick and Jane"* they begin participation in learning how to read Mom and Dad's business letters and documents. From the earliest age they are taught to participate in the family's businesses – progressing through their 18th birthday. They become excited and enthusiastic that they can do like mom and dad. Doing for them such things as letter writing, research, participate in problem solving and called upon for recommendations. Here is why this is so important.

In a public school they learn and participate in gangs, using drugs, sexual promiscuity, football, basketball, singing, hanging out and many other desirable and undesirable activities. You have in effect substituted the following for the above: sports include swimming, golf, skiing, boarding, hunting, scuba diving, hiking and all other activities that can be done life-long as a family or with a partner. Educationally they major in survival courses: reading and writing contracts, leases, purchase offers, mortgages, trust deeds, business journals, taxes, financial books and prospectuses, investing, etc. In travel they learn: moving around foreign countries with special emphasis on the country in which they were born, vacations in Spanish speaking countries if that is the chosen family second language – don't overlook the opportunity for the family to live for a month or so with a family that speaks the language – sort of like a private student exchange program for families. October / November (2006) Robert was in Frankfurt, Germany for four weeks of German language study. Heide desires to attend an eight-week intensive course in Spanish. We are or will be in a year both 80+++ and when it comes to learning, we never stop and neither should you.

FUTURE GENERATIONS: Pause here to appreciate and understand that what you will be offering your children is good and what you will avoid is exposing them to what is harmful. You will quickly understand the values and appreciate the benefits.

THE CONTROLLING DOCUMENT

We deliberately did not discuss this section earlier as we needed to first walk you through the case file. Regardless of your past and current business acumen, you must acknowledge that memories, at best, are fraught with the danger of changes due to the passing of time. Any successful operator will understand that people's word is no longer a valid commitment that can be relied upon. That a contract setting forth the rules, who does what, when and how and what is expected of other parties to a contract is superior. For simplicity we need a simple name for this document, so how about "OPERATION-PRINCIPALITY"? Good, glad that you agree.

OPERATION-PRINCIPALITY

WHAT IS THE BEST FORM OF GOVERNMENT FOR YOU?
We have a list to choose from. Autocracy – one person rules; Oligarchy – power limited to a few families; Plutocracy – ruling by the wealthy; Democracy – rule by the majority; Republic – power by representatives; Principality – each person or family is its own sovereign and rule themselves.

WHAT WE FIND – *Justifying Principality*
We find a document, detailed, clearly written, a vision for a new Nation. It is called *the Constitution of the United States of America.* It is the writing of citizens visualizing a dream that was radical in all aspects. While it was ratified, there were many who felt that the masses were ill equipped to govern themselves – better they be governed by an educated elite. Those on either side of this matter were simply men and women like you and we. Was all this an illusion in so far as there were at the same time logically those who disbelieved strongly and were prepared to find ways over-under-around-or through the intent of the Constitution? This vision, the Constitution, was created with the greatest of enthusiasm and belief. For over 200 years we have held these beliefs and to this day we continue to hold them as sacred. Anything or anyone who intentionally attempts to undermine these values and

beliefs must be suppressed and contained. There is no other choice for we must not abandon what we believe in and trust. It would be nothing less than catastrophic to deliberately deny the Constitution as a massive deception meant to deceive all the people. To believe in the Constitution is similar to believing in a particular faith. There is no conclusive evidence that either is right or wrong, only faith, trust and determination to make it work. Faith in our forefather's judgment is our faith and is better than any faith in political panderers, for they [the true anarchists] are horrific and attempt to negate our Constitution. The whole point about our republic is that it offers hope and direction to help us understand where, how and why we are going. However, there are those who would sneak around the Constitution, like a thief in the night, wanting to revise its intent. This would truly be a devastating blow to individualism and the freedom it begets. For over 200 years there has always been those who were loyal to the Constitution and fought to prevent it being hijacked by those with power and money. Those hijackers believe they are endowed with the responsibility to save us all, even if it means first destroying us in a Vietnam-style death process, body bags and all. Post-modernism science, philosophy and education don't contribute to the efforts of those wanting to defend their Constitution. We (all of us) are partly to blame because of our excess nitpicking, quarrellings, like degenerates running around 'in your face', too much greed, ego, ambition, and petty internal rivalries. Are we making mistakes? Of course we are – remember we are all human and that our mistakes hinder us for they detour around the real issues facing our country. We are guilty of tolerating the horrible acts, shameful behavior and conspiring to 'cover-up' those sins with greater sin. Americans have always been slow to face up to the real issues. This time the rapid change is submerging us like a tsunami and leaves us vulnerable to making even greater mistakes. Our republic has become greater than anyone would have imagined and for it to fall and fail now would be catastrophic. We know that our forefathers wrote this document for they have signed their names to it and pledged their lives and their fortunes to this belief. The people need an honest government now – not later. Look, listen, read and think. You will see the corruption, lies, anger, infecting the country from the very top on down. Look at the values, the ones we have abandoned and the ones we have substituted. Observe the moral vacuum, intellectually hungry for the truth and the substitution of new values for the tried and true values. The people grow cynical, fatalistic and disillusioned by government corruption. We steal, kill, rape and mutilate each other at an unprecedented rate and with no reasonable purpose as we don't believe that apathy, lack of caring for others, and the general lack of moral values is a reasonable purpose. Corporate governance has taken a page titled 'corruption and how to get away with it,' from the political book of lies. What excuse is acceptable for such behavior? Or maybe we must wait longer for a medical term to be coined to explain and justify our gross misbehavior. Our mental capacities have expanded greatly during the past decades, but good character has moved inversely. The Constitution is there for the people; however, the politicians are not defending it for the people. We use the Constitution to justify more wars, bloodshed and violence and all the while America is dying a slow and painful death. Despite the corruption and lies, government remains a major part of our lives. We continue to rely on our government, as our addiction to co-dependency with government is stronger than addiction to drugs. This is how we justify our Principality. Granted, our Principality rests within our mind and is invisible to others. We express it as a metaphor and we understand our responsibility to guard that document. We remain silent, knowing that the politicians will never reform their own corrupt behavior, but we remain vigilant and prepared to put the pieces together again after the fall of empire.

In a Principality, a written agreement should be signed by every member of the family, even the young as they reach the age of understanding, outlining how the Principality is created, how it functions and each member's responsibility to the Principality. In signing, they state that they understand and, of their own free will, participate in this operation. They do however always retain the right of self-determination. The purpose of the written paper is that successive generations grow up learning from that generation forward. We will also pledge our lives, our fortunes by signing our names to this declaration. For example, our children have not the slightest ideas of the impact the Depression and WWII had on our minds and our values. They grew up during the roaring 60s and the birth of 'political correctness' and its causal relationship with an ensuing struggle between secularism and religion. They had little knowledge of how we earned our wealth and the struggles that we fought to succeed.

At or near the top of priorities is concern about the US$ and other country currencies being printed without control as to the numbers, thus devaluing each of the previous dollars. All currencies, just like the US$ is based upon faith, trust and confidence in our government. The US government in turn exchanges US$ with other currencies, also because of faith, and trust in those countries. The problem arises when we understand that all monies are vulnerable to manipulation and that the managers that manipulate these currencies are lacking in the qualities that we believe are necessary for the US to justify their faith, trust and good intentions. For most of us, for we are not multi-millionaires or billionaires, we can only wait and pray that those idiots managing currencies will not bring upon us all another distressing collapse of the economic systems. This play money is completely vulnerable to manipulation of all sorts. We are thinking first of central bank lending rates, currency market intervention, capital restrictions, trade barriers, margin requirements, lack of access to some international investment opportunities. When we, one day, wake up and find that large investors are fleeing from the US$ we will, or should be, frightened. We will watch large denominations flee from property into bank deposits. Once the money is on deposit it can be exchanged into other currencies and from there into hard assets such as precious metals: gold, silver, aluminum, copper, platinum, palladium and uranium or again back into property. We can describe this plight as *"Get out of Dodge"*, but once free of Dodge where do we want to be? The answer, of course, is we want to be in our private-personal Principality. The safety and security of our Principality rests with our opportunity to do like the *"big boys,"* albeit on a much smaller scale and to have implemented the ideas that we have discussed above. It is similar to the concept of Noah's Ark, a place to ride out the economic storms and paper money devaluation. All of this could reasonably trigger a repeat of the government confiscation of gold. The reason for confiscation of gold is to deny people the opportunity to flee from the play money every country uses and to literally hold them hostage for ransom. In this case the ransom is that they must hold their wealth in US$ denominated investments. Can you imagine a more evil policy that can be made a requirement? If you have any item that can be confiscated that is in any way movable, be sure you have placed it beyond the evil reach of the above.

These books, actually they are personal letters to each of you only in book form, are our way to pass feelings and impact events forward to those yet to come. They are the written Constitution for our *Principality*. Our grandchildren began their lives well into the age of the cold war, the growth of wealth for the many and materialism. They know little about their parents' struggles and even less about ours. Probably, there is not much interest in grandparents or great grandparents, which is a shame for we will carry to our grave a great deal of experience and knowledge that is now called history. History is important for it tells those coming along later what happened, often why it happened and how it influenced our lives. We were into our fifth and sixth decades before we had put together what our parents did, did for us, and their sacrifices. There was much we didn't know and again, we are desperately working on these four books so that many of you can read about the past as experienced by us and begin adding to this information before you are out of high school and literally passing it on to your children. *Pause*

When these books are finished and available to you, we will have finished what we believe was one purpose in life. We both worked as employees in the private sector and government. When we freed ourselves from those restraints, we became free labor real estate investors, for we knew that our past experiences would never lead to freedom and thus wealth. Becoming *'real estate professionals'* permitted us to move forward to where we now are. Fortunately, real estate in Arizona was a free wheeling activity. We made our mistakes but real estate had a built-in forgiveness for our errors, and we had the opportunity to learn from our experiences. We acquired business knowledge that we carry forever in our heads, and many times found it useful in making good decisions. Our discovery of *'free labor'* was to learn that there was another and better way to reach our goals. At first the responsibility and opportunity seemed overwhelming and frightening, for this was our first trip down this road. But it is amazing the manner in which success brings confidence, and confidence brings courage, and courage begets the desire for total freedom. That was how we created and entered our principality from which we will never leave. We pray that many, actually most of you, will also find your home in your principality. One final thought. We love America and the opportunities it offers. We also distrust and fear our government. Our forefathers knew clearly that governments are or quickly become evil. We still are never sure if our leaders and politicians are themselves evil or only purveyors of the evil of government. But the question is mute - stay clear of them for they are toxic in nature and will enslave and destroy you. The likes of we are the true patriots for we defend America and its Constitution. It is they who believe they guide and lead, who betray their oath and our Constitution and offer us a new direction. This ends the pause and we now resume.

Each child has engaged in paid labor; meeting the minimum hours necessary each quarter to, by age 18, qualify for Social Security and Medicare. Circumstances may be such that they never work again as an employee. Mom and Dad have set up limited partnerships for each of their business activities being a minor partner in the other's partnership. So it is natural that having reached age 18, the legal age to own their own partnerships, maybe Mom and Dad will be minor partners, pursuing the business activity of their choice that is most likely a spin off of some facet of the parents' businesses. The reason this works is that from birth the child is immersed in the parents' activities. They learn how to perform each aspect of these activities. They understand the why and the how, and they become good at it. They share in the benefits while learning from Mom and Dad. It is only normal that the children will continue in the path of Mom and Dad.

Remember that the children were paid a going wage for those ten years. Before they receive their first earned paycheck, you have had many discussions about money, what it is and isn't, how to make money work for you, the value of regular savings and compound interest. They must determine how they will allocate their wages between savings, which always comes first, expenses for items of necessity and lastly discretionary spending. Just as the parents decided on 2m$ in 40 years, the child will set a $ amount to be achieved by age 18. Think of your child starting out in business with a new partnership, payroll taxes paid for initial qualification, and say a $25,000 nest egg with all taxes paid on it. Education expenses to qualify for a job or skills to perform a task are not tax deductible. If however, the child, now an adult, decides to go to college to *continue the education in the chosen field*, these expenses are tax deductible. Talk to your personnel and administrative family staff member.

Fun games that parents can play with their children are to challenge them to solve problems. Let's take an example from the tax code. The difference between owning a car in your personal name and owning it in the business for the production of income is that certain expenses and depreciation are deductible. It is the task of the child to research this issue, say in a J. K. Lasser annual tax guide. Go to the past years income and expense worksheets and itemize all of the expenses that they found that they could deduct. Give them the information that these taxes fall into the 15% tax bracket. Find the amount of tax dollars saved for one year. Find the amount of total tax dollars for 40 years, assuming no change in the value of the dollar. Find what percent this number is to a $5m goal. Find how much remains to be gained and recommendations of where they can locate other deductions.

Assume the worst-case scenario that government declares insolvency and is unable to print enough money to make good on all their promises to the workers. Government confiscates all gold and seals all bank accounts pending devaluation of the dollar. I'm sure that you are happy having used the children's dual citizenship to have alternative arrangements in the investing of your wealth. Government debt, of less than 30-year term, can arbitrarily be converted to 30-year term. Government blames the rich and poor, never pointing a finger at themselves. All hell has broken out around your principality, but others don't know of your principality, as you had learned to keep your mouth shut, so all is well. It is now 2007 and no substantive action has yet been taken

REBALANCING DEBT FINANCIAL ALERT

In 1971 the Bretton Woods International Monetary Standards were implemented, setting up the process for the world to trade exports for paper dollars that could be issued without limit. This year, 2006, the G7 countries announced, with little publicity, that it will be necessary to have another Bretton Woods type meeting to deal with the United States' inability to curb or even think of repaying its debt to the world.

PRESIDENTIAL EXECUTIVE ORDER 6102

BY VIRTUE OF the authority vested in me by Section 5 (b) of the Act of October 6, 1917, as amended by Section 2 of the Act of March 9, 1933, entitled, *"An Act to provide relief in the existing national emergency in banking, and for other purposes,"* in which amendatory Act Congress declared that a serious emergency exists, I, Franklin D. Roosevelt, President of the United States of America, do declare that said national emergency still continues to exist and pursuant to said section do hereby prohibit the hoarding of gold coin, gold bullion, and gold certificates within the continental United States by individuals, partnerships, associations and corporations and hereby prescribe the following regulations for carrying out the purpose of this order.......

Franklin Roosevelt – April 5, 1933

FUTURE GENERATIONS: It is important that you understand that an offshore account is not a tax shelter action. You still report the account on the bottom of schedule "B". You pay tax on the income from the money you have re-invested. The purpose of the off-shore account is to protect your after tax wealth from confiscation by government through devaluation and / or rebalancing of government debt within the international debt accounts. It also protects you from frivolous lawsuits by the greedy.

Continuing...

Every down turn that the economy takes creates again winners and losers. The winners as usual will be those who put together and manipulate the terms of a rebalancing implementation. The losers will be the usual suspects, you and we, unless all of us do something to protect ourselves. Whenever debtor's liabilities are rebalanced, such as occurs in most bankruptcies, there is also a revaluation of the currency to *force fit* the rebalancing. To us it means that any US dollars that we hold in any account in America will be devalued. The only manner that you can avoid such an event is to place your money in a bank, in a different currency, maybe in the country where your child was born. Why? Suppose that you have $100,000 on deposit in a bank in another country, where your child was born. Say that the US$ dollar is devalued by 25%. If that money had been in a US account, it would then be worth $75,000. If it is in another country, with a stronger currency, your account would remain more of its pricing power value than the $. For example, if you had your money in euros and the dollar plunged against the euro, you can then exchange your euros for a greater number of dollars.

FUTURE GENERATIONS: By age 18 you should be able to solve even more complicated problems, have developed a large vocabulary of business terms, read and understand contracts and other legal documents, write business correspondence, read and prepare annual reports. For the last years of working for the parents, you should have been doing the books, writing correspondence as well as Mom and Dad. Don't try to tell us that with this training and motivation you will not succeed. If you deny this, we shall rise from our graves and come after you.

COMPARISON OF WAGE
AND FREE LABOR

Compare the status of your 18-year-old with their peers who attended public school. Your child has for 10 years participated in the parents' home-based business and has formed a clear opinion of what he /she wants for the rest of his life. The peers when asked what are they planning for a career, will all too often answer, *"I don't know."* At age 18 your child has a business, a business plan, venture capital, knowledge of how to make it all work and future education in their field that is considered continuing education. Their peers have no sense of business, free labor, no venture capital, no knowledge about business matters and they are faced with college loans to obtain a higher education. Your child knows how to properly select a mate, a partner, a person that shares similar values and character. The peers will all too often end up marrying the first girl that they can get into bed with, called the lust marriage. Those don't work.

Your children understand the intricacies, innuendos and subtleties of the relationships to government. They are prepared to play the game and win because they know the rules and how to play them for their benefit. Their peers believe the propaganda pounded into their heads, the one side of every issue – essentially the government line, they have no idea what they don't know. Unless they change they are damned to be *'stupid'* all their life. What did Clauswitz say about this when discussing his principles of war?

[Editor's note] As you read Clauswitz think of education, experience, economy, government, taxes, regulation and why your own decisions regarding your business life and family life should be followed, as you will know and understand both sides of the issues confronting you in your lifetime.

The natural timidity of humans, which sees only one side to everything, makes this first impression incline toward fear and exaggerated cautions.

Therefore we must fortify ourselves against this impression and have blind faith in the results of our own earlier reflections, in order to strengthen ourselves against the weakening impression of the moment.

These difficulties, therefore, demand confidence and firmness of conviction. That is why the study of military history is so important, for it makes us see things as they are and as they function. The principles which we can learn from theoretical instruction are only suited to facilitate this study and to call our attention to the most important elements in the history of war.

Your Royal Highness, therefore, must become acquainted with these principles in order to check them against the history of war, to see whether they are corrected or even contradicted by the course of events.

In addition, only the study of military history is capable of giving those who have no experience of their own a clear impression of what I have just called the friction of the whole machine.

Of course, we must not be satisfied with its main conclusions, and still less with the reasoning of historians, but we must penetrate as deeply as possible into the details. For the aim of historians rarely is to present the absolute truth. Usually they wish to embellish the deeds of their army or to demonstrate the concordance of events with their imaginary rules. They invent history instead of writing it...

But so be it – we are certain that you get the point.

Life, in competition with government for control over your freedom, is a game of incomplete information, making the best choices and the fewest mistakes. In this game you will prevail and your children in turn will make you very proud of them. For example: A common phrase to use when assessing risk for the country is, *"we are all in this together,"* but what about economic risk in particular. What if we did have an economic meltdown? Would we all be hurt similarly or would some suffer more than others? Our leaders in all of their cleverness have not forgotten to *"spread their risk."* They have done this by the benefits that they have provided for themselves, which the average Joe is at risk of losing. When mortgages begin to be called or foreclosed, we should not be surprised that those, the elite, have greater access to some form of consideration or forgiveness than others, like maybe you and we.

We do have one quiz for you. Near the end of this book you will find a draft of a partially completed *"Declaration of Independence"* written for the 21st century. Your mission, if you chose to accept it, is to finish that declaration in your own words and build a plan that will achieve it. Again, we apologize for leaving you with failures of our making. We have left you with one hell of a mess, we do not beg for forgiveness as we confess our guilt as charged. Please do a better job with your lives than we did with ours.

BACK TO OUR EXAMPLE OF 'FREE LABOR FAMILY'.

Initially, the mother and father will likely share the five staff functions of responsibility. As the children arrive and grow, their skills will be developed by participation and when ready they will be given individual responsibilities within the *"free labor family"* enterprise. The leader(s) will be the wisest and the one with calm and reason that will lead him/her to a sound decision. Leader(s) will be the source of guidance and the tasking of others as they are joined as part of the family. The leader(s) will be expected to develop a working knowledge of each of the four other activities.

Personnel/administration will carry out the guidance from leader(s) regarding the education of the new members [children] of the family. It will liaison with the Social Security Administration to obtain a SSN for each new arrival. It will coordinate the numbers of hours needed to work to complete each credible quarter of coverage for the newcomer. That goal will begin before the child is eight as this is the best time to reach the mind and soul of the child. From ages eight to eighteen the child will be an employee of the home-based business, to be described in greater detail later. As the child progresses from doing janitorial service, he/she is trained in each of the four sections so that the child can perform them all satisfactorily and be a viable candidate for leader. This section will also manage the tasks of bookkeeping, accounting, tax preparation and other administration tasks.

Information/intelligence will study the operation of federal and state government and the public business section to ascertain their capabilities in bringing either unintended consequences or consequences of deliberation to the family. An assessment of government level, manner and means of corruption will be best if corroborated by two viable sources. From this exercise, this unit will prepare an outline of government's past corruption identifying the betrayers and losers of these acts. Regular intelligence briefings will be disseminated to others setting forth likely directions and action that government is probable of taking, its potential to harm the family, and courses of action that the family can take to protect or take advantage of for the benefit of the family.

Plans/operations will evaluate the recommendations of information/intelligence and select and recommend to leader the implementation and course of action that is best suited for the family and has a high probability of success. Upon approval by leader, plans/operations prepares a scenario for accomplishing the mission, advises and trains those selected for the mission and sees that the mission is carried out according to the plan.

Supplies/service fulfills the needs of the plan by acquiring the supplies necessary and developing a service plan for support of the plan.

FUTURE GENERATIONS: As our children grow up and pass into adulthood, they often come face to face with a fact that makes many of them very uneasy. This occurs when the grown child first realizes that he and his parents have reversed their roles.

AFTER COMPLETION OF THE EXIT PLAN

Free Labor Family is a euphemism for a family that is dissatisfied with the status quo, believes that it, the family, is being denied opportunities to enjoy fully its rights and just Constitutional claim to life, liberty and the *pursuit* of happiness. It is the embodiment of freedom.

We might say that everyone in America is free, but that does not mean that each of us has freedom in an identical measure. Look around at society; do you see others that enjoy greater freedom than you? Do you see others who enjoy less, often far less, than you? Ever ponder how freedom is distributed among a population? Or, why others have more or less than some? Obviously, freedom is not automatically allocated to everyone in equal shares. If equal means same, and equality means each of us is the same, then to believe that is to claim a truth that does not exist. Actually, each of us is different from everyone else in some form or manner, be it fingerprints, genes, DNA, or some truth yet to be discovered. So, what is equality other than the equal opportunity to use our rights in either the best or not the best means to benefit oneself? The euphemism described above is that opportunity that each has to move forward toward personal and family freedom. It is how that opportunity is utilized that determines the degree of freedom that each of us attains. Notice how quickly equality becomes inequality despite all the laws of man. This appears to be a paradox in conflict between two forces. If man's law is one force, then natural law must be the opposing force. Seems that somewhere it says that for each and every force there is an equal and opposite force. Man's law has never achieved anything resembling equality making it more of a vision than a fact of life. Natural law, however, has provided a pathway for individuals to pursue individual life, liberty and the *pursuit* of happiness, by the wise and proper use of their inequality.

Inequality must be understood if it is to be used properly and effectively. How do we measure the distinct differences between people in consort with the above? Here we subjectively assign words to define these differences. Character is a broad use of a term to denote difference – it can be labeled as good or bad – and that is very subjective. Character brings to mind other words like interest, determination, steadfastness, willingness to sacrifice, courage, compassion – and on and on. Each word may have either a negative or positive connotation depending upon its use or misuse by each person.

There are words to also describe the differences between individuals in *pursuit* of their happiness that are invoked, usually by a third party, often for a reason understood best by that third party. Just as each individual's DNA and genes are different, each also selects a different plan for their respective *pursuit,* albeit often minor in nature but in its own pertaining to those words like character. As each individual plan is prepared and executed, the success of each plan owner will define them as either being among the fortunate or the less fortunate – the willing or the unwilling – the haves or the have nots – the lucky or the unlucky – the deserving or the undeserving. Only an individual can judge oneself and often without much accuracy. When judged by another, it is usually for the *'another's'* benefit and purpose. For in the end, each of us will receive what we deserve – not what we want – unless the two are compatible, which they seldom are.

Facing each is an imposing array of obstacles better known as temptations. St. Augustine named seven of them and called them deadly sins. Engaging oneself in any or all of these deadly sins will immediately, like an anchor, slow down your *pursuit* for happiness by offering you a different type of happiness from a sin, allegedly of greater importance. This happiness is immediate, gratifying, and unfortunately, defeating your intent and purpose.

Survival in the business sense, as well as its relationship to freedom, is the act of surviving, that which threatens you, and the fact of having survived and saved your freedom. Stay with us for an example.

The threats include: First, a political body that has the authority and the will to use it for the purpose of taxation, regulation and punishment. The purpose in mind is, through incentives and disincentives, to gain your compliance for the purpose of eliminating you as a threat to them or what they believe that they stand for. Second, other threats to your business and family survival will include customers [class action suits], employees [lawsuits], products [liability], plus an array of criminals, terrorists, con artists, and everyone who envies you and wishes you misfortune. Your freedom and your wealth are their primary target. When you enjoy freedom, you are outside established norms relating to groups; this poses a threat to them because you are beyond their ability to coerce, intimidate and confiscate your actions and your assets. This freedom begins where limited government ends. The illusion of the nature of your social, economic and political relationship with your government and the middle-class majority is something you can only defend through due-diligence and understanding, and avoiding the addictive nature of co-dependency.

2004 FRAUDULENT ELECTION. It does not really matter which pair wins the elections for the White House, for whoever wins *"we-the-people"* lose. One would continue his attacks on threatening windmills, and the other would attack everyone who had the strength to become successful. There will be no changes in the direction that we have been traveling for the past two hundred years. With the fall and demise of common-man democracy, we have embraced the Reign of the Oligarchs. At the end of this journey, American Empire will pass into the history books in the same manner as all empires that preceded ours did. So, we talk truth to you, and if you don't like it, so be it, and good luck. If you wish to avoid this debacle, you must pay attention to the following. Another way to view the election is as an intramural kickboxing match with few, if any, rules. We have the defending national oligarch champion, a graduate of Andover Academy, New Hampshire, Yale and Harvard, a multi millionaire attempting to defend his throne. We have the international oligarch challenger, a graduate of St. James, New Hampshire with roots from education in a Swiss private academy and Yale, a multi millionaire married to a multi billionaire, attempting to unseat the reigning oligarch. Either way we will have an oligarch reign for the next four years and neither of them has even a simple idea of how you and we live or the needs of the working class. They do not feel our pain. They are both deceiving frauds.

What fraud? Take two people earning the median income for their years working and they want to retire at 65. We need to look at the numbers. The Urban Institute values their joint Medicare benefits at $283,500; however, they contributed only $43,300 in Medicare taxes [2004 dollars]. Taxpayers get stuck with the remaining $240,000 – sweet deal for them, lousy deal for us. They will each qualify for $22,900 in annual socialist security benefits, rising annually with the CPI. Present value of their socialist security benefit is $326,000. Actually, they paid $198,000 for this income stream. Taxpayers get stuck with the remaining $128,000. Thus, taxpayers must pony up this additional $348,000 to cover the loss to government. Will you agree that America's lavish entitlement programs are on a collision course with financial reality? Is it your intention to go down with that version of the Titanic?

When inventory of an item builds up and becomes excessive, the market answer is for the retailer to discount the price and give it lots of attention. When a commodity is deeply discounted and you are a user, you take the opportunity to increase your inventory. Wage-labor is similar to any other commodity. When it is in surplus, the employer discounts the cost by laying off workers. When labor is scarce it increases in cost, and the user of wage-labor must find alternatives; i.e., part-time or temporary workers. In 2004, wage-labor was in surplus, but wage labor is a living, breathing human. The unemployed search for new jobs at the old wage rate and within easy commute. They face a number of difficulties; namely, minimum wage, unemployment rates and welfare rates. If one is wage-labor, one must be prepared to compete in the market, which is now a global market. Most will fall back on the old method that the government will fix it, but that was how you got into this mess to begin with. Politicians are great at making promises, but when those promises don't work out, they are not prone to repudiate their promises. They take the course of least resistance. If they are afraid of public opinion if they take a benefit away, such as, lowering the minimum wage, reducing unemployment benefits, etc., they consistently turn to that old tried and true deception. Tell the people that they will print more money, increase benefits, blah-blah. What they are really doing is devaluing the value of each dollar. That is like cutting benefits. They give you more dollars, but you lose more than you gain through the inflation created by devaluing the dollar.

We are talking about an alternative to wage-labor that for some will make life much more pleasant.

Wage-labor vs. Free-labor has been beaten to death in this book. If you haven't got it yet, then we doubt your candidacy for entry into free labor will succeed. So, we move on to those items that lend themselves to deconstruction. First, it is nil to none that government has the ability or the *will* to reform itself. *Reformation,* therefore, must proceed by a different route. Deconstructionism is a means to partially accomplish this for the family.

President George W. Bush was reported to have said that after the first five or six years of life, we become prisoners of our peers. We also know that forces are moving to take control of our children's minds away from parents at age three. **Education** is the responsibility of parents. Our president is correct – the question you must ask and answer is who shall control those minds for the first eighteen years of their life, and what do you wish for your personal relationship with your children? Look! In 2002, non-high school graduates had a median annual income of $18,826; those with a high school diploma had a median annual income of $27,280; those with a college degree had a median annual income of $51,194; and, those with advanced degrees had a median annual income of $72,824. Anyway you wish to figure these statistics [source: U.S. Census Bureau], these incomes are peanuts compared to what it takes to survive in the 21st century. We grossly misuse the word *education* giving it a spin synonymous with knowledge or intelligence, when what we in effect have is the value of a resume. How can you purchase [acquire] knowledge tailored to survival [higher incomes] without investing $30,000 a year to get a resume, and simultaneously become free?

Your difficulty in answering that question is related to president Bush's statement. You are a prisoner of not only your peers, but also your employer and government, and all of those listed as **threat** to you. So, step one is for you to decide the relationship within your family, how to develop for yourself and your children the nature of that relationship, and build it together as a total family unit – free of excessive peer influence and all other threats. We mentioned earlier that there is a way to hide in the open.

Hiding in the open seems at first like an oxymoron. To hide this way you arrange to publicly be like everyone else, except for one item that we will discuss later. What does everyone else look like that we desire to hide among? Most are middle-class, live in the suburbs, have at least two cars one of which is an SUV. Their children attend public schools, that often being a major reason for living in the burbs. They have a mortgage on their house and car and carry some revolving debt on credit cards. They brag about their family, complain about government taxes, etc, and have a quick answer for every problem, like the government should do something about this - ha – ha. You will look and appear exactly like them except for that last item. Imagine that your mouth is attached to your brain by something called a transmission. The average Joe and Jane usually have their transmission in overdrive when it comes to social, political and economic matters. Here is where you part company.

The standard transmission has R for reverse – D for drive – N for neutral – plus a D1 and D2 for uphill driving. Most are in D or D1 and when the discussion gets hot and heavy they shift into D2 with a roar, literally, with their mouths, getting maybe 500 words to a bottle of beer. What you do differently is keep your transmission in either R or N. We say that N is to be quiet, careful and attentive listening to the Joe's and Jane's rhetoric. You find out everything about their values of social, economic, political and religious matters. When the discussion begins to wane and you think that maybe they will begin to question you, place your transmission into R. This position is where you continue to listen attentively and encourage them to talk by asking simple questions of who – what – when – where – why and how. You have made yourself essentially invisible to onlookers. When you wish to disregard the rules of 'hiding in the open,' you first make sure that NO Joe's or Jane's are present. Now you are among family and trusted friends [they think like you do] or maybe you just desire to mull things over with your mind, alone. Now, no one knows you, who you are, what you are. You have entered the sanctity of your principality, you are the prince, and your classified thoughts are safe from the thought patrols that seem to be everywhere. In short – shut up and listen.

When weighing the nature of this relationship, the item of **wealth** must be defined as to its nature and degree to which it supports your lifestyle. For most of us, we arrange wealth in priority with family, God, country, and money. Money and its equivalent play a role. Sit down, take a deep breath, and ask yourself how much money is enough, and how will it be obtained? Your purpose for the use of money is to fund that decision; therefore, the amount you select must be reasonable within those parameters. When is enough – enough? When you have enough why do you need more? To help you get started, let us toss on the table the number $2,000,000. Your task is how to create it, and how long will it take. It is not necessary that you work two jobs or eighteen hours a day as you must not lose sight that your greatest wealth is your family; so, participate by being the example and directing.

As you ponder the question 'how', you must keep in focus the importance of **location.** The first location question is the broad one of where do you want to live, work and play geographically, such as in East or West, urban or rural, etc. The second location question is do you want to work from your home or from a distant business location. If you have chosen to take direct responsibility for your children, you would likely favor conducting your activities from your home, that way you solve one argument, dealing with raising the children, as opposed to letting caregivers manage those minds.

How you hold title to your home will determine whether you have *"office in home"* or *"home in office."* Before the advent of suburban popularity, many business owners lived either above or behind their business place. With the advent of our electronic generation, intellectual businesses can be managed from any place. Just look at how many different activities are being outsourced to distance lands.

Important in your planning is the type of business. Do you want an *employer,* non-employer or both, but at different times and for different reasons? A non-employer business will normally be either a schedule "C" sole proprietorship or partnership, as both can be used as a pass-thru for tax purpose.

That leads directly to the possibility to deconstruct [at least in part] elements of government, such as the departments of labor, HHS, education, etc. This is important from the twin standpoints of cost and freedom. The cost results from the requirement of *compliance,* which indirectly denies you part of your freedom.

HHS has recently medicalized gluttony under the term obesity and extended Medicare coverage for them. Gluttony is one of St. Augustine's seven deadly sins. Greed, pride and lust have already reached the level of acceptability removing them from the taint of deadly sin. Wrath has moved into the early stages of medicalization by renaming it as rage, and prescribing drugs to the alleged victim. Sloth is practiced by many – maybe even a majority – so medicalization of all deadly sins will occur prior to the fall of the American Empire.

One of the leaders in cost compliance emerges with the IRS. Fifty years ago we began to hear the argument that one should not plan their activities exclusively to save *taxes.* Today that *'old-saw'* is as much wrong as it is right. Taxes from all taxing authorities take fully 50% of your gross wages. *Systemic fraud, waste and abuse [corruption]* have been credited with wasting between 25% and 40% of the tax dollars collected. Corruption like everything else is subject to inflation or devaluation. It took one dollar in 2000 to buy what a nickel bought in 1900. Those of us who have knowledge of government operations are fully aware that corruption exceeds 50% of what government spends. So yes, taxes are important when planning your life. Different sources have different character, and thus different rates to be taxed at. What is a business expense for one might be a costly luxury for another. The most popular method to avoid taxes is, of course, not having any income, for then you become a beneficiary of that system. You always have the opportunity, when your annual income is rising rapidly, to stop working for the balance of the year and take the family on an extended vacation. You have no obligation to neither support corruption with tax dollars nor conduct your affairs in a manner that benefits government or their constituency of *the unwilling.*

And finally, you need to design a *product* and *service* that fits all of the decisions you have made from the above issues.

You may wish to consider a product that is intellectual or knowledge-based. Examples include *"real estate professional,"* a term coined by the IRS or trade your own portfolio. Today, many professionals like lawyers, doctors, insurance agencies, etc., operate from a residence. How to use this knowledge can become your service.

For many, the *greatest gift* they can give their child at high school graduation is not a new car, but their own spanking new partnership and the knowledge of how to make it work for them. In planning this gift, you give the child a real shot at his/her own freedom. Imagine solving their questions about why they should learn certain things – like reading that is necessary in evaluating contracts, leases, mortgages, etc. – or math that is necessary in calculating present and future values, interest rates, amortizations – or the actual experience of investing their own money [they work for you for salary], seeing it grow and planning for its ultimate use – doing their own taxes – helping with your taxes - doing accounting for you – recommending investments to you – and best of all, eligibility for future socialist security benefits, albeit minimum, and full Medicare coverage at age 65.

The earlier that the child decides what it is that he/she desires to do to provide the means for a life they want, permits the child to assess those items of knowledge that must be learned to be successful. Knowing what knowledge you must have and what knowledge is more of the *'nice to have,'* the child [with parental guidance] now determines where and how to obtain this knowledge. At this stage in planning, it is obvious that public schools fail the child in two major areas. Those are 1] failure to adequately make available to the child that which the child wants, and 2] failure to focus on the important item [knowledge desired by the child] that is taught, but for reasons such as the social engineering and extracurricular activities are taught in a manner that makes the material near worthless to the child.

You need to also visualize those overseas trips with the whole family [what a wonderful opportunity to learn another language, like Spanish or Mandarin Chinese]. How about skiing the Alps – scuba diving at Cozumel – golfing along the Caribbean coastline – maybe some mountain climbing in Nepal; nothing is now beyond your reach.

At eighteen with their own for-profit business, they are making money, doing something that they know how to do and enjoy doing. Most of us instead of retiring as we age, downsized and kept our fingers in that pie. Turn loose your imagination, throw away your fears, and be about the life you had dreamt about.

BUMPS IN THE ROAD TO PRINCIPALITY

Misused tax code implemented in a manner violating the 14th [equal protection] amendment.

Onerous regulatory system that takes peoples freedom in exchange for false socialist promises.

Failed public education that denies the masses knowledge and the truth of corruption in government.

A system of labor that smells and walks like the old master/slave system.

Evil election system designed to permit socialists and fascist to alternate in controlling the levers of power and the purse.

Denial of a system of self-determination and choice through the use of illusions that coerce people into a system of dependency.

To answer the questions that are already swirling around in your head, we look at examples of what and how.

FREE LABOR INSTRUCTOR AND COORDINATOR NON-EMPLOYER BUSINESS

What. Develop and implement a program based upon the information in this book.

How. Conduct the proper research of the technical items by study and consultations with professionals. Develop a curriculum for presenting to those we will call, *persons of interest.*

Note: This activity is key to the continued conversion of other wage labor to non-employer businesses, predominantly their children.

SMALL BUSINESS WITH SEVEN EMPLOYEES

General situation: Case study of a small electrical service company. Staffing consists of an owner [master electrician], five employees [master electricians], one employee [administration and accounting] and one employee [supply and requisition]. Owner desires to restructure the business to convert all employees from wage labor to free labor. The owner has in the past, procured contracts from third parties and assigned the employees their daily tasks. The administration and accounting employee had the responsibility of processing those regulations and mandates from federal, state, county, city such as, withholding payroll taxes, payment of unemployment insurance, coordinating annual and sick leave, implementation of any other mandates. The supply and requisitions employee ordered and stocked for issuance to electricians on an *as needed basis,* managed inventory control.

The owner has consulted with the free labor instructor and coordinator. The seven employees will be asked to each become an independent contractor, recommending to them to use limited partnerships with pass-through features. Owner has previously functioned as an owner/broker in obtaining contracts and assigning them to employees. Owner will become exclusively a broker and sub contract to independent contractors. The other two employees will also be encouraged to restructure. If serious opposition arises instructor will assist in doing what in the real estate business is know as a *"condo conversion."* This could result in the original corporation being dissolved and a new limited partnership created. Instructor will have a training responsibility to the seven employees in how to restructure and manage their limited partnerships.

Benefits to owner: All mandated responsibilities to the other seven as employees is eliminated and passes to former employees in their capacity as owners of new limited partnerships. Owner now has a non-employer business.

Benefits to new owners: Their contracts are designed to transfer a portion of the administrative costs of the former owner to them for their use in providing for their own benefits. The seven employees are restructured as seven new non-employer businesses.

Think your way through this and then compare to the analysis citing threats from government listed above.

REAL ESTATE PROFESSIONAL

General situation: Case study of a family enterprise in real estate covering buying/selling/exchanging/ landlording and financing/maintenance of/legal/license.

A family real estate enterprise should include both mother and father and the children who will join later. The ideal is for either the mother or father to select education as a real estate attorney. To learn real estate you have to study, think, and be literally in the market. Start by researching the IRS designation of *'Real Estate Professional'* and *passive income and losses.* Both of these can be studied in J. K. Lasser's annual guide to tax preparation. Visit *'open house'* opportunities on weekends. Pick up the information sheets for future reference and comparison with other houses. Study rent rates by calling ads and viewing the houses to learn what one is likely to get for the type of houses you are considering buying.

You will need two types of purchase money contracts, one for buying and one for selling. If neither is an attorney, pick a qualified real estate attorney to write a simple buy and/or sell contract that covers current state law. In addition you will eventually need a mortgage and/or trust deed form for when you may wish to sell and carry back. You can start with the legal documents for the house you bought to live in or borrow a friend's legal file. Read all of the documents noting those sections that you do not understand. Research those sections until you can accurately speak to each and every paragraph as to its meaning.

Learn some of the better means of gaining knowledge by talking to others who are in the same business, attending seminars on buying foreclosures, exchanging, tax implications and benefits, managing property and maintaining your houses.

Listen closely – pay attention. We have talked elsewhere in this book about entrepreneurs, private venture capitalists and other forms of shuffling money around. When you purchase property as an investment, you will always be aware of what the property is worth. The slogan goes this way, *'buy as cheap as you can – add value to the property – and sell it for a big profit.'* Thus you do exactly as a multi-billion dollar hedge fund or private equity fund does. You buy cheap, add value, and sell for a good profit.

You must become a negotiator; the better you become the more successful you will be. Keep in mind that a seller's asking price is in effect the most that he/she will take for the property. Negotiating therefore is to lower the price for the house you are looking at. This house will appraise for a comparable value so ask yourself how much rent you will expect to earn. Be conservative so that the surprise will always be on the upside. After evaluating the price, the rent and the annual maintenance determine the cash flow potential. Don't forget to calculate a P/E. Remember P/E from buying stocks. A stock with a P/E of 15 means that the yield from that stock, reinvested will pay for the cost of the stock in 15 years.

Learn the tricks of the trade. For example, after you have learned both from others, books and experience, you can begin to make multiple offerings to buy subject to the acceptance of another offer. Try to determine the seller's true motivation for wanting to sell. Then, you begin making low-ball offers to purchase. A true low-ball offer is one that you don't expect the seller to bite on. When you know how to buy right then calculate what the property will do for you and begin to understand how often you need to buy another rental house. For example, if you buy one house per year [average] in 30 years you have a portfolio of 30 rental homes. The reason for this is to caution your anxiety so that you do not become an anxious buyer, for if you do you always pay too much for that investment.

SMALL MANUFACTURING BUSINESS

INTERNET MARKETING

Use these for personal exploration and study. You will find other ideas in the yellow pages.

EPILOGUE

CLEAN UP YOUR ACT, PUT YOUR AFFAIRS IN ORDER

We are not in the business of making predictions. We are lucky if we get the trends correct. There are a variety of possible, but not entirely probable, trends that may materialize. We want to look at one; it may come in your lifetime - or in your children's lifetime, but it must come eventually. Its name is INSOLVENCY, the party insolvent will be government and the big loser will be the people.

Government insolvency comes when government reaches the point were it cannot pay its debts as they come due and outsiders, our creditors, raise the stakes by refusing to buy our debt or demanding excessive interest rates to compensate for the risk factor. Government is at the point that even if it could sell all of its assets it would not have enough money to pay off its debt. A large array of problems facing us in the 21st century, most of which will have to be resolved or rolled over to the 22nd century, and it might be your great grandchildren who have to solve them. Your great grand children are also our great-great grandchildren. What are these problems?

We will list them here but not in any order of preference or risk except for the number one. It is our government, with bloated bureaucracies; spending money like it was paper, which it is, with no intent to pay off its debts or to ever balance the government books. They roll over debt like water over a dam, their lies have reached the highest magnitude, they are politically corrupt whores, none of who will speak out regarding their own malfeasance. Our problems defy solution having that type of government. It is they who created this monster. By the time this book is published, we will know the results of the 2007 elections. Our comment is in the form of a question – which flavor of corruption do you prefer – is the color of the hand in your pockets relieving you of your money significant – do you prefer the lies told you to be flavored RED or BLUE? You actually have no choice, in this election, between corrupt government and honest government. Your only choice is the color of the corruption you find least disgusting. Pity the poor people who vote for their own executioner.

THE TRUTH ABOUT SAFETY/SECURITY/SURVIVAL [SSS]

The police car drives by and usually has the slogan *"Protect and Serve."* Neither of these words are correct. Their responsibility is to investigate the crime, determine the perpetrator, gather the evidence and present it to the District Attorney for prosecution. We are concerned about the time period leading up to the commission of the crime. Protection for all is limited and random, there is just not enough money to hire the manpower needed to protect all of us. Therefore, our safety rest with ourselves and our family, and very close friends and neighbors.

Safety requires that we analyze all situations to determine if and how a threat may exist. When we are in our cars, walking on the streets or among a group of people that we do not know, we are always in potential threat condition. If we detect a threat, we assess it and take immediate action to eliminate or reduce the threat.

Security begins with securing our home, or as it once was known, 'our castle.' We need perimeter defense primarily for early detection. Fences and walls are the primary examples.

Observation and fields of detection includes the ability to cast immediate light on the area between the fence and the home. This will give early warning to both the people inside and the guard dog that sleeps in the bedroom.

Early warning permits us to reach down along side the bed and remove the 20-gauge pistol grip shotgun from its place with out getting out of bed. When you immediately *"jack"* a round into the chamber, you are giving notice that you are armed and ready. You tell your spouse and she executes movement from the bed to the safe room. It is now you or they. They have been duly warned and you shoot first and ask questions later. Never shoot to injure only, as the next shot heard will be coming at you, RIP. The police will sort out the details when they arrive to investigate.

Guard dog[s] are recommended. A trained German Shepherd will hear the intruders long before you will. The dog will, if necessary, also attack on your command.

Weapons may be guns or knives. You should, if your state permits, obtain a concealed carry weapons permit [CCW], understand how to use it, the necessary safety precautions, and your legal responsibility connected with the permit.

Survival is the ultimate purpose of SSS. Many people have created safe rooms to conceal themselves or gain more time. In your safe room you must have a cell phone to call 911. It will help if you have extra weapons and ammunition in the safe room. If your location is isolated, provide limited amounts of food and water. Your survival will depend on your plan and your ability to execute your plan. There is a side bar discussion necessary at this point.

Cho and Virginia Tech. We have, like so many others, debated this matter in terms of the 2nd amendment, privacy and the right to defend. After a hot and heavy debate, we agreed that we were both wrong. We had used the political correct approach instead of logic and reason. Here is what we agreed to. There were two gun platforms used, one to fire 22 cal. projectiles and the second to fire 9mm projectiles. There was one person in charge of these two gun platforms. Cho. We know who, what, when, where and how. The question before us is why. Cho sent information to NBC expressing his feelings, particularly his personal feelings toward the rich. While all of the information is not available from the police investigation and may never come to light in our lifetime, we can begin to connect the dots that we are aware of. Cho hated the rich and their way of life enough to massacre 32 people. This in effect makes the massacre a *"hate crime."* This hate crime can be further explained as hatred between classes. So where did Cho find this information? Who made it available to him and today continues to reinforce it in peoples minds? Cho probably began his mental process as *'schadenfreude,'* hoping that another will get their cum-uppence. Cho could not wait for some event to occur and decided to initiate one. Cho had the opportunity almost daily to hear this hatred of the rich spewing forth from the television, newspapers and magazines. Politicians from both the Red and Blue camps daily argue over the issue of taxing the rich and laying claim to their labors and wealth. Yes! It is clear that our dear friends the lying politicians created this mindset for hate crime. While the 16th amendment permits government to tax any and all income throughout the world it is silent on the matter of progressivism in tax rates. We have to go back to the Constitution for that guidance. The Constitution states that the government must treat all people equally and especially, *"do-no-harm."* This issue has always been a hot bed of debate and will continue in its present form as a hate crime – committed daily by politicians and government. Therefore we find that those who preach class warfare, in this instance hatred of the rich, contributed to the slaughter at Virginia Tech and they should be called to answer for this crime. Hatred is a cowardly act and perpetrators of hate will always seek their revenge on those least prepared and able to defend themselves. That is why they select schools, churches, universities, post offices, work places, etc. Cho was both a physical coward and a mental coward for the means he used upon the helpless. This side bar defines the purpose of the entire issue of safety, security and survival and should reinforce in our minds where and who the real enemy of the people is.

THE TRUTH ABOUT INTEREST RATES AND POLITICAL DOLLAR DEVALUATION

Interest rates can be seen as the cost of renting money from another [borrower] or the return you expect to receive from lending your money [lender] or if you simply invest your money in a venture from which you expect a return. Earlier we said that during Greenspan's tenure as Fed. Chairman [1987-2005] that the purchasing power of the dollar was devalued by 50%. This quandary is stated as either, what cost 50 cents in 1987 costs a dollar in 2005 or what cost one dollar in 1987 cost two dollars in 2005. The glue that holds those three factors together, sort of a bear hug, is the growth of money supply in circulation. Gary Dorsch, of sirchartsalot.com identifies money growth as *"explosive."* Similarly, John Williams at ShadowStats.com puts current US money growth at 11%. On your calculator divide 72 by 11% and the answer is the number of years it will take for money supply to double. Paul van Eeden says that to calculate real, inflation-adjusted interest rates, those that determine your buying power, you combine the two inflations. The first is monetary inflation [11%] and second price inflation [3%], which when added up comes to 14%. Real interest rates are calculated by subtracting inflation [14%] from interest rates as set by the Federal Reserve [5.25%], lo and behold we find that real interest rates are a negative [-8.75]. The *"official GDP report"* from government for Qtr. 4 of 2006 was 3.5%. Today, 02-14-2007, that GDP number was revised down to 2.5%. We hope that now you understand that the $10,000 you had in your savings account a year ago will today buy measurably less in goods and services. Do you have that funny feeling that your retirement saving plan is going in the wrong direction? If it will make you feel better you are in good company. In Australia monetary growth is 13%, China 16.9%, Euro Zone 9.3%, Great Britain 13%, Korea 10.3%, Russia 45%. We know what we are going to do – have you made your plans?

THE TRUTH ABOUT POLITICAL ECONOMIES

When we talk about the economy in today's world, we have to understand that there are really FOUR LEVELS to the economy or if it is easier to understand we can state that there are four distinct economies. Of course, the one that comes to mind is the one we, middle-class, participate in. So we call that the *"common-man economy."* The middle-class can look down and they will see what is known as the *"poverty-man economy."* They are also known as the cash economy for cash leaves no prints. If we look up we will see the *"elite-man economy."* Finally, above the clouds we find the GOD-like economy created and controlled by life long power brokers whose history goes back to our colonial days. This economy is a gathering of the wealthy and powerful – the private equity firms, hedge funds, arbitragers, financial institutions, and all of the other type of money managers. These participants need a very large volume of money to finance their activities. The additional money supply is provided by the Federal Reserve by means of *"money supply growth."* We discussed money supply in the previous paragraph. As the monetary growth enters into the economy it first appears in the elite-man economy. It is used to finance private equity firms, hedge funds and all of the other hands that operate in the above ground economy. Some trickles down in the form of additional money used to fund and finance housing or student loans, et cetera. People who saw the value of their home increase by 50% or more and sold into that market were momentarily wealthier. If they sold their home and received a 50% or more gain and then either rented or bought down [buy a lower priced home], they captured this new-found wealth and were able to do something else with it. Hopefully they invested it wisely for their retirement. Far above these economies resides the apex or *"SUPER elite-man economy."* SUPER Elite-men are few in number but powerful beyond our imagination. It is they who devise the schemes and implement the actions that affect wealth at each level. The elitist-men, few in number, skim a *"vig,"* or vigorish of disproportionate size from the total before the trickle down begins.

THE TRUE GREENING OF AMERICA

Today, those of the elite and super elite are turning totally green, green with more money than one can imagine, while the middle-class turns green with envy. The rich provide financial services for others that are not so rich. They lend you money to buy homes. You refinance, when rates go up, with the lender down the street. You invest your money with a private equity firm. They take their company private, paying off the shareholders and you. You take your money and invest it with a hedge fund. When the company that was taken private is put back on the market your hedge fund buys it, at a higher price, with your money. Everybody that participates in that shuffle of money gets a nice piece of the action. Too bad that you were not one of them. Of course, all of this money originates with the Federal Reserve. They keep money supply increases at a steady 10%. But don't worry, in Europe it is also 10% and in

Asia it is 14%. Everybody is chasing the green stuff, except you and your friends. But, then you can take pride in your patriotism in making the wealthy – wealthier. It becomes a bit obnoxious when the whores of DC talk about stopping doing tricks, for then the worst is yet to come.

THE TRUTH ABOUT PRICE ESCALATION [inflation]

Historically the world has experienced on many occasions a change from stable prices to a slow and gradual rise in prices over a long period of time. **Demographics** play a role when the birth rates are high or migration increases the population. Both of these we have experienced in America. First, with the baby boomers and more recently with illegal aliens flooding across our Southern border into the Southwest. This increases demand for not only the basics of food, water, clothing and shelter, but also impacts pricing in other areas such as border control, transportation and so forth. A heavy pressure begins to appear in the production of resources needed to meet these new demands. The 1940 census placed the population of America at 140 million people. The 2000 census, plus the interim censuses, has placed our 2007 population at about 300 million, an increase of 160 million. **Wealth effect**, such as we experienced in the 90's and 00's, drove people to not only want more of everything but of better quality. This effect was driven in large part from a relaxing of credit qualifications and bad judgment of lenders. Continuous **domestic migration** from rural and less populated areas into larger urban areas continued as people sought to find employment. As people became aware of this steady increase in prices, they demanded to know why this was happening. We heard members of our Congress talk about trade laws similar to those of the 20's. Government responded by increasing the **money supply.** During the period beginning in 1971, the money supply has been increased to meet the necessary demands of commerce. It is when money supply exceeds those needs, such as flowing into the hands of the elite-man economy to supposedly filter down to everyone, that imbalance begins to appear. All economists speak too simplistically when they allege that price increases are driven by more money available in the economy. Money supply cannot be the primary villain as they paint, for it is illogical and nonsensical to believe that an effect can precede a cause. Money supply does of course drive prices higher but not until prices have first begun to rise. **Wage labor** begins to fall behind the price increase while the wealthy-man and elitist-man economies ballooned to preposterous levels. Real wages actually fell during the 90s and 00s and only recently have they begun to play catch up. People with few if any skills or who had little or none in savings suffered disproportionally. By comparison, landlords, merchants, professionals and capitalists benefited greatly. **Inequality** increases during these periods when the gap between the rich and poor, for who there never was equality, grow farther apart. Again, government believes that expanding the money supply is the correct remedy. Monetary theory can explain why an increase in the money supply can drive up prices. What they can't explain with their theories is why the price of goods and services increased in the first place. Recognizing that price increase is a complex circumstance in which many factors play their roles without us being able to understand them. The straw that breaks the back of the above situation lays itself directly at the feet of our politicians. Our best minds cannot explain this with any consensus, so what do our politicians do? It depends whether the socialist or the fascists are in control. Those who control fall back on their respective ideological values and pass legislation that supports those values. That is why we label our politicians, fools, idiots, incompetents acting in corrupt manners with corrupted ideals. They choose pure political action for it preserves their positions, gives them plausible deniability. Who is, then, responsible for the unintended consequences that fall heaviest on the lower classes? David Hackett Fischer in his book "The Great Wave," quotes George Hackwill who said, *"The plenty of coin and the multitude of men...either of which asunder, but much more both together, must needs be a means of raising prices of all things."*

THE POLITICAL TRUTH ABOUT POVERTY

All countries **must** have a poverty class for without them there would not be a middle or upper class. Leaders must have the poor for without them there is no scapegoat, no illegitimate argument to use against the wealthier. All of us, yes, all of us, must have the poverty, the down and outers, or whatever name you wish to give them, for without them we would all be the same, and everyone knows that means mediocrity and we all are really number one.

THE POLITICAL TRUTH ABOUT DRUG WARS

The inception of the war on drug use was around 1914 with legislation making some drugs illegal without a medical prescription. From day one we have been on the losing side of that war. Today there is more usage, more money spent for enforcement, more arguments used by politicians to justify their own value system. In the actual business there are more pimps and more product. Those marketing the crop are paying off the ones supposed to stop the trafficking of drugs. It is a sick game of payoffs, bribery, scams, skimming and all the while we are the losers as our children are addicted to trying anything that parents say is bad. Most of us never knew about addictive drugs until it became an open subject for discussion and that were mostly political lies on both sides.

THE POLITICAL TRUTH ABOUT TAX COMPETITION WOW!

We start with class warfare as to who will pay taxes, who will pay little or no taxes, and who will not only pay no taxes but will receive benefits directly from the tax code. We next turn to special interests that claim to represent and speak for the weak, the oppressed, the wealthy and any other class of life or condition such as environment, animals, and so forth. The *Big Kahunas* are the political ideologues that rant and rave that their values represent mainstream America, and then vote for outrageous expenditures for which there is no legitimate purpose. They do this to stroke their egos, get re-elected and convince themselves they are the second coming of Christ. In reality they are useless, worthless, and we all would be better off without them. States, counties, cities compete among themselves to attract business, especially manufacturing, to locate in their political jurisdiction. This is politician and labor wanting the taxpayers to foot the bill for more jobs. A great many people would beg them to stop, for adding jobs and growth creates urbanization with all of its malaise. We compete between states in that several states have no state income tax, other states offer low tax and several offer higher taxes and are proud of it. Crawling up this ladder, we find at the top, tax competition between countries. Most countries seek investment from the wealthy of other countries by offering tax breaks, residency or even citizenship. Interesting that the two largest panderers of tax breaks to individuals and companies are the [UK], United Kingdom and the [US], United States; for they are also the largest complainers and belly achers in opposition to small countries, such as some Caribbean island countries. Yet – the big countries absolutely prevent their citizens from participating in globalization as individuals when it would benefit them the most.

HEIDE SAYS TO ROBERT

Heide always reminds Robert that anyone can win at the casino, however, only a few will walk out the door with their winnings. For the homeowner, when the market was hot they could have sold their house and won, but only a few walked out the door of the office where their transaction was closed, with more wealth and less debt. That is why we say there are winners and losers. The winners are called fortunate. The losers cry out in the dark of night that it wasn't their fault. They are the less fortunate. The reason it is said that beggars can't be choosers is because when they made their choices they left [lost] their money in the casino of chance or the casino of money managers. That is why we also must remember that we do not necessarily get what we want, but we always get what we deserve. Casinos use the exact same strategy to seduce guests that the market gurus use to seduce investor money. Enter the casino and you can visualize three risks, so to speak. The first is the one-cent, two-cent and five-cent machines that you can play three, five, fifty or a hundred hands simultaneously. These machines entice people to believe that they are playing for pennies. The middle risk is the twenty-five cent, fifty-cent and dollar machines where you can play five coins at once and be eligible to win the big jackpot. This is also more enticement to take your money. Then comes the upper risk. The five-dollar, twenty-five dollar and the sky are the limit. More enticement. Additional problems include: demographics, cultural deterioration, preemptive wars, increase in violent crimes, a middle-class lacking the education to compete, withering of individual entrepreneurial skill, destruction of the monetary system, grouping and labeling people and then encouraging incivility between them, excessive taxation, non representation, growth of political families, and on and on. We have lived this charade since 1971. With the closing of the gold window by Nixon, the control of the dollar was given over to government control along with control over the printing presses. They created *unrealized* appearance of greater wealth for everyone.

There will be a massive shift of wealth when solutions are imposed from outside. We will refer to it as a mini-Armageddon and search for answers as to how to survive this thing – not if - but when it comes. Debt is the poison that will create an Armageddon so we must first deal with that. For us there is no such thing as a *"get-out-of-debt"* card that comes with a free ride or a bye. It must be done by you step by step. Expenses must be paired to the bone and income maximized at each opportunity. Start with the most costly of debts – the credit card – cut them up and pay them off and stay on a cash and carry system. After debt begin accumulating cash in your accounts. Study the value of cash and how to protect and grow your cash. One source that we use is William O'Neill's program featured in his newspaper, Investor Business Daily [IBD]. Your children should be exposed to this type of program as soon as possible. Remember, above, we talked about the salary they would receive from their work for your business and that they would learn to invest their own money. Your accounts will grow in size and then they become vulnerable to threats against your wealth. Your children were born in a country that recognized birth as automatic citizenship. This is your camel's nose under the tent. The threat we refer to is government's unlimited authority to, at any time for any reason, seize your assets. The second threat is from those who envy you, your wealth, and want to see you lose it, preferably to them. When your assets reach a point that they will attract the envious like flies to a manure pile, legally move your money to that country, invest it, declare it, and pay taxes on it. This money is now beyond the reach of government and enviers.

POLITICAL TRUTH ABOUT CONDUCT, BEHAVIOR AND CHARACTER

In all sincerity we speak to our future generations of conduct, behavior and character, recognizing our own faults and weaknesses. We don't expect you to be perfect, just try to be better than you are or the others that you observe and hear.

- Begin with **impulse control**. If you want to learn impulse control, drive the interstate in the right or slow lane, and set your cruise control exactly on the posted limit. We dare say that every car behind you will pass, going at a speed well above the posted limits. Impulse control is vital in every aspect of your life. Learn it and practice it.
- It is mere **illusion** and **petty sentiment** to expect equality from a government, if it forgets the Constitution and the people, and governs for power and prestige. Knowing this allows you to understand the enemy and its capabilities.
- **Political power** --- is in its essence --- the main condition to generate great passion among the masses. It places in the hands of the powerful the means to make men and women destructive and combative. Of all the wars of the past century, each with its great slogans, has really achieved nothing close to the claims that were made. But hindsight is superior to foresight. Who among us would have believed that the millions of deaths, millions more injured and trillions of dollars later the wars we fought resembled fighting windmills? We fought first and afterwards searched for plausible claims to justify the wars.
- All political power is based on **deception.** If the enemy seeks control over us, when we are capable of standing up to them, we must seem passive. When we wish to use our forces, we must make the enemy believe we are distant, when we are close, and close when we are distant.
- If the enemy is secure, having created legislation that ties our hands and feet, we must avoid them. We may seek to irritate him, pretend to be weak so that he will grow **arrogant**. When he takes to rest, give him no time to rest, appear where he least expects to see you.
- No government will survive **prolonged struggles for freedom** from its people. Husband your resources and forage upon the enemies' excesses and pride.

This book only scratches the surface of this subject. We feared that you would overdose if it were too long and too much. We are constantly researching the subject and documenting our thoughts and ideas. One thought that persists is the effort made by our institutions to place an authoritarian label of *truth* to that which they speak and write. The Constitution is a document that we believe in. The writers of the Constitution believed with a passion, but history shows that many today don't. We watched a panel discussion the other day debating fiction versus non-fiction. One argument is that literally the Bible and the Quran are works of fiction as they are based upon belief and faith, but again believing is not the same as knowing.

Let's take a peek at globalization.

From the long travail of the 20th century, a new social order must be born to facilitate our arrival, as individual sovereigns, to survive and prosper in this next phase of globalization.

> "Globalization is like rain. It is a force of nature. It comes and you can't do a thing about it. However, like rain, you can channel it into beneficial courses and uses. Or, if you want to, you can take personal shelter for yourself and who ever else you wish to include. However, one must realize that this shelter, by necessity of the nature of globalization, can only be localized and perhaps only of short duration."
>
> 05-07-2005, P. E. @ Riol Germany

PRACTICAL APPLICATION

Today you are faced with an actual situation that will challenge everything that we have taught you. We speak of the 2008 national election. Remember that our position remains one of neutrality for it matters not whether the *Radical Socialist* or *Radical Fascists* are in control of government for each has an ultimate goal and each, to succeed, must deny the people their rights to life, liberty and the pursuit of happiness. To put everyone on the same page, we furnish the dictionary definition of each.

SOCIALISM: A social system in which the producers possess both political power and the means of producing and distributing goods. In Marxist-Leninist theory, the building, under the dictatorship of the proletariat, of the material base for communism. Editors note: Communism is a word not used by socialists nor do they like the word liberal; their preference is some variation that has the word democracy in it. But democracy remains as whatever those of influence wish to call it.

FASCISM: A philosophy or system of government that advocates or exercises a dictatorship of the extreme right, typically through the merging of state and business leadership, together with an ideology of belligerent nationalism. Editor's note: Fascism is a word abhorred by the conservative right for its connotation is just as divisive to the right as communism is to the left. Both are today labeled as radical in their use of power.

This is where your *Plans and Operations* section earns their keep. They must bring together other factors; e.g., *Illusion and Co-dependency*. It is their job guided by the leader to identify the problems, state the tasks, and coordinate the use of all resources. Here are some of the considerations you must understand. In an earlier section we said that you survive very well if you understand the origin and flow of money and power within a corrupt government. Under fascism, government works closely with business granting them tax advantages, privilege and access to the power that government wields. The socialists now control both houses of Congress, albeit by very narrow margins. Money flowed from lobbyists, special interest and elite wealthy through the hands of republican fascists and influenced the tax and regulatory laws passed by government. Under socialist control the money will continue to originate from similar sources, but will primarily flow through the hands of the socialists in their attempt to rewrite tax legislations. Think of it in this manner. Under Bush there was clear knowledge of who were the winners and who were the losers. The socialist leadership of the Congress must reverse engineer the present flow of money and whose hands they flow through. They will do this by redefining who will be the new winners and losers under the new balance of power in government. Today's winners know that they will become tomorrow's losers and their task is to change their spots and reappear as part of the new winners. These are some of the considerations that you must master to survive. The majority of Americans will sit on their hands and limit their efforts to criticizing, complaining and just plain bitching about how the country has gone to hell in a hand basket. They will think that they are now the winners, but for them it is only an *Illusion*. We want you to be real winners – so remember the difference between the fortunate and the less fortunate. Thanks for listening and good fortune to all of you.

PROFITING FROM GOVERNMENT STUPIDITY AND CORRUPTION

We introduced this subject earlier in the book. Now we want to be more specific in what this means.

1] **When government devalues its paper money,** as it is doing in the early 2000's, you must look to foreign currencies that are appreciating in value because of the dollar devaluation. You will also look for methods of holding these currencies off shore. Remember that off shore simply means *"safe haven"* for what you value most, yourself, your family, your freedom and your wealth.

2] **When government makes health care more expensive than it should be.** As government prices more people out of the health care market, you must take your health into your own hands. This means proper diet, exercise and control over what you do.

3] **When government threatens to raise taxes.** They always announce that they must tax the best producers more to provide for the poorer producers. Seek legal methods of reducing certain character of taxable income. Look for off shore tax advantage.

4] **When government refuses to create a sensible energy plan.** Buy fuel-efficient vehicles and light bulbs. Invest in energy, especially uranium, as the tide will turn in favor of this inexpensive form of energy.

5] **When government redistributes tax dollars to favored groups.** Relocate when possible to share in this largess.

6] **When government redistributes tax dollars taken from disfavored groups.** Where possible abandon your position in disfavored groups by relocating to your safe haven.

7] **When government tells you that they are here to protect and serve.** Quickly recognize that this is an illusion.

They are pretty much limited to investigating and prosecuting, and they don't usually do that well. Take steps to protect yourself and your family.

8] **When government threatens war and violence against a real or imagined enemy.** Consider buying those stocks that will do well in wars such as with Iraq or Iran.

9] **When government next raises payroll taxes.** Change from wage labor to free labor, reduce your taxable income, increase your normal, necessary and appropriate expense deduction. Look off shore for cheap medical, but of good quality, service.

10] **When government gives titles to laws such as "Patriot Act."** Recognize that this is an illusion to deceive people into believing what they want them to believe and what they don't want them to know. This act on their part must be taken seriously so activate your safe haven plans pursuant to your Principality Constitution.

11] **When government drives the CPI to 3% or higher.** Convert your dollar investments to gold, silver, platinum or stronger currencies. Stop all unnecessary spending, pay down debt, and become niggardly tight with a dollar. You have no actual right to your social security says the Supreme Court. In the case of *Helvering v. Davis* they made it quite clear. They said, *"Neither you nor any American has any legal claim on a single penny that you've paid toward Social Security."*

12] **The deceit and lies of elections.** Hardly a day passes that we do not read, collect and analyze ideas and information. Evaluating and understanding the promises of the 2006 election was like crawling out of the sewer, and in just months, we will be reburied with the lies of the coming 2008 presidential elections. One reason for labeling them as idiots and truly dishonest is that they tend to put effect ahead of cause when legislating. They are unable to predict consequences of their acts for they are blinded by their pet ideology. They claim that the unintended consequences are the fault of the other party. These idiots remind us of the fool who ran backwards down the aisle of a speeding train and believed that their ideas were gaining. Do we really wish to stay on that train with ideologues making decisions based upon results that they cannot see and run the country blindly into oblivion? It is important for voters to decide if they want to continue on this train with this crew. Next, they must decide what train they will take if they choose to get off this one. It seems that when too many politicians think and act alike, they really are not thinking at all.

WHOM DO WE FEAR THE MOST?
a. Terrorists
b. Pompous politicians seeking self gratification
c. Our own wavering confidence regarding our courage and conviction.
d. Devaluation through rebalancing
e. All of the above

The correct answer is [e]. We prefer to label it *GRAND THEFT GOVERNMENT*.

GRAND THEFT FRAUD

FUTURE GENERATIONS: In this section we describe how your government cheats and steals your wealth, your future and your freedom. We have chosen as the vehicle to do this the Bretton Woods Agreement and what it intended and how it began to fail almost before it was signed. Countries proved they could not be trusted to fulfill an obligation to which they signed their name and good faith. Following the signing it became a game of who could manipulate their currency for their gain only.

In July 1944 the Bretton Woods Agreement was debated and signed, at the Mount Washington Hotel in Bretton Woods, New Hampshire. WWII was still in progress when 730 delegates from 44 countries met. This Agreement established the rules for commercial and financial relations among the world's major industrial states. This agreement set up the International Monetary Fund [IMF] and the International Bank for Reconstruction and Development [IBRD], now one of five institutions in the World Bank.

Each country was expected to adopt a monetary policy that maintained the exchange of its currency within a fixed rate, plus or minus 1%, in terms of gold and the ability of the IMF to bridge temporary *imbalances* of payments. Until the early 1970s, the Bretton Wood system was effective in controlling conflict and in achieving the common goals of the leading states that had created it. This system, under increasing strain, collapsed in 1971 following the United States' suspension of convertibility from dollars to gold. The dollars value versus other currencies was as follows;

December 1945 one dollar bought 119.11 francs;
June 1948 one dollar bought 3.33 Dmarks;
November 1947 one dollar bought 575 lira;
April 1949 one dollar bought 360 yen

WHAT WENT WRONG?

Several years ago the Prime Minister of Malaysia proposed backing the dinar with gold. He was stopped dead in his tracks by the IMF, International Monetary Fund. Their rules don't permit any currencies that are exchanged at the consumer level to be backed by gold or silver.

If Congress actually introduced real reforms it would probably fail. More and more voters depend on some form of government handout and they will not allow it.

Deception for the greater good: In *United States versus Russell* allowed the police to use deceptive procedures to obtain evidence. The justification? Without it they might never make a case.

Competition between countries encourages every country to devalue its paper currency faster than the others, for this gives them an advantage.

The US dollar was designated the world's reserve currency because other countries believed that the US would maintain the value of the dollar and their devaluations would benefit them.

ECONOMIC SECURITY: The foundation of the agreements was a shared belief in capitalism ranging from France preferring greater central planning and state intervention to the United States favoring limited state intervention. Cordell Hull, US Secretary of State, believed that the cause of the two world wars lie in economic discrimination and trade warfare. He specifically identified trade and exchange controls [bilateral agreements] of Nazi Germany and the imperial preference system practiced by Great Britain [by which members or former members of the British Empire were accorded special trade status.]

THE RISE OF GOVERNMENTAL INTERVENTION: The developed countries also agreed that the liberal international economic system required governmental intervention Following the Great Depression, public management of the economy had emerged as a primary activity of governments in the developed states. Employment, stability and growth were now important subjects of public policy. In turn, the role of government in the national economy had become associated with the assumption by the state of the responsibility for assuring for its citizens a degree of economic well-being. The welfare state grew out of the Great Depression, which created a popular demand for governmental intervention in the economy, and out of the theoretical contribution of the Keynesian school of economics, which asserted the need for governmental intervention to maintain an adequate level of employment. This occurred before the ink was dry on the writings of the Great Depression. The 1930s saw government policy that used currency devaluations to increase the competitiveness country's export products in order to reduce balance of payment deficits – worsening deflationary spirals – plummeting national incomes, mass unemployment, and an overall decline in world trade. We find thus that the agreement established a limited government policy in name only, for they refused to acknowledge that government had in fact created the Great Depression, and that those acts are the very ones mentioned in the agreement that should not be repeated. The phrase that best describes this is *"dead-on-arrival."*

The rules of the Bretton Woods Agreement provided for a system of *"fixed exchange rates."* The rules further sought to encourage an open system of committing members to the convertibility of their respective currencies into other currencies and to free trade. What really happened was the establishment of the *"reserve currency."* This meant the US dollar would be the reserve currency and other countries would peg their currencies to the US dollar. Once convertibility was restored countries would buy and sell dollars to keep exchange rates within a plus or minus 1% of parity. Thus the dollar took the place of gold and earned the name, *"good as gold."* At this point the US currency was effectively the world currency, the currency with the greatest purchasing power and the only currency backed by gold. This led to the creation of the IMF [International Monetary Fund] with an economic approach and political ideology that stressed controlling inflation and introducing austerity plans for fighting poverty.

Post war Europe suffered from economic doldrums - world capitalism suffered from a huge dollar shortage. The US was running huge balance of trade **surpluses** and US reserves were immense and growing rapidly. It was felt that it was necessary to reverse the **surplus** flow and replace it with a **deficit** flow. George Marshall defined it thus;

"The breakdown of the business structure of Europe during the war was complete ... Europe's requirements for the next three or four years of foreign food and other essential products...principally from the United States.... Are so much greater than her present ability to pay that she must have substantial help or face economic, social and political deterioration of a very grave character."

From 1947 until 1958, the US deliberately encouraged an outflow of dollars, and, from 1950 on, the US ran a balance of payments deficit with the intent of providing liquidity for the international community. The primary conduits for this liquidity included various US aid programs, the Truman Doctrine entailing aid to pro-US Greek and Turkish regimes, aid to various pro-US regimes in the third world, and the Marshall Plan [from 1948 to 1954] when 16 Western European countries received $17 billion in grants.

In 1945 Roosevelt and Churchill prepared the post-war era for the cold war by bad negotiating with Joseph Stalin at Yalta, creating zones of influence and dividing Germany up among the Allies. A series of wars [the domino theory] were fought by the US increasing the flow of dollars into economies and growing a larger balance of trade **deficit.**

The fiscal discipline imposed by Bretton Woods made it fiscally impossible for the European nations to both rebuild their economies and retain their colonies. Only the US could afford large-scale foreign deployments within the Western Alliance. The price America paid for this position was the militarization of the US economy, also know as *"the military-industrial complex."* A trade surplus made it easy for the US to

keep armies abroad and to invest outside the US. Being the
only country able to do this saw the decision-making process
become a US prerogative. The dollar was the compass to show
the world the economic way. Thus we had *Pax Americana.*

The gap between free market gold prices and central bank
gold prices tended to widen. This created a temptation among
countries to exploit this imbalance by considering a *'carry-
trade'* by buying gold at the Bretton Woods price and selling it
on the open market. The dollar, because it earned interest,
proved somewhat more desirable. Robert Triffin was early to
notice that the reason dollar holdings were more valuable than
gold was because constant US balance of payments **deficits**
helped keep the system liquid and fuel economic growth. Later
he noticed that if the US failed to keep running **deficits** the
system would lose its liquidity, not being able to keep up the
world's economic growth, thus bringing the system to a halt.
Yet, continuing to run these **deficits** means that over time the
deficits would erode confidence in the dollar as the reserve
currency creating an imbalance among countries of relative
exchange and risk considerations.

In 1967 there was an attack on the pound, and a run on
gold in the *"sterling area,"* and on November 17, 1967 the
British devalued the pound. LBJ was faced with a conundrum,
either he could institute protectionist measures, including
travel taxes, export subsidies and slashing the budget – or he
could accept the risk of a *"run on gold."* The country would
have had better odds if he had only made a throw of the dice.

However, as everyone knows, LBJ was wedded to his legacy
program *"The Great Society."* He substituted *"guns and butter"*
for his biased belief that the world supply of gold was
insufficient to be relevant to our budget, and it was off to the
races. This was to lead to the deterioration of the US balance of
trade position.

By the mid 60's, Germany and Japan had become
international powers eroding US hegemony. Their total reserves
exceeded the US reserves, and they narrowed the gap with the
US. America's role as the world's *"central banker"* and
privileged role as the international currency was under serious
challenge. By 1970 the US held under 16% of international
reserves – down from 50% with the creation of Bretton Woods.

In sum, monetary interdependence was increasing at a faster pace than international management in the 1960's, leading up to the collapse of the Bretton Woods system. Amid these problems, economic cooperation decreased, US leadership declined, and the system broke down.

The *"Nixon shock"* came on August 15, 1971 with the closing of the gold window. By March 1976, all the major currencies were floating – in other words, exchange rates were no longer the principal method to administer monetary policy. The fundamental point of agreement, as to why Bretton Woods failed, is that the US ran an increasing balance of trade deficit, and that, in the end, the US could not be trusted to reign in their deficit. So where do we stand today – September 2006?

One US dollar now buys 0.7839 euros – note that the euro has been substituted for the former German Dmark –, which was at 3.33 Dmarks.
One US dollar buys 0.5259 British pounds.
One US dollar buys 116.48 yen compared to 360 yen

Bretton Woods I, Bretton Woods II and the Smithsonian Agreement between the *'Group of Ten'* failed, and with it currency management passed into the ether of history. When a political event such as this dies, the death does not take with it a body as in mortal death. Political death usually leaves behind that which caused its death and is yet to be resolved.

We offer the following time and ratios to attempt to make this remaining problem more clearly understood. For the hundred years preceding the creation of the Federal Reserve System [1913], the value of the dollar remained relatively constant. In the period since 1913 that which the nickel bought required in 2005 a dollar. The closing of the gold window preceded the inflation of the 80's. During the reign of Alan Greenspan [1987-2006] the purchasing power of the dollar was cut in half, thus requiring 2X the dollars to buy the same amount of goods and service. This explains somewhat why the working class has not kept up their standard of living during this period as their wages and benefits would have had to double in those 20 years to just stay even. The government has, with some success, avoided a hard landing recession by flooding the economy with additional dollars [this produces a symptom called inflation] and is preparing even now to use this technique to mute the next recession that comes our way. The government has already passed *"peak-borrowing,"* that being defined as people, institutions and foreign countries losing faith, trust and credit in the US government and beginning to decline the opportunity to buy US debt.

We have seen the most massive shifting of wealth between workers and owners and are seeing this trend continuing. This 50% devaluation in twenty years goes almost unnoticed among the rank and file. Life is the same, work hard, pay your taxes and if you have money left over enjoy it. Devaluation is measured first by the buying public in the normal course of living – or at least it should for it is obvious. Second, by the devaluing of the dollar against other currencies. Remember in 1948 one dollar bought 360 yen. Today one dollar buys about 16 yen – now that is devaluation. Imagine if you had used all of your money in 1948 to buy yen at 360 to the dollar and today you sold those yen and bought dollars at 107 yen for each dollar. My little calculator, when I divide 360 by 107, tells me 2.36. For each thousand dollars invested in yen in 1948, your return today would be 3.36 thousand dollars. If, instead of investing, you hid your money in the mattress, that thousand dollars [laying there for 56 years] would be worth a few hundred dollars at the most. Since the end of WWII, you have been ripped off, by the smoothest grifters the world has even had – *the US government.* The good news, for the government, is that they know or believe that most of you lack the intelligence or will to make the effort to recognize that you are being raped.

So what will government do when foreigners decline to buy our debt? We pose this question at this time [May 2007] for in a few years the baby boomers will begin to retire and by 2020 they will all be drawing Social Security. Because the true federal debt is about ten times the published debt [$ 8 trillion] or approximately $72 trillion dollars, there will be no one to buy the new debt offered by government each month. The government has a real Houdini escape plan. The Federal Reserve will offer new debt; if no one comes forth to buy it, the Federal Reserve will buy their own debt by printing the amount of paper [funny money] necessary to make these purchases. The value of the dollar will plunge like a lead balloon. Where will that leave you?

Instead of acting stupid, we need to act intelligently in our own way for our own future. We need to seriously reduce and / or eliminate outstanding personal debt.

We need to recognize the herd mentality and identify the proper contrarian actions. For example – for decades people have been carried away with the desire for a bigger, larger, better, newer home. The contrarian opposite action is to sell that big house and downsize. This reduces debt service, cost of operation and maintenance compared to the bigger is better house. We did this.

You need to appreciate exactly what devaluation of the dollar is doing to your wealth balance. The dollar has been falling for decades, and will probably stop only when it hits bottom. Bottom is when no one trusts the dollar and countries are fleeing to other currencies. The smart thing for you to do is get rid of as many US dollars as your situation permits. If you have $100,000 or more, legally move it out of the country, convert it to a stronger currency, and wait for the final gasp of the dollar, then it will be time to consider bringing some money back. If you have between $25 and $100 thousand consider converting your dollars to Swiss Francs by buying the currency through a broker. If you are living from paycheck to paycheck, consider converting small amounts of US dollars by purchasing gold or silver coins. If the government is in full panic they will consider making that illegal. So be prepared to put them in a small section of PVC, cap the ends so they are water tight, and bury in your flower garden.

Consider having a moving sale and dump all household items that you don't need and have a large garage sale for the lesser items.

During the 80's and 90's, investing in debt was a popular investment – we did it – but we haven't for some years. So what is the real deficit? The answer is which accounting system are you using, so let's talk a moment about systems.

The official deficit tally for each fiscal year comes from Congress and the White House. Most of you wouldn't trust any of them to babysit your dog.

The audited version is from the Treasury Department and follows standard accounting principles.

The third figure is based on accounting rules like those used by corporations and includes the costs of Social Security and Medicare.

Here we quote from the USA Today from the third week of September 2006.

"The federal government keeps two sets of books. The set the government promotes to the public has a healthier bottom line: a $318 billion deficit in [fiscal] 2005. The set the government doesn't talk about is the audited financial statement produced by the government's accountants following standard accounting rules. It reports a more ominous financial picture: a $760 billion deficit for 2005. If Social Security and Medicare were included – as the board that sets accounting rules is considering – the federal deficit would have been $3.5 trillion."

Secretary of the Treasury, John Snow, was cashiered for contracting an audit of the true debt and deficit and making public the results. How he must be smiling now and saying, I told you so! But back to the USA Today article.

"Congress has written its own accounting rules – which would be illegal for a corporation to use because they ignore important costs such as the growing expense of retirement benefits for civil service and military personnel. Last year [2005] the audited statement produced by the accountants said the government ran a deficit equal to $6,700 for every American household. The number given to the public put the deficit at $2,800 per household."

FUTURE GENERATIONS: Everything preceding is to give transparency to the swindle that is being perpetrated upon all of us. Well, maybe not all of us, those with the greatest wealth have already maneuvered to protect their precious millions and billions from past and future devaluations and defaults. After the coming debt rebalancing debacle, and when the dust has cleared, they will stand tall virtually untouched by the fall-out. Oh-oh, we didn't tell you about the debt rebalancing that will ultimately bring this fraud to an end, leaving us little guys to pick through the rubble for survival while the leadership is emerging unscathed from their *"debt rebalancing bomb shelter."* Can you hear them crying that it wasn't their fault that all governments were doing it. Sure they say, we made a few mistakes, but bankrupting the country – don't look at me – and they point their finger at those who are to be the scapegoats. If you wish to tar and feather them [politicians] you have our permission – but in the meantime act and act quickly, fully and forever and let them rest in hell. Without you and we.

So let's discuss this coming debacle. We set the stage. Following WWII the US was the big dog on the block, it did what it wanted, paid the bills of the world, converted its *"world's largest creditor status"* into the *"world's largest debtor status,"* started wars – finished some and cut and run on others, spent money on anything and everything, bought goodies it didn't need – with money it didn't have, and to hell with the world and we-the-people. The problem with that tirade is that it isn't a sneak attack like 9-11. Government knew it would eventually come and simply said, *"We'll cross that bridge when we get there."* Well we are there.

Read the next paragraph and tell us where we are wrong!

Foreign governments for most of the past 3-4 decades have developed a dislike ranging up to hatred for America. Not unlike a case of good envy turning into bad envy. Our enemies and even our friends want us taken down several notches or even made to squirm and grovel. We have lost their trust and respect, and now we pay the piper. After foreign governments stop buying debt [except if the interest rate is raised to outrages height], then US financial institutions cut back and stop buying US debt and the people scorn their politicians, the creditor world convenes a *"debt rebalancing session"* like the creditors and debtor in a bankruptcy. They do not intend to destroy the American economy, only cripple it badly so that America becomes a second rate power both financially and militarily. The crown now passes to another country or countries that take over dictating how the world will be governed. Creditors at a bankruptcy seldom anticipate getting anything near what they are owed. Therefore, one popular alternative will be to force the US to make a major devaluation of its currency. When we say major we remember that Greenspan maneuvered the dollar into 50% devaluation in two decades and the people didn't catch on – therefore a one time further devaluation of 50%, while not predicted, would certainly not be out of the question. They don't literally want to kill us just cripple us so that any return to power is remote by putting out the fire in our bellies that drove us to great heights of success.

WHAT OTHERS THINK AND SAY ABOUT AMERICA

Our North American editor, Mary Coons, has periodically spent many months in Bahrain, where her husband works as an engineer. She forwarded to us an article out of the Gulf Daily News, dateline Monday April 2nd, 2007. A Mr. Paul Balles who writes a column for this paper, titled *Of the people*, wrote, *"Yesterday an Arab friend sent me an email full of photos of Americans holding up signs saying, "We're sorry." These were people who felt guilty about what the American government has been doing around the world.*

Presumably, their purpose was both to assuage their guilt and to let people outside of America know that not all Americans are warmongers. I also assume that my friend's purpose in sending the photo collection to me was to let me know that not all Arabs think all Americans are as bad as their government.

Considering what the Bush regime has accomplished in terms of its own carnage and that of its Israeli puppeteer, for my Arab friend to express a view often heard 35 years ago was – under current circumstances – quite generous. Much too generous from this American critics point of view.

Arabs tend to forget at times that America still lays claim to being a democracy, proud to have embraced Abraham Lincoln's reference to a government **"of the people, for the people and by the people."** It's no longer any of those things.

Joel S. Hirschborn recently asked, "When you can no longer trust the elected representatives what happens to American democracy?" His response; **"It becomes an oxymoron."** *An oxymoron is a contradiction in terms, like "military justice" or a "just war." Hirschborn added:*

We have arrived at a delusional democracy. Delusional because Americans overwhelmingly cannot admit the painful truth that their limited democracy no longer works for the good of most citizens. Instead, through corruption and dishonesty, our representative democracy has morphed into a plutocracy that serves the wealthy, power elites and corporate masters that control the political system and through that the economic system.

If the government is not "for the people," how did it become a plutocracy that serves "the wealthy, power elites and corporate masters?" Could that happen if the government was "of the people?"

It should be clear from the inaction of a Congress recently voted to represent the electorate's wishes to leave Iraq that the government is not of the people.

When 2 per cent of the American population controls the country, no one can claim that America has a democracy "by the people." The Jewish population in the USA is 2 per cent, and it is represented by the lobbying power of the American Israel Public Affairs Committee [AIPAC].

Is it a democracy when 2 per cent of the population effectively controls the government and media? This is the democracy that the plutocrats in charge want to impose on other countries.

According to George Soros, in an article on "Israel, America and AIPAC," it is a lobby "which strongly affects both the Democratic and the Republican parties. AIPAC's mission is to ensure American support for Israel but in recent years it has overreached itself."

Later, Soros added, "Any politician who dares to expose AIPAC's influence would incur its wrath; so very few can be expected to do so."

If AIPAC, representing 2 per cent of the American public controls the American government, how can anyone claim that it's a government "by the people?"

Some still call it a "democracy." Is it a democracy for, of, or by the people when a presidential candidate must humble himself/herself before an AIPAC that yields the power of life or death for his/her candidacy?

Photographs of ordinary citizens holding placards saying "we're sorry" to the offended, wherever else in the world they may be, achieves little, if anything, but a weak expression of guilt by a dozen or so peaceniks.

[PROPOSED-NEW]
DECLARATION OF INDEPENDENCE

By the People

WHEN in the course of betrayal of our Constitution, it becomes necessary for *"We-the-People"* to dissolve the political, regulatory and tax laws that have connected them with another, and to assume among the Powers of the Country, the separate and equal Station to which the Constitution had granted and the Laws of Nature and of Natures God entitle them, a decent Respect of the Opinions of Citizens requires that they should declare the causes that impel them to this separation.

WE hold these truths to be self-evident that all Americans are created equal, that they are endowed by their Creator certain unalienable Rights and Responsibilities, that among these are control over their bodies and minds, thoughts and desires, and the Pursuit of happiness in manners that are fair to all, that each has the same opportunity to do with their lives, and each accepts the results of their actions as just and deserving, as intended in the Constitution. Government was instituted among us, deriving its power from the consent of *"We-the People"* and has betrayed the People by establishing itself as *"We-the Government,"* thus placing itself as a Power over the People to be used as government dictates, and is prepared to abolish people's rights, in view of government becoming destructive of these ends. It is now and always will be the right of the people to institute new government principles and organizing its Powers in such form, as to them shall seem most likely to effect their safety and happiness.

Having shown, that working Americans are more disposed to suffer, while evils are sufferable, than to right themselves by abolishing the form of government that has emerged and which they have become accustomed to. But a long list of abuse, fraud and corruption, pursuing invariably the same purpose, evinces a pattern to reduce people to absolute serfdom beholden to the whims of *"We-the-Government."* It is *"We-the-Peoples"* right, it is their duty and responsibility to change such government, to provide new controls for their future security. Such has been the patient suffering of these people; and such is now the necessity that demands them to alter their former systems of government. The history of Reign-of-Oligarch is a history of repeated injustices. Lies and deceptions having the purpose of the establishment of a government, unaccountable to *"We-the-People."* To prove this, let the following facts be submitted to an angry country.

Government has refused to make laws wholesome and essential for the public good.

For taking away our Constitutional rights, legislating to favor special groups at the expense of others, resulting in our Republic altered into something called a democracy concealing the bitterness of ideologies favoring race, sex, religion, workers, business until the bureaucracy has become unmanageable from its original intent.

For denying us the right to petition government through referendums and declaring themselves invested with the Power to legislate for us under the false principle that government knows better what is good for us than we do.

Government is, at this time, moving large numbers of troops and ships in pursuit of Super Star status, establishing a hegemony over the planet, spreading our culture like an AIDS epidemic, all totally unworthy of a civilized Nation and in complete disregard for the words of warning given us by our founder and first president.

Government professes that we are in a war versus terrorism and the evil of police states. Government claims that democracy (?) is superior to police state tyranny. Why then do we create a police state of our own to fight another police state? If democracy is so *'all powerful'* why are we not fighting the enemy police state with our greatest weapon, democracy? People know that what you take from us either through persuasion or compulsion you have no intention to ever return it to us. The U.S. Constitution was once the brightest star in our universe. Today it is but a dim glimmer of its former self, and our generation will live to see that star die, leaving behind a *'black hole.'*

Government has condoned domestic violence among us failing to take necessary action to protect our lives and properties, actually seizing in some matters our property for private use.

FOR creating a national debt of 51 trillion dollars of unfunded obligations, apparently with no intent to repay, by rolling over the obligation to repay to our children and grandchildren.

WE, therefore, the citizens of the UNITED STATES OF AMERICA, appealing to the Supreme Power of this Super State for consideration and resolution of our freedoms, by authority of the good people of these states, solemnly publish and declare that these people are, and of right, ought to be FREE INDIVIDUALS AND FAMILIES, and that they have the full power to change their form of government.

/s/ Robert Egert-Budik
/s/ Adelheid Egert-Budik

FUTURE GENERATIONS: Some will agree with us while many others will not. Regardless, your opinions are requested that we may further study this issue. Government is so full of good intentions; it can now pave the road to hell – four lanes – itself. If knowingly violating the Constitution is evil, then government is evil. If violating the Constitution in conjunction with other branches of government (who are supposed to check and balance), are they not then betrayers of the Constitution and thus traitors acting in treacherous warp?

The following reprint appeared in the May 26, 2007 *"The Northwest Valley Republic"* as an insert in the Arizona Republic for the same day. This clever article puts the *'stupid-idiotic-asinine"* flavor into our reference to the stupid – idiotic – asinine attitude our socialist and fascist government uses to keep power over the common – man.

COMMUNITY COULD PROVIDE BALANCED TREATMENT

"Women should receive smaller Social Security checks than men. It's simple – on average they live longer than men, so they receive more checks over their lifetime. It's only fair to make their checks smaller.

Mormons should pay higher property taxes than the rest of us. On average, they have more children than non-Mormons, and property taxes finance our schools. It's only fair to make them pay higher property taxes.

Asian-Americans should pay higher tuition at state universities. On average, they score higher on IQ tests and college admissions exams than the rest of us, so they have an advantage when it comes to receiving scholarships. Since they are more likely to get scholarship money, it's only fair to make them pay higher tuition.

Outrageous? Sure. These proposals are fiction, nothing more. But they show how ridiculous it is for governments to punish citizens on the basis of gender, religion, or ethnicity. Most people would see these ideas as obviously wrong and unfair. Americans don't punish people for their religion, gender or race.

Governments discriminate all the time. They award athletic scholarships, give senior citizens tax breaks, offer preferential hiring to veterans or bilingual applicants. These policies, unlike those fictional ones, are aimed at qualified individuals not groups. The benefits are available to anyone excelling at sports, living to a certain age, serving the nation or learning a language, regardless of their race or gender.

It's not the same when governments reward people just for belonging to a particular group. The policies are always promoted as giving something to certain people but not taking away from others. That's nonsense, of course, because governments don't have limitless resources. Scholarship money set aside for only one type of student limits what's available to everyone else. Exempt some people from a tax and everyone else must make up the difference.

When government benefits, or tax dollars go to citizens based on race or gender, politicians call it affirmative action. But they ignore the negative consequences for everyone who doesn't receive the benefit. Precisely because state contracts, school admissions and state jobs are limited in number and paid for by all Arizona taxpayers, they belong to those taxpayers. Their award could and should be based on many different factors, but not on race, religion or gender. That's unfair, just like levying higher taxes against LDS church members.

How's this for a proposal? 'The state shall not discriminate against or grant preferential treatment to any individual or group on the basis of race, sex, color, ethnicity or national origin in the operation of government of public employment, public education or public contracting.'

It seems pretty straightforward and simple. It's called the Arizona Civil Rights Initiative. It will be attacked here as racist, unfair and divisive, and many elected officials and would-be officeholders will condemn it. California, Michigan and Washington have already approved similar proposals. It likely will be on our ballot in November. I think it will pass.

Thanks to Gene O'Neil

CLEANING HOUSE / THROW THE BUMS OUT AMENDMENT
[PROPOSED]
New Amendment XXVIII To The
CONSTITUTION OF THE UNITED STATES

Section 1. The Congress shall surrender its Constitutional authority on the following matters and said authority shall pass to the citizenry in the form of direct democracy.

Section 2. The right of citizens to establish term lengths and term limits for Senators and Representatives, through direct democracy, shall not be violated by any branch or agency of the Federal Government.

Section 3. Effective immediately the special retirement plans enjoyed by the Congress shall be terminated and rolled into the Social Security program where Congress will be treated as are all other citizens.

Section 4. Effective immediately all salaries of Congress shall be frozen. The right of citizens to determine if Congress be entitled to a raise in their salary or in the event that the citizenry feels that they deserve, for action unbecoming an officer under oath, a decrease in their salary, said action shall become law.

Section 5. Effective immediately all perks presently furnished Congress shall be withdrawn. The citizens by direct democracy will establish a fair and equitable membership fee for the use thereof of any and all perks. An independent Citizens Congressional Oversight Board will rule, define and regulate all perks.

Section 6. Effective immediately travel by Congress shall be reduced by 50%. Travel expenses for first class transportation and luxury accommodations will be denied. Travel expenses [per diem] shall be identical to those regulations published by the Internal Revenue Service for non-political business travel.

Section 7. All attachments to spending bills, commonly referred to as *CONGRESSIONAL PORK* shall not be permitted. These bills that do not benefit the country as a whole and equally must be submitted as separate, stand alone bill, for the scrutiny of the citizenry.

Section 8. The XVI, income tax amendment, is herewith repealed.

Section 9. Redistribution of funds from one group to favor and benefit a select group, commonly called special interest groups, shall be prohibited.

Section 10. All off-budget, commonly referred to as emergency spending, shall be discontinued and made a part of the uniform budget. Emergency funding for wars and disasters shall be provided for, in advance, by the federal and state governments through prior proper planning and establishment of emergency accounts fully funded on an annual basis, and invested. These funds *shall not* be invested through purchase of debt instruments of state or federal governments.

TO THE GOVERNMENT WE SAY:

The time has arrived for all people to realize and understand that our present form of government and the individuals elected and appointed to carry out our instructions has been corrupted beyond reason and acceptability. We-the-People of the United States do hereby give notice to our politicians that their corrupt behavior is considered by the people as failure on their part to fulfill their respective oaths of office. This will no longer be tolerated. We have above set forth our demands that are not negotiable but to be taken as the people's orders and instructions regarding how government is to carry out the will of their superiors.

To our government we say, *"If you continue to be part and parcel of the problem and refuse to obey our instructions and be part of the solution your refusal and attitude will be declared treasonous and you shall be dealt with as a traitor and if found guilty by the people your punishment will rise to the level of a capital crime."* You are hereby advised that we-the-people of the United States not only demand that our will be carried out and that we take no options off the table as how and when we will exercise our Constitutional rights as your employer and that you must do as directed, or you will face the consequences of all Betrayers, of a determined populace. Enough is enough and lying, cheating deception, b___ s___ing, out of control egos, personal goals and vendettas, lust, pride, gluttony, wrath, sloth and disgusting behavior will end. We-the-People of the United States have spoken, that we do not trust you in your present attitude and behavior, and make no mistake that both individually and collectively we will oppose your treasonous attitude.

Furthermore, the Constitution makes no provision nor offers any comfort to liberal / socialist and conservative / fascist ideology and this war of ideologies, special interest, and personal gain must end immediately as it will not be tolerated.

These are not threats but statements and orders of the people's wishes as to what you must do, and do beginning immediately, or we take matters into our collective hands.

FUTURE GENERATIONS: We have said the above so that there will be no opportunity nor excuse, for any one to wonder or question what we say and what we mean. God help us if we-the-people fail in our rights and responsibilities under our Constitution. Our government has currently exiled the Constitution to file 13, it is now the duty of the people to reclaim, reinstitute, replace all incumbents, and exercise our *"due-diligence"* as the rightful owners of America. So help us God.

You as the future generations that will run this government and country must consider the above proposed Declaration and proposed Amendment XXVIII. In addition, in the event that government spurns these demands and continues to illegally take from us and you our rights and freedoms, then you must consider forcing a call for a second Constitutional Convention, withholding your vote, demonstrations near voting places, calling for state and / or federal referendums demanding the above, and any other peaceful means to achieve those demands. If push comes to shove, we must be prepared to shove with all our force, for to fail at this means serfdom and slavery for our future generations. Our Empire of Greed, Ego, corruption and our efforts to war with the planet if for no other reason than we are being bankrupted by borrowing money for the purpose of these wars. Never lose sight of the fact that, *"a flawed economy and debasement of our currency, as a strategy, is a strategy for our own destruction."*

Think tactics and strategy. We know that government will stonewall our efforts and from time to time take retribution in the form of new onerous laws; therefore we propose the following or something similar. We know that the best defense is a good offense. We are guessing that phrase was coined by either Sun Tzu or Clauswitz.

INTRO TO OFFENSIVE OPERATIONS:

We must think back to the indoctrination we received in schools, churches and various forms of media. This indoctrination channeled the majority of us into wage labor. Therefore we think like an employee giving only lip service to what an employer is faced with. Upon receipt of an application for employment the employer will go through a process including a criminal background check and follow-up on your references and former employment if applicable. We forget that regardless of who we are that we are the employers of those we elect to office. The reason we elect so many fools and idiots is that we have not done our due-diligent responsibilities under our Constitution. Failure on our part provides us, not with the government we want, but the government we deserve. Our failure in due-diligence allows the politicians to label opponents and other significant issues. Therefore we get the crap from Washington that we deserve. That is what we want to reverse by going on the offensive. Here is how we do it!

PHASE ONE: Within each Congressional district a small non-partisan group forms for the purpose of engaging the services of a private investigator [spread the cost] to investigate in detail the background of your Congressperson and cooperate with other district groups in doing the same investigation on both senators. Make certain that the information is verified and then publish this information for everyone interested to read. Make sure that the criminal record for each is thoroughly investigated, that their sexual behavior passes the test, that their financial records are thoroughly scrutinized and that they themselves, as citizens, are in compliance with the IRS code and other legislation passed by

Congress. [This phase should be handled through a non-profit, non-partisan, tax-exempt organization].

PHASE TWO: Set up email addresses by groups on your computer so that with one push of the button you can reach all 535 suspects, another to reach both senatorial suspects, another to reach your Congressperson, and of course, do not forget the media.

PHASE THREE: Refuse to vote for those that fail to receive a clean bill of health from the investigation. Prepare and demonstrate on the day of election, making certain that you do not violate any election laws regarding proximity to the polling places, and use signage to alert voters about the evils of the candidates. This alerts us to include in the investigations all candidates and their backgrounds. In those situations where both candidates fail the investigation, point out to other voters that voting for the lesser of two evils is not a constitutional choice and neither candidate is eligible for your vote.

PHASE FOUR: Be sure the media gives you equal time for interviews and use paid advertisements to keep all voters up to date of any and all lawbreakers, or those with identified criminal intent, or enlist their membership in your non-partisan effort.

ATTACK, ATTACK and then ATTACK AGAIN.

FUTURE GENERATIONS: The true odds that government will reform itself or cooperate with the people to change government is virtually nil, but it deserves the opportunity, to succeed or fail on its virtues and the will of the people. Remember to keep up to date your *"Get Out of Dodge"* plan and settle into your principality. The Bush family has allegedly purchased a ranch in Paraguay that works for them.

FUTURE GENERATIONS: In 2008 we again will be faced with either extreme liberalism or extreme conservativism, as our choices on the ballot for president. Politics has passed the phase of two siblings fighting over the family fortune. It is like a marriage that is irretrievably fractured and will never lead to happiness and security. This is today's version of the struggle between the *Red* and *Blue* states - the heartland and the ocean states. It is time to begin thinking of what is next for America. In 1861 America in total insanity warred internally and tore the heart out of the country – never to be the same again. The ideological and cultural differences between the two extremes of thought, has literally torn America asunder. It appears that the inevitable divorce of the *Red* and *Blue* states is being baked into the cake. We talk about it here to alert you to the fact that something – no one knows yet – will occur like an explosion upon society and government and things will change in a yet to understand manner.

Since the 60's we have watched the deterioration of truth, honesty, integrity, self-responsibility sink to levels seldom seen in history. Change is inevitable but is yet a mystery to all. We hold our breath and actually hope that we will live long enough to see how nature deals with those who preyed upon the stupid or the stupid who fell for the hollow promises of those who preyed. There will not be winners and losers as in a zero sum game. Everyone loses, yet some will lose everything and others will lose only a little. We think we know who will be the big losers but wish to see if our analysis is correct. After that we will feel a need to lay down and sleep – a long and lasting sleep – grateful that we will not have to do another trip down life.

ADVICE FROM MOM AND DAD!

07-04-2006
We sit enjoying *"Independence Day"* yet wondering where the independence has long ago gone and what do we do when we find out *"it ain't coming back?"*

We then began to reminisce about old America when it was a *"cash and carry economy."* It worked very well until we were induced to *"buy things we didn't need – with money we didn't have – sinking deeper into debt until we find that there is no way to escape."* But maybe there is a way. Cut up all credit cards and don't spend a dime without sleeping on why you want something [you won't be tempted as much] if you ain't got the cash don't buy it. Ya! – that is the old cash and carry way. It still works.

Your ancient and old-fashioned parents, of a sort, had an interesting debate the other day on relationships between people. In Martin Luther King's *"I have a dream"* speech, he said, *"judge us not by the color of our skin – but by the content of our character"*. Skin color was the subject of our research debate. Throughout the planet there exist people of various colors – yet their skin color is not a consideration in judging them. We just finished watching Tiger and Vijay go head to head for a golf championship. Vijay is as black as they come; he is a Figean, yet not a derogatory comment is made regarding him. In fact he is consider an example of good character. Tiger is of course about 50% Thai with the balance made up of black, Indian and a couple others that we don't remember. He also is considered a man of good character. We are searching for an answer to, when judging people is their skin relevant, if so, why is skin color not relevant equally across the world? We find it hard to understand America's hang-up and our obsession over the color of another's skin – all in contradiction to the dream of MLK. A person of good character is a good person without regard to skin color.

Government, for the past several decades, has fallen in love with the cliché; it's an investment, when referring to voting for a pet project. That is a bunch of you know what – you know the smelly stuff we shovel out of the cow barn. A true investment will carry with it several specific considerations. 1] return *of* investment – how will the appropriated money come back into the treasury, 2] return *on* investment – how much benefit [in dollars] will it bring, 3] what is the nature of cash flow accounting that gives confidence that it can repay this investment. Our bureaucrats, with straight faces go to church on Sundays, say that the program is compassionate and it will make people feel good about themselves, and all this while they have no intent of ever repaying the debt.

WHAT IF:

What if we were 30-40 years younger and had the strength and fire to run for public office. What would we say to you to get your vote? We shamelessly borrow from President Klaus of the Czech Republic for his outstanding plan that he submitted for the reform of Europe. The only change in his six points is the first word in each point is Europe and we have substituted

America. The same problem that Klaus sees in Europe we see in America. Therefore we would run on the following ideas.

1] America must be free, democratic and prosperous. It will not be achieved by democratic deficit, by super nationalism, by statism, or by an increase in legislating, monitoring, and regulating.

2] America needs a system of ideas that must be based on freedom, personal responsibility, individualism, natural caring for others, and a genuinely moral conduct of life.

3] America needs a political system which must not be destroyed by a postmodern interpretation of human rights (with its emphasis on positive rights, with its dominance of group rights and entitlements over individual rights and responsibilities, and with it denationalization of citizenship), by the weakening of democratic institutions which have irreplaceable roots exclusively on the territory of the state's by the continental-wide rent seeking or various *non government organizations'* [NGOs].

4] America needs an economic system which must not be damaged by excessive government regulation, by fiscal deficits, by heavy bureaucratic control, by attempts to perfect markets by means of constructing optimal market structures, by huge subsidies to privileged or protected industries and firms, or by heavy labor market legislation.

5] America needs a social system that must not be wrecked by all imaginable kinds of disincentives, by more than generous welfare payments, by large-scale income redistribution, or by all other forms of government paternalism.

6] America needs a system of relations and relationships of individual countries that must not be based on false internationalism, on *super national'* organizations, and on a misunderstanding of globalization and of externalities, but on the good neighborliness of free, sovereign countries and on international pacts and agreements.

NOTE: The matter of separate countries within America will be thoroughly discussed in the fourth book of this series titled, SELF-DETERMINATION.

Following is the gist of our *"stump speeches"* which we will express over and over until death do us part.

Ladies, gentlemen and especially the children of America, we stand before you to share with you the truth of what America is, has become, and why the direction must be changed.

Two-hundred-thirty years ago our forefathers signed their name to the Declaration of Independence and two-hundred-eighteen years ago our Constitution was ratified. Today, both of those documents have been exiled and no longer do they provide for a free and independent community of individuals to live in peace and harmony in this great country.

Today we speak to you about a more hopeful country that is within the reach of every individual, a principality that is each individuals castle, standing strong against not only threat from without but especially of the threats and fears of our government that has changed America from a free republic to a state of Federalism that treats its people with scorn, lacking respect and dominating our personal lives. Your principality is a *"SAFE-HOUSE"*, a world beyond terror, where ordinary men, women and children are free to determine their own destiny, where the voices of true freedom are empowered, and where the radical-extremists of Federalism are marginalized by our peaceful majority. America can again belong to the people if we seek it and offer to others our voluntary cooperation.

Imagine what it's like to be a young person living in America where each successive generation has less freedom than the previous, where schools graduate children into society less literate than their parents and grandparents. You are 18 years old and you are not sure of what you want to do or can do. Government's net of regulations and taxes is literally strangling the life from your veins. You feel powerless to change the course of your government. You are filled with the lies of government propaganda and conspiracy theories that blame one group for the failure of other groups. That tells one group that they are entitled to more from government than other groups - while telling the other groups that they must share the fruits of their labors with those who march to the drummer of government lies and misbehavior. We are not a village, we are each a principality, we are not a slave - we are free, we desire voluntary cooperation between us.

In America's early days, government work was not considered a career and each citizen was expected to give a few years of their life to serving their country. But now we wonder why so many of us despise our leaders. Is it because they have in fact made government service a lifelong and a family tradition that places their goals ahead of the country or citizens? Today there are approximately 50 persons elected or seeking election that are of a family of elected. They must be seeking these positions of power for self-gratification. We are not and should not become a multi-monarchy where elite families rotate the holding of power and authority. We should say good-bye to them and take charge of our individual lives and live in a castle within our principality.

Elections are not necessary for you to have the opportunity to again be free. Your vote is all too often an excuse for not doing for yourself but delegating your life to corruption by these elite. They did not make slaves out of you against your will – they exchanged worthless promises to you – you became a willing serf to the will of the elite minority. You are concerned about the voting process and are there any threats to this system? If so – who, what, etc? A new paradigm, actually it is an old one, is regenerating itself to prepare for globalization. The following quote is attributed to David Rockefeller. The who is not so important as the what, this is what David said in June 1991. *"We are grateful to the Washington Post, the New York Times, Time Magazine and other great publications whose directors have attended our meeting and respected their promises of discretion for almost forty years."* He went on to explain. *"It would have been impossible for us to develop our plan for the world if we had been subjected to the lights of publicity during those years. But, super national sovereignty of an intellectual elite and world bankers is surely preferable to the national auto-determination practiced in past centuries."* Reread that paragraph every so often and ponder just what it means to people in general. Individualists will have a good chance of circumventing   this   terror   and   horror.

OUR NEXT BOOK

Originally we planned to write two additional books titled, GLOBALIZATION and SELF-DETERMINATION. These two proposed books will be combined into a third and probably final book. At this moment we are preparing to submit the manuscript for SURVIVAL to Trafford Publishing.

We sat on our patio in our back yard, fully understanding we had to think even more clearly than we had believed we were. We had to define what is before all of us with globalization and self-determination, and then how do we outthink those who are manipulating the people and the economy. We must do this without panic and in the context of we and many of you having created your own principality, aka, *SAFE HAVEN.* Continuing as a faithful foot soldier of a government that has put us at great risk could violently upset the delicate balance between us. Our definition of safe-haven is: *a place of refuge or sanctuary affording protection from danger, injury or hazard.*

Without breaking the rules, we must define the means and methods available without the risk normally associated with globalization and self-determination, between socialism for years than a switch to fascism for years. The risk of violence would generally be expected to appear when one or the other decides to *"go-all-in."* We must move quickly to achieve **control**. Control over our lives and the means and methods of controlling our future. It is a simple word but the demand it makes is incredible. Control will be our means to guide us from this utter emptiness that our leaders have created. It is like a vacuum into which will rush either violence or safety – safety in our *safe haven.* If you can survive the creating of your safe haven – done quietly and carefully they will not see you – but you will see them. Keep your eyes and ears focused on them – every damn one of them - every damned minute. They will terminate you to stop and thus prevent you from your thoughts and your plans.

Book three has the working title of "SAFE-HAVEN." It will include how to use it with globalization and self-determination, plus those two items discussed in detail. Publication will be delayed until after the 2008 election and we have had the opportunity to study and understand, on the basis of who are the winners, what will likely be the political scenario, and what actions we must consider.

"GLOBALIZATION" OR "WHAT'S IN IT FOR ME?" PROLOGUE

Globalization is coming – and – it is accelerating. It brings with it changes of great immensity that will affect peoples' lives forever. You don't have to be a rocket scientist to see distortions not only in jobs, but also especially in the manner that people and their government interact with each other. This process that we refer to today, *globalization,* probably occurred steadily since the first humans crawled out of their valley and found that others existed on earth, that they were different in many ways, speech, etc. This process has crept along slowly until the end of the 20th century, and we find a massive acceleration to the process as we proceed through the 21st century. It is therefore nothing new, just larger than life, and life will again learn to live with change. Those who do not or refuse to understand this movement will later regret it.

Changes in lifestyles and interaction with other cultures have always existed and will exist until the end of mankind. The future will continue to bring the rise and fall of empires; ours is not excluded. Best to prepare for this change and move quickly into whatever succeeds it.

Freedom is our passion and we want everyone else who yearns for freedom to have the chance to seize it. Even a minor examination of what has happened in regards to the Constitutional guarantees granted to the people should be enough to sober up the addicts to conclude that the future bodes great losses of freedom as the New Order takes control.

INTRODUCTION TO GLOBALIZATION

[**] *Globalization is about worldwide economic activity – about open markets, competition and the free flow of goods, services, capital and knowledge. Consumers are its principal beneficiary. Its benefits in terms of faster growth, quicker access to new technology, cheaper imports and greater competition are available to all. Globalization has made the world economy more efficient and has created hundreds of millions of jobs, mainly, but not only, in developing countries. It generates an upward spiral of jobs and prosperity for countries that embrace the process, although the advantages will not reach everybody at the same time.*

We must first recognize and remember that globalization is not and never will qualify as a merger of equals. Therefore those who are ahead will be asked to carry the less fortunate countries. This immediately puts us back into what we detest so much in America; socialism in control of capitalism and guilt and fear dispensed by political correctness.

Globalization will have many profound impacts upon governments and their societies. The major change will appear in how governments are restructured and how they view their citizens. Stock or shareholders hold a completely different attitude and perception of government than the formerly passive and obedient attitude of people deigned to follow, without question, their ordained leaders. Understanding the nuance, of new terms and phrases will make it easier to make your choices.

Our jobs will be organized differently than they are today – how we don't know yet – but if we keep our sense tuned, we will recognize the change when it comes. Many argue that international government is unstoppable. This may appear to be true but that type government could hold it together only with an increase in violence and moving towards total autocratic power. The peoples of the world are just too different in culture, beliefs and lifestyles to fit into one universal, global state and government peacefully. Just the thought of uprisings throughout the planet brings memories of the worst of Iraq and Afghanistan or plain anarchy. Just the thought of this condition descending upon us should be more than enough motivation to spur individuals to immediate action to defend themselves against this unknown.

SELF-DETERMINATION

Self-determination is based on a theory that is stated as: a macro-theory of human motivation concerned with the development and functioning of personality within social contexts. The theory focuses on the degree to which human behaviors are volitional or self-determined – that is, the degree to which people endorse their actions at the highest level of reflection and engage in the actions with a full sense of choice.

It is a general theory of motivation and personality that evolved since the 70's as a set of four mini-theories that share the organismic-dialectal meta-theory and the concept of basic needs. Each mini-theory was developed to explain a set of motivationally based phenomena that emerged from laboratory and field research focused on different issues.

Cognitive evaluation theory addresses the effects of social contexts on intrinsic motivation; **organismic integration** theory addresses the concept of internalization especially with respect to the development of intrinsic motivation. **Causality orientations** theory describes individual's differences in people's tendencies toward self-determined behavior and toward orienting to the environment in ways that support their self-determination. And **basic needs theory** elaborates the concept of basic needs and its relation to psychological health and well-being. Together these mini-theories constitute self-determination.

Attribution for the above to: Deci, E. L, and Ryan, R. M. found in: *Intrinsic motivation and self-determination in human behavior [1985]; Psychological Inquiry [2000]; and, American Psychologist [2000].*

What does this mean to you and us? We are all concerned about our health and well-being. Each of us is aware of our differences regarding self-determination. Some are highly motivated while others are passive and go along for the ride. This difference in motivation arises from how each internalizes society and government and the degree to which these relationships are either good or evil. [Editor's definition] In essence man rebels [seeks self-determination] against the 'social controls' that society in general and government in particular attempts to force conformity in behavior, even when it is clear that that behavior is neither Constitutional nor equal.

Self-determination must include the right to conduct legal business any where in the world, even if it allows the individual to reduce their taxes by virtue of the existence of tax competition between countries.

DETERMINATION *by* SELF *for* SELF

The secret of self-determination *IS* determination by self. When you reach this stage, you truly understand and know the evil of co-dependency and are prepared to go forward with your life in quest of freedom.

FUTURE GENERATONS: As we grow older, it seems that there are more and more dead people that have gone before us. Many of these deaths were unnecessary and could and should have been avoided. At the same time, we have more and more people joining us to fight for limited space, clean water and non-polluted air. We have no answers to these thoughts. Best that we leave it alone and let time and circumstances deal with it. As mean, ugly and violent as some among us are, we know of no one that we disliked so much that we wanted them dead. We were satisfied just being as far away from them as possible.

Survival is the only thing – for everything else is political/ideological dung spread over an infertile field by others of ill repute.

Sleep well in your personal Principality and may the force, always be with you!

Love you all, Heide & Robert

POSTSCRIPT: In the past 35 years, our country, we don't know what name to give it at this time as we are no longer a republic, led both Sweden and Japan in increasing health benefits for everyone. Actually they grew at double the rate of socialist Sweden. It appears that it is now too late in the cycle, our conversion from a republic into whatever it should be called, so our traditional patriots really have nothing to save, for the republic literally does not exist. Our patriots, like everyone else, are trying to save themselves from a decaying empire by escaping from the decay and dissolution of empire that destroys everything they get their hands on. We call this looting and hoarding. Insofar as the government has neither the intent nor the means to pay its debts, the only course remaining is to print more $100 bills. We calmly wait for the day they print $500 bills when a $100 bill won't buy a decent meal. This of course will dramatically raise everyone's expectations of higher, much higher, inflation. By now you should be aware of what is recommended as a means for survival.

POTPOURRI
02.05.2007: Sovereign Society Offshore *A* letter. *Classified secret*

Biometric and biometric travel database; recommended by DHS [Department of Homeland Security]. Every time you cross a border, every time your machine-readable passport is *scanned* at a hotel, bank or other location, your movements will be recorded in a global database. Mark Nestmann – www.nestman.com

CLIMATE CHANGES
An excellent article by Ralf Tiedemann, in German, discussed ocean and climate histories. While his original article ran a hundred plus pages, he did provide a brief summary for those of you who don't read German, in English. The title is *"Summary: Deep-Sea Sediments - Witnesses of the Ocean and Climate History"*. It reads as follows: *"Growing interest in global climatic changes and the need for more precise modeling of past and future climate has increased the demand for a better understanding of how ocean circulation and its chemical cycling are linked to climate fluctuations. Deep-sea sediments provide the most important database for global environmental reconstructions and predictions. This archive holds a variety of*

tracers which can be used to reconstruct paleoclimatic and paleoceanographic variables, such as continental aridity/humidity, global ice volume, sea level, ocean temperatures and nutrients, CO2 contents and other parameters related to past global environments. It has been shown that the long-term evolution of these parameters undergoes rhythmic changes with periods of 100,000, 41,000 and 23,000 years. These cycles are considered as a product of Earth-Sun orbital variations, which link the climate response to orbital-driven changes in the insolation. The spectral relationships between the different climatic and oceanographic parameters provide basic insights into the processes and causal chains that control the climate system today as well as during the past."

IMMIGRATION

What if we have it all backwards? Politicians and special interest groups talk about the benefits to be had if their version is passed. Yet, the Constitution addresses the issue that government should do no harm. Either version of fairness will produce harm. Maybe we should look at these versions and determine which does the least harm. After all – no one bothered to place a statue of liberty on either the Northern or Southern borders. Just a thought for you to mull over.

SOURCES

The following books, tapes, CD's, and periodicals have been sources of information and background for setting the perspective of what manner of truths and untruths have befallen us.

The following is a partial list of the research attributions and reference material used in formulating our ideas.

The point of view presented in this book is today decidedly out of favor in America. For young people whose outlook has been formed entirely by the views that have been dominant during the last twenty years, this will scarcely be sufficient to provide the common ground required for profitable discussion. But although unfashionable, the views of the author(s) are not as singular as they may appear to some readers. Our basic outlook was formed over many decades beginning with President Coolidge, the Great Depression, WWII, the Cold War, emerging global economies and the approach of mankind into the 21st century. We wish to thank the authors of the following books, magazines and papers, all of which were used in our research. The reader who would like to acquaint him/herself further with what they may have found unfamiliar, but not an uncongenial climate of opinion, may find useful the following list of the more important works of this kind.

Printed by authority of H. Con. 172nd Congress, "Our American Government", 1993 edition***
American Institute for Economic Research, various pages*
Allen, James, "Freedom and Truth", 1971 edition***
Andrew, Christopher and Mitrokhin, Vasili, The Sword and the Shield, [The Secret   History of   the KGB as taken from the Mitrokhin Archive] *****

Baldwin, W., Battles Lost and Won, Great Campaigns of WWII Hanson***

Bauman, JD, Robert, Where to Stash your Cash Legally*****

Bauman, JD, Robert, The Passport Book ***

Belloc, Hilaire, The Servile State Introduction by Robert Nisbet****

Beschloss, Michael, The Conquerors****

Bogle, John C., Bogle on Mutual Funds*

Boorstin, Daniel J., The Seekers, The Story of Man's Continuing Quest to Understand His   World, **

Braudel, Fernand, A History of Civilizations***

Bray, R. S., Armies of Pestilence, The Impact of Disease on History***

Bresheeth, Haim, Hood, Stuart and Jansz, Litza, The Holocaust***

Brzezinski, Zbigniew, "The Grand Chessboard", 1997 edition*

Burke, Edmund, A Vindication of Natural Society***

Carey, George, In Defense of the Constitution***

Carter, Jimmy, Our Endangered Values

Celente, Gerald, "Trends 2000", 1998 edition**

Chodorov, Frank, Fugitive Essays

Clausewitz, Carl von, Principles of War

Condon, Gerald M. and Jeffery L., Beyond the Grave**

Constant, Benjamin, Principle of Politics Applicable to All Governments*****

Davidson, James Dale & Rees-Mogg, Lord William, The Sovereign Individual

de Jouvenel, Bertrand, On Power****

de Jouvenel, Bertrand, The Ethics of Redistribution****

De Sota, Hernando, The Mystery of Capital

De Toqueville, Alexis, "Democracy in America", 1984 edition****

Duncan, Richard, The Dollar Crises

Economist Magazine**

Flynn, John T., The Roosevelt Myth*****

Fischer, David Hackett, The Great Wave*****

Garrett, Garet, A Bubble that Broke the World*****

Gibbon, Edward, "Decline and Fall of the Roman Empire" ***

Goldberg, Bernard, Arrogance

Greider, William, "Who Will Tell the People", 1992 edition*

Hine, Robert V. & Faragher, John Mack, "The American West," 2000 edition*****

Hayek, Fredrich A, "Hayek on Hayek", 1994 edition***

Hayek, Fredrich A., "The Road to Serfdom", 1994 edition*****

Herbert, Auberon, The Right and Wrong of Compulsion by the Sate, and Other Essays****

Hustad Burleigh, Anne, Education in a Free Society, Libert Fund***

Internal Revenue Service, Package X***

Investment U Course, Investment University***
Johnson, Chalmers, The Sorrows of Empire
Lasser, J. K., Annual Income Tax Guide*****
Leuchtenburg, William E., The Supreme Court Reborn
Levien, J. R., Anatomy of a Crash – 1929****
Levitt, Stephen D. & Dubner, Stephen J., Freakonomics
Macmillan, Margaret, Paris 1919*****
Mansoor, Peter R., The G. I. Offensive in Europe
Morley, Felix, Essays on Individuality****
Mosier, John, The Myth of the Great War ****
Naisbitt, John, "Megatrends", 1984 edition**
Nestmann, Mark; "Lifeboat Strategy" *****
New Individualist Review, Volumes 1-5, 1961-1968**
Nietzsche, Friedrich, Human, all to Human
O'Neil, William J., The Successful Investor
Opposing Viewpoints Series, Crime and Criminals***
Phillios, Kevin, American Theocracy, The perils and politics of radical religion, oil, and borrowed money in the 21st century.
Patterson, James & Kim, Peter, "The Second American Revolution", 1994 edition**
Pirate Investor's Bible, Pirate Investor LLC***
Macmillan, Margaret, Paris 1919*****
Moynihan, Daniel P., Maximum Feasible Misunderstanding
Radzinsky, Edvard, Stalin*****
Ross, Stewart Halsey, Propaganda for War
Schoeck, Helmut, Envy****
Shils, Edward, The Virtue of Civility***
Smith, Hedrick, "Rethinking America", 1995 edition**
Stansberry & Sjuggerud, The Pirate Investor's Bible
Sterling, William and Waite, Stephen, Balantine, 1998, "Boomernomics: The
Stewart, Jon, America – Teachers Edition
Sumner, William Graham, On Liberty, Society, and Politics, Edited by Robert
Sun, Tzu, The Art of War
Stinnett, Robert B., Day of Deceit, The Truth about FDR and Pearl Harbor *****
Suskind, Ron, The Price of Loyalty
Taylor, John, Tyranny Unmasked, 1821, Edited by F. Thorton Miller**
The Summa Theologica of Saint Thomas Aquinas; Volumes I, II and III****
Thoreau, Henry David, Walden and Civil Disobedience***
Waitley, Denis, "Empires of the Mind", 1995 edition*

567 SURVIVAL

future of Your Money in the Upcoming Generational Warfare" **
George Washington in His Own Words*****
West, E. G., Education and the State****
C. Bannister****
White, Bouck, The Book of Daniel Drew***
Wolfram, Herwig, The Roman Empire and Its Germanic People
Yellow Pages, your local phone company****

* INTERESTING   ** GOOD   *** VERY GOOD
**** REMARKABLE   ***** MUST READ

Great Courses on Tape. The Teaching Company

1] The Great Ideas of Philosophy – Part I – Professor Daniel N. Robinson; Georgetown University
2] The Great Ideas of Philosophy – Part II – Professor Daniel N. Robinson; Georgetown University
3] The Great Ideas of Philosophy – Part III – Professor Daniel N. Robinson; Georgetown University
4] The Great Ideas of Philosophy – Part IV – Professor Daniel N. Robinson; Georgetown University
5] The Great Ideas of Philosophy – Part V – Professor Daniel N. Robinson; Georgetown University
6] Power over People: Classical and Modern Political Theory – Part 1- Professor Dennis Dalston; Barnard College/Columbia University.
7] Power over People: Classical and Modern Political Theory, Part II – Professor Dennis Dalton; Barnard College/Columbia University
8] Thomas Jefferson: American Visionary – Professor Darren Staloff; City College of New York
9] Hell, Purgatory, Paradise: Dante's Divine Comedy, Professors William R. Cook and Ronald B. Herzman; State University of New York at Genesco
10] No Excuses: Existentialism and the Meaning of Life – Part I – Professor Robert Solomon; University of Texas
11] No Excuses: Existentialism and the Meaning of Life – Part II – Professor Robert Solomon; University of Texas
12] Einstein's Relativity and the Quantum Revolution: Modern Physics for Non-Scientists – Part I – Professor Richard Wolfson; Middlebury College
13] Einstein's Relativity and the Quantum Revolution: Modern Physics for Non-Scientists – Part II – Professor Richard Wolfson; Middlebury College
14] The History of Hitler's Empire, Professor Thomas Childers;

University of Pennsylvania

15] Explaining Social Deviance, Professor Paul Root Wolpe; University of Pennsylvania

16] Business Law: Contracts, Professor Frank B. Cross; University of Texas at Austin

17] Business Law: Negligence and Torts, Professor Frank B. Cross; University of Texas at Austin

18] The Will to Power: The Philosophy of Friedrich Nietzsche, Professors Robert Solomon and Kathleen Higgens; University of Texas at Austin

19] The History of the English Language, Part 1 – The Origins of English, Professor Seth Lerer, Ph.D.; Stanford University

Part 2 – Making Modern English

Part 3 – English in America and Beyond

20] The Life and Writings of John Milton, Professor Seth Lerer; Stanford University

21] Must History Repeat the Great Conflicts of this Century? Professor Joseph S. Nye, Jr.; Harvard University

22] The Soul and the City: Art, Literature, and Urban Life, Professor Arnold Weinstein; Brown University

23] Alexander the Great and the Hellenistic Age, Part 1, Professor Jeremy McInernery; University of Pennsylvania

24] Alexander the Great and the Hellenistic Age, Part II, Professor Jeremy McInernery; University of Pennsylvania

25] Ancient Greek Civilization, Part I, Professor Jeremy McInerney; University of Pennsylvania

26] Ancient Greek Civilization, Part II, Professor Jeremy McInerney; University of Pennsylvania

27] Argumentation: The Study of Effective Reasoning Part I, Professor David Zarefsky; Northwestern University

28] Argumentation: The Study of Effective Reasoning Part II, Professor David Zarefsky; Northwestern University

29] Biology and Human Behavior: The Neurological Origins of Individuality, Professor Robert Sapolsky, Stanford University

30] The Ethics of Aristotle, Professor Joseph Koterski; Fordham University, New York

31] A History of the U.S. Economy in the 20th Century, Professor Timothy Taylor; Macalester College

32] Joyce's Ulysses, Part I, Professor James A. W. Heffernan; Dartmouth College

33] The Iliad of Homer, Professor Elizabeth Vandiver; University of Maryland

34] The Odyssey of Homer, Professor Elizabeth Vandiver; University of Maryland

35] The Passions: Philosophy and the Intelligence of Emotions, Professor Robert C. Solomon, University of Texas, Austin. Parts 1 & 2

36] World War II: A Military and Social History, three parts, Professor Thomas Childers, University of Pennsylvania.

CHANGE

The people clamor for change in government. Politicians offer promises of change, but do not reveal the exact change they have in mind. The voters and candidates are like two trains going in different directions on different tracks for different reasons.

We reduce this issue to an analogy. There was a time when spring planting seasons arrived and farmers reached into their previous harvest for seed corn for the new planting. Their harvest, or yield, remained constant over these years. Those farmers who sought change through the use of new types of seed from other sources saw their yields increase. Selecting a president is similar to the corn planting analogy in this manner. If voters continue to reach into career government(s) for a president, they will never see change from the welfare and warfare government(s) we have had to live with. This is the condition we want changed. Change means to reach out and find a candidate that is **NOT** embedded in government ideology. An example of real change is the concept offered in ***"YOUR PRINCIPALITY"*** discussed in ***"SURVIVAL"***. If you reach into your bag of talent, skill and knowledge, you too can have the freedom from over-regulation outrageous tax-policy, out-of-control government spending, the horrors of political correctness, and politicians pandering lies and deceptions. The thoughts of our politicians come through loud and clear: ***"If the voters are stupid enough to believe what the candidates pander, then they deserve more of the same failed government."*** The voters will harvest that which they sow. In this case risk is who ultimately gets stuck with the bill and has to fight the wars. This is known as ***"THE SOCIALIZATION OF RISK"***. Anything else is pure **"bull-crap"**.